ROCK CHICK
A Girl and Her Music

"A treasured collection, the personal voyage of one of the First Ladies of Rock Journalism. Patricia Kennealy-Morrison takes us on a delicious journey through the dawn of rock and the rise of its greatest artists—an unapologetic first-hand perspective of the landscape of the Sixties."

–*Kathleen Quinlan, Academy Award nominee*

"Patricia Kennealy was *there*. As a young girl in love with the brand-new late '60s rock music that was magically liberating our lives; as a top writer and editor on the subject of that music (and one of the very few young women in that role at the time); and as the lover and wife of one of the most iconic rock gods of that era, she lived it and wrote it from the most intense and singular of perches. **ROCK CHICK**— including writings from the time and her wise thoughts decades after the fact — is like a letter in a bottle washed up onshore…the rare real deal. Read, savor, remember (or learn) — and enjoy!"

–*Sheila Weller, author of* Girls Like Us: Carole King, Joni Mitchell, Carly Simon—And the Journey of a Generation

"The most overused words in the annals of rock criticism? *Ethereal*, sure. *Jangly*, that's a good one. And, of course, anything *-esque*. Right up there, too, is *pioneer*. Without Patricia Kennealy-Morrison, though, those of us who took up the calling of rock critic may well never have had a place to overuse those words. Sure, today the landscape is littered with semi-literate bloggers who wouldn't know an Airplane from a Grape, but in the days she so colorfully, insightfully chronicles herein, the ground was trampled under no foot. From a Saturday night at the Fillmore East as Janis Joplin takes the stage, to her 1969 account of her famed-to-be first meeting with one Lizard King, to strategy sessions with David Bowie, she isn't a reporter or critic as much as a witness, not just to the music but to new frontiers of culture. What else could we call her *but* a pioneer? Patricia *is* Rock Chick. All others can only aspire to be, uh, Rock Chick-esque."

–*Steve Hochman, veteran music journalist, Los Angeles Times, Rolling Stone, KQED, KPCC, etc.*

ROCK CHICK
A Girl and Her Music

The *Jazz & Pop* Writings
1968 ~ 1971

Patricia
Kennealy~Morrison

Lizard Queen Press

This book is a compilation, with new commentary, of the articles, interviews, columns, features and reviews I wrote for Jazz & Pop magazine, as editorial assistant and Editor in Chief, during the period 1968 – 1971. I retain original copyright in all pieces.

On the Web:
www.facebook.com/patriciakmorrison
pkmorrison.livejournal.com
mojohotel.blogspot.com
myspace.com/hermajestythelizardqueen

Jacket design by Lorrieann Russell
Jacket photograph by Michael Rosenthal
Production by Lorrieann Russell and Jesse V. Coffey
Interior book design by the author
Author photograph from the author's personal collection

ISBN-13: 97806-1585-2324 Lizard Queen Press
Printed in USA August 2013

Author's Notes

These are my writings from my days as a rock critic — one of the first such, and one of the very first women ever to write about rock music, a Founding Mother of the genre. From 1968 to 1971, I was the editor in chief of Jazz & Pop magazine, and save for three pieces in the two years following, my work there constitutes the sum total of my rock journalism career. From there, I went on to write ad copy at two record companies, and then to write novels — fifteen as of this year of publication, eight in one series, THE KELTIAD, six in another, THE ROCK & ROLL MURDERS: THE RENNIE STRIDE MYSTERIES, and one standalone historical — and a memoir, *Strange Days: My Life With and Without Jim Morrison.*

But my years in the music biz are very close and dear to my heart, and I got to thinking that it might be instructive to assemble my Jazz & Pop pieces together in a book for those readers who weren't around to actually have read the magazine in its original shape and form. And also to preserve them for history: not so much like flies in amber but more like amber beads, adorning viewpoint and viewer alike.

I was twenty-one when I started work at J&P as editorial assistant; a year later I had been named editor and met Jim. And so my views and writing were those of a young, educated, passionately opinionated person in a time of stupendous social change on all fronts; like the rest of my age cohort, I was experimenting with attitudes, language, even, a little, with power — the power of the word, the power of youth, the power of being a woman. I think the views were accurate and the writing was reflective, and I am pleased to see, upon reappraisal, that I am ashamed of neither.

I have left everything exactly as it appeared in Jazz & Pop's pages, no matter the evil, terrible temptation to edit. (You have no *idea*. No, really. You don't.) Well…I've fixed typos and erring punctuation, and perhaps one or two small but egregious errors that somehow had managed to slip through. (And oh how I cry out to the goddess Pedantica, deity of editing, that I *could* revise things! Because I was young, and sometimes I was an idiot, as one sometimes is. But I didn't.)

Any new typos or omissions are strictly my fault—it got very tiring retyping all this, and my attention, not to mention my fingers, may have slipped from time to time, as I refused to use a scanner or have someone else do the typing. Old-school all the way!

I did disitalicize venue names (Fillmore East, Madison Square Garden, etc.) and song titles. Pauline Rivelli, Jazz & Pop's publisher, loved italics for everything, and it had been house style from the first, but I preferred them for album, book and movie titles only. We had some spirited discussions about this; in the end, it was her magazine, so she won. Here, now that I can, I've gone with my own preferences. So song titles and venue names set roman, and song titles also take quotation marks; itals for everything else.

On nomenclature: At the time, I was of course using my birthname and its original spelling, Kennely, so you may occasionally see that here; I haven't bothered to alter the spelling. Also Pauline, in a vain and misguided effort to informalize and "friendify" to readers the people who appeared in the magazine, liked to shorten names. She kept insisting that my name was Pat. It isn't, and wasn't, even though she sometimes snuck it in, much to my annoyance. So you *won't* see *that* here, occasionally or otherwise.

Back in the day, nobody minded how many lines of song lyrics or other quotations rock writers borrowed for use in a review or feature; at least, if they did, they never complained to us about it. Nowadays, legal departments are rather more strict, and I cannot reproduce all the quotes we used even though they appeared in the magazine. I have therefore been obligated to redact when they exceeded the fair use allowance, and have indicated these redactions thusly: [...]
Just so you know. You can always look up the omissions online, where lawlessness still prevails.

My thanks to old and dear friends: Marion Harris for permission to use her late husband Bruce's piece, "*Morrison Hotel* Revisited"; and Thomas Courtenay-Clack and Kurt Brokaw for elucidations on, respectively, studio techniques and David Bowie.

In the interests of reminding my possibly forgetful peers and informing the younger generations who won't have a clue who the hell I'm talking about (and probably still won't even after I've elaborated), I have on occasion glossed references with bracketed and italicized clarification and commentary. Bracketed copy that appeared in the original piece is left roman.

A small caveat up front: being the editor of the magazine, I basically wrote about, interviewed and reviewed only the bands I truly loved—which basically meant the Doors and Jefferson Airplane in a photo finish for the win, and coming in a few lengths behind, in a multi-way tie for show, the Beatles, the Rolling Stones, Big Brother and several other bands and artists who shared third-most-favored-nation status. There's a few instances where I diverged from this policy: it's pretty easy to tell when my heart wasn't in what I was writing about. This didn't happen so much in my Pop Talk columns, where usually I just ranted until the steam stopped coming out of my ears and I ran out of rant, which was pretty much never; but in my reviews and features, it occasionally did. Still, I thought it was important to include pieces that I wasn't in love with, just for the record(s).

Anyway, this is just by way of warning you that if you dislike the bands I chose to write about, you probably won't enjoy yourself here much.

In the end, though, these are indeed period pieces, true to their time. They have a political and societal subtext, sure—how not?—and they will absolutely *not* reflect 21st-century tropes, political correctness, sensibilities, language and trigger-points. They were moderate in their day, not wild-eyed revolutionary, because that was how I was and how I wrote. It still is. But this is meant to present a picture of a time and a mindset that are gone, that I loved and still love, a time and a mindset that made the present possible. If you were there, you'll know. If you weren't, maybe it will help make the backward glance a little clearer.

This book covers roughly the same ground as *Strange Days* did. Both books were written so that people do not forget. But it was all for Jim and the truth, and out of love and fury, that I wrote *Days. ROCK CHICK* is more for me and the memories, and written out of love and wistfulness. I like the idea of making those long-gone days more accessible and more understandable to everyone who wasn't there for them. So that they can hear tales told around the campfire by someone who actually *was* there, tales about who we were and how we were thinking, how we felt when we first heard *Abbey Road* or *Morrison Hotel* or *Cheap Thrills* or *Volunteers*, to hear about what we wore and where we lived and what we did…to hear what it was like to be present at the creation with a front-row seat, to have been lucky enough to have had a small speaking part in it, and even a tiny bit of power, at a very young age.

I wouldn't trade it for anything.

Come Up the Years

Pop Talk was the monthly column I wrote. It was just a compilation of press release clips before I came to the magazine in February 1968—and it retained that nature and configuration for several issues thereafter, as we all found our feet. But then it started changing; and so, thank God, did I...

1971

"A critic...rock and roll critic...I don't know, that seems like a pretty nutso thing for anyone to be doing."

— Rob Tyner,
MC5

"I want to thank you for the article, which I consider to be the most brilliant, witty & amusing. ... Let me hear from you sometime. Please."

— Jim Morrison,
The Doors

"Why did you get into all this to begin with? Surely not just to meet musicians!"

Rennie smiled and patted his arm. "Couldn't care less about meeting musicians. I got into it because I wanted to meet the music."

— Patricia Morrison,
California Screamin': Murder at Monterey Pop

For the music

And the people who played it,
and the people who loved it

Jazz & Pop 4Ever!

I would guess that most of you who are here reading this have read at least some of my work before: my Keltiad science-fantasy series, or Strange Days: My Life With and Without Jim Morrison, *my memoir about Jim and me and our relationship/marriage, or my Rennie Stride rock and roll murder mysteries, or by now (or if not, then shortly), my Viking historical novel; or even just my online writing presence, in my website, Facebook and assorted blogs.*

But some of you might go back with me a lot farther than that, back to the writings in these pages, collected for the first time... and if not, if you weren't there for any of what follows, maybe you'll find something here to interest you, something you didn't know before.

Some people might call this merely a vanity production, me boasting of my youth in Arcadia, most excellently misspent, or well-spent, depending on how you look at it; and well, yeah, maybe, there might be a little of that—I really did enjoy myself tremendously, probably way too much, and I'm not going to pretend that I didn't.

But only a little of it: I prefer to perceive this book as a time capsule, preserving things that are gone, and as a personal life diary, chronicling days both strange and wondrous that are no longer with us—sadly, to my way of thinking—both simpler and far more complex than you could possibly imagine.

Because you people absolutely couldn't have what you have in 2013 without us having done all this stuff in 1968 and the handful of years before and after...so here it is, for you, as it was for me.

On the top floor of 1841 Broadway, an old beige-ish brick office building at the northwest corner of Broadway and West 60th Street, with the New York Coliseum across the street to the south and Central Park across the avenue to the east, were the offices of Jazz & Pop magazine.

Born in 1962 as Jazz, the brainchild of Pauline Rivelli, a longtime jazz aficionada and sometime songwriter with many, many industry connections and credits, the magazine was founded as the less stuffy counterweight to Downbeat, which for many years had been the official jazz publication of the music world. And for five years, Jazz counterweighed it, with a masthead and advisory board boasting great names. And then the music changed. And then Pauline changed the name to Jazz & Pop, to reflect that. And then I came to work there.

She's Leaving Home

But before I did any of that, I was a journalism student at St. Bonaventure University, way out in the hills of western New York State. SBU had a great journalism program, and it was one of the chief reasons I chose the school. I had considered Cornell and *their* journalism program, but the more I thought about it, the more I saw that a school like that wouldn't be the right fit for me: a huge, impersonal place with a lot of competition and little individual attention and, frankly, a lot of snobby legacy preppies looking down on my middle-class origins was not my idea of a great college experience.

I wasn't about to be a commuter, either, still living at home with parents and siblings—that would be just like high school, only harder, and I would have to drive, which I hated to do, and in fact I have never gotten a driver's license, from that day to this. No: I was getting the hell out, and I wanted someplace to get to that was small and old, someplace beautiful and rural, someplace tucked away among mountains, someplace where I would get the kind of personal attention and confidence-building care that a big school could never have given me—and the kind of classical-humanities education (Latin, Greek, languages, literature, history, philosophy) that at that date only a Catholic college and Oxbridge were still supplying. Oh, and of course it had to have a journalism department. And because of my Regents scholarship, it had to be in New York State. And to please my parents, it had to be Catholic. That pretty much narrowed it down to one place, and in September 1963, at the age of 17, that was where I headed.

Bona's is a small school in a lovely, wooded, deeply rural mountain valley setting, on the banks of the Allegheny River in the snow country of Cattaraugus County—the most beautiful place I've ever lived. With wonderful old Italianate tile-roofed brown-brick buildings, sixty miles south of Buffalo and a couple of miles from the Pennsylvania border, on the northern fringe of Appalachia, the school is just west of the small city of Olean, an old oil town, in a tiny village called Allegany. A Franciscan institution, founded in 1858, SBU had about 1,500 students when I was there, and it was 100% Catholic and 90% male—women, or "coeds" as we were called, had only started being admitted a few years before I arrived, and things were still shaking out.

As students, we had 8 a.m. classes. We had Saturday classes. We had 8 a.m. Saturday classes. And we shouldered *serious* course loads: in my freshman year alone, I coped with English literature, junior-year French, Latin, math (always my downfall), sociology, world history and theology; plus mandatory work on the school newspaper to satisfy the journalism major, formal classes in which didn't start till sophomore year, though we got personal coaching and hands-on experience from day one. Not a creampuff course in the bunch. And I even learned how to use a linotype machine—etaoin shrdlu lives!

Unlike high school, where I had had an extensive extracurricular life—newspaper columnist, yearbook literary editor, literary magazine editor-in-chief, National Honor Society, choir, student government, several different clubs and sports teams, so nerd *and* jock—in college I chose not to be a joiner, and at Bonaventure did pretty much nothing beyond my coursework and an active social life except for working on the newspaper, joining the Press Club for j-majors and pledging a sorority (Theta Lambda Chi! Rushrushrush!). Oh yes: I also founded and captained a rifle team for women students, which I had to fluently persuade paternalistic administration sorts as well as the campus military hierarchy (big ROTC presence) into allowing; learning to shoot was extremely satisfying, in several unexpected ways, and I enjoy it to this day. Other than that, I just lived in the library stacks and read my little heart out.

Bona's journalism department was a very small place back then: maybe fifteen or twenty students in each year. The vast majority of the professors were friars—it was a Franciscan school, after all, the hippies of the Catholic Church—though there were a few white male laypersons, and there was one woman on the faculty. One. Teaching philosophy (she was my apologetics and logic prof). And she was a Franciscan nun. (Known as either The Nun or Motormouth, depending on how you were feeling about her at the time.)

The j-school head was a civilian: Dr. Russell J. Jandoli. The only other prof in the department was capable but rather uninspired (and uninspiring). But Dr. J. was the goods, and today the Dr. Russell J. Jandoli School of Journalism and Mass Communication, with more than three hundred students and a whole splendid building of its own with state-of-the-art facilities, is one of the proudest boasts of the school, and rightly so.

A Notre Dame graduate, he had been a reporter for, among many other places, Time magazine; as a staffer for the Stars & Stripes military newspaper, he had been stationed on Kwajalein during World War II. After the war he had made his way to Bonaventure and founded this new and then-tiny department; he would be its head and guiding force for the next thirty-four years. But what he brought to the students who were lucky enough to be under his tutelage, and who universally adored him, was considerably more than just the nuts and bolts of journalism.

Without being preachy or arrogant or condescending, he called out in us the most admirable ideals of journalists: honor, courage, objectivity, dispassionateness in the heat of passionate tumult, outrage in the face of iniquity. He taught us how to observe and how to write down what we observed, how to listen to the inner voice that tells us what's important or what's not. He gave us the tools of our trade: organizing, structuring, editing, revising, proofing. People aren't taught like that anymore; times, and media, have changed too much.

I am proud to be a Jandoli journalist, and I was prouder still when the j-school dean, my old friend and colleague Lee Coppola, who'd been a senior when I was a freshman and is just recently retired, invited me back to be the Communications Day speaker in 2008, to give a speech to three hundred high-school future journalists—and staggered, not to mention profoundly humbled, when they gave me a standing ovation after. But the real tribute was to Dr. J: I was just paying forward a little in his name. I consider myself incredibly lucky to have been there to benefit from his presence, advice, teaching and example, and everyone who was likewise taught by him feels the same.

If I had to characterize myself as a journalist, I'd say I was born to be a feature writer; I guess because features are stories, and I've always loved stories — hence my novelist career. Features are reporting just as much as news pieces are, of course; they're just presented and told differently. If straight reporting is like being a witness and a prosecutor, feature writing is more like being the judge and jury. And occasionally the executioner.

I wrote all sorts of things when I was back there in journalism school, putting forth propositions (and prepositions) all over the place. Which is strange, my affinity for features, because I can't write short stories for anything, and that's really what features are. I've written only two so far in my whole life, and they are more novellas than short stories: everything else has been epic-length novels, songs, the occasional poem, commentary of various sorts, scripts, even one-liner ad copy. But a short story is the hardest fictional medium to write, requiring you to be well into the event even before the first sentence, *in medias res* — there's nowhere to hide — and it takes me about fifty pages just to get my typing fingers warmed up. Features require that same sort of organizational immediacy; you don't have the luxury of stretching out over a few expository chapters, you have to be right in there introducing your subject or subject person from word one. But for some reason it seems easier for me; I have no idea why.

I moved on from journalism long ago, of course, but my training has completely informed my writing from that day to this; you can see it especially in my memoir, as my British publisher once told me. And now, as a novelist, I tell stories all the time. Feature articles are true stories; sure, you can paint them any way you like, but beneath that, you have to be factual, just as you do in straight reportage. I always tried to be as truthful and accurate in my articles as I could, because that's being a good reporter, that's what I was there for—I owed it to my subjects, and I owed it to myself, as Dr. J. taught me. And even in my fiction I strive for accuracy and truth within the fictional framework. Because if it's not there, people notice. And judge you for it. And so they should.

The Other Side of This Life

I stayed at Bonaventure for only two years. Though I loved the school, and my friends (some of whom I'm friends with to this day), and more than anything the spectacularly beautiful location, the enforced Catholicism and petty restrictions (girls couldn't wear trousers on campus! Not even in the bitter winters of Western New York, when it was 20 below zero outside with three feet of lake-effect snow on the ground and a northwest wind that never quit and my stockings actually disintegrated on my legs once while I was walking home to the dorm!) were driving me mad.

Not to mention that the virulent hating sexism displayed to us by, yes, I'm sorry to say, some not inconsiderable proportion of the friars, who bitterly resented females coming into their little He-Man Woman-Haters Club, or possibly their Not-So-He-Man Boy-Lovers Club (coupled with the bullying we got from the guys, who then rather cluelessly turned around and wanted to *date* us...), was appalling.

By the time of my arrival, coeds had been at the school for only a few years, and things were still shaking out: my first semester, I had a friar history prof with a face like a fist who told one girl, who was sitting with her knees *slightly* apart and completely covered beneath a below-kneelength skirt, "Close the gates of hell, bitch!" And this same devoted servant of Jesus and St. Francis used me as a demonstration of high and low relief, putting me up in front of the appalled class next to the podium moving me forward and back, illustrating his point by how far my breasts jutted out past the podium line. All the upperclass girls warned incoming freshman girls about him, so it was well known among the students, and therefore must have been something the administration was aware of. Nowadays, of course, he would have been bounced out of there so fast it would have been a miracle of some sort, probably credited to a joint production of St. Joan of Arc and St. Philomena…not to mention sued. A true fell beast, a total pig, and a disgrace to his order. He was clearly among the most egregious offenders, but he was by no means alone.

Anyway, after two years I figured I had picked up enough journalism tricks to go on with. Also my then-fiancé had been expelled, so I transferred to Harpur College, in his hometown of Vestal, N.Y., near Binghamton. As it turned out, we broke off the engagement a year later; but even though Harpur (now Binghamton University) was a big new school, and fairly unlovely, and less rurally situated than Bona's, and lacked a journalism program — all these things I had said I didn't want, or had to have — transferring there was still the absolute best thing I could have done for my own personal development.

For one thing, I got to meet people who weren't like me. I had grown up in a white, Catholic, Irish-American middle-class bubble — with a not insignificant Sloane Ranger behavioral component added to the mix from Victorian great-grandparents, you'd think I'd been brought up by Mary Poppins — and Bonaventure had been a bubble of its own, full of people pretty much like me, though as soon as I got there I had ditched even lip service to the Catholicism I hadn't believed in since I was a beady-eyed six-year-old, wondering aloud why there were seven sacraments for men and only six for women, and getting my knuckles rapped for my brazen attitude.

At Harpur, I was surrounded by edgy, smart, driven kids from New York City. The fierce academic competitiveness was a problem, sort of, and so was the loneliness of the transfer student—I made very few friends, and no close ones, socializing mainly with my roommates and floormates and their circle and staying tight with the friends I'd had at Bonaventure, two of whom I moved in with in Manhattan after graduation. But by this point I'd decided I had better things to do than try to be top of the class, which considering the amount of work I was willing to put in—not more than strictly necessary—wasn't going to happen anyway. I figured if I stayed on the dean's list for four years, kept my scholarship and spent my time reading, that should be enough for my academic pride. And it was.

Harpur was a very politicized place in those days: I joined Students for a Democratic Society, SDS, as soon as I got there, which made me a radicalized sorority girl who knew how to shoot guns—it's a wonder I didn't end up like Patty Hearst. But it did open my eyes to a lot of things, and chiefest among them was rock and roll. I'd always been a folk-music fan, and a classical-music fan (symphonies mostly), but even though I was familiar with the dance music of the era (loved the Ventures, and Buddy), in my personal musical preference list, rock and roll had always come in a distant third.

By 1964 that had all started to change: with the Beatles, of course (whom I had heard for the first time in the Bonaventure snackbar, asked "*Who* is THAT?"—one of many such music-induced moments—and on receiving the information I immediately hopped a bus to the only music shop in Olean and bought three albums on the spot), but also with the other bands of the British Invasion—the Stones, the Kinks, the Hollies, the Zombies, all the rest of that early pantheon.

It was becoming rock now, not rock and roll: by the end of 1965, Dylan had gone electric, the Byrds had covered "Mr. Tambourine Man" (*huge* revelation, that was), the Stones and the Beatles were omnipresent, and bands like the Beau Brummels and the Four Seasons were new favorites (and remain so to this day). Then, in the fall of 1966, as I was beginning my senior year at Harpur, the current boyfriend dragged me to the Vestal mall for this newly released album he said I needed.

It was called *Jefferson Airplane Takes Off*. And so did I.

I don't think I can accurately convey to you just how hard that record hit me. From the first rumbling riff of Jack Casady's almighty bass on "Blues from an Airplane", it changed *everything*: my musical tastes, my attitudes, pretty much my whole LIFE. I had never heard anything like it; no one had. But that could be said of all the music you could hear around then. Every day there was something new and equally amazing, every week something better than the week before. And there hasn't been an output to even come close to it from those days to these.

Anyway, after that, there was no stopping me: *Rubber Soul* and *Revolver*, the first Cream album, *Aftermath* and *Between the Buttons*, the first two Byrds albums, *Surrealistic Pillow*, the first Doors album, the first Grateful Dead album, San Francisco bands like Quicksilver Messenger Service and this other one called Big Brother and the Holding Company, with a singer name of Janis Joplin... *SGT. PEPPER*...

Reader, I had become a rock chick.

Starry-Eyed and Laughing

And so *much* had I become a rock chick that I got a weekend job go-go dancing in front of bands in local Triple Cities roadhouses, which did wonders to further my musical education and even taught me a little rock guitar to add to the folk. Scorning the white boots and pastel-microdress go-go girl template that was prevalent across the land, I went Dark Side, wearing a black leather-look fringed bikini, black fishnets and black knee-high boots; I had hair down to my rear end and I looked like Zorro's kinky girlfriend. I loved it. (So did Jim, when I told him about it a few years later...)

I shared gigs with another Harpur girl (who danced in a long-sleeved leotard, so I leave it to you to judge who was the more popular with the mostly male, mostly drunk bar crowds), and we would switch off all night long, dancing half sets alternately with the band and to records so we each got a chance to dance to both. I helped her with her classwork essays, and in return she taught me how to bellydance...win-win.

I'd have made a terrible waitress, so as a part-time job this was *great*, and, I thought, a rather creative solution to the spending money problem—though I never told my parents, from that day to this, exactly *how* I supplemented my allowance. I'd bring my Shakespeare textbook or whatever so I could study between sets, sitting in a corner wearing a red-and-black buffalo plaid lumberjack shirt over my costume. The local married couple who booked us into the places chauffeured and chaperoned us, keeping the drunks away and making sure no one hit on us. Plus I made thirty bucks a night, which was six times my weekly allowance (yes, your math is correct: my college allowance was $5.00 a week—take *that*, millennials!), more if I danced both weekend nights, so it was a positively sumptuous income supplement, which enabled me to buy books, records and clothes.

And drugs.

It's become fashionable for people of my dowager boomer vintage to beat themselves up for their Sixties drug use, loudly bemoaning their weakness, or claiming they didn't inhale, or other such after-the-fact abasements (probably made only for the benefit of their children or grandchildren) that really don't fool anybody. Well, they can just put a sock in it. If they didn't enjoy themselves or get off on drugs, that was their own damn fault.

I did drugs from time to time, of course, just like everybody else I knew: I *tried* a lot of stuff, but I never *did* a lot, because it got very boring very quickly and I had better things to spend money on, like books, records and clothes. I pretty much limited my infrequent intake to weed, even though I hate smoking anything and have never in my life been a cigarette smoker. I tried mescaline and psilocybin once or twice, and would sometimes indulge in a bit of speed, or, later, coke or Quaaludes. Never acid and certainly never heroin. I used drugs as they were meant to be used: to have an occasional (as in a couple of times a month) bit of fun with. When they stopped being fun—the year 1979 comes to mind—I stopped doing them: just walked away and haven't done them since.

But in the early days of the music, it was extremely pleasant to roll a joint, pass it around amongst your friends and just happily zonk out listening to the Airplane or the Byrds or the Stones or even (my roommate's choice, God help me) Leonard friggin' Cohen—who sounded like Eeyore on acid and whose muddy nasal monotone never failed to pitch me straight into unconsciousness, like getting pistol-whipped by a sloth. But a nice companionable buzz was all we were ever looking for. Sure, there were people even then who were looking for other things, moods that nastier drugs could supply; we tended to scorn them. We treated pot like beer, as opposed to hard liquor: mellowing, not serious as long as you didn't abuse it. We didn't drink a couple of sixpacks every single day and we didn't do a lid of grass every single day either. If some people did, well, that was their business.

To paraphrase dear Mr. Keith Richards: I didn't have a problem with drugs, I had a problem with the people who had a problem with drugs.

It's not like that now, of course. These days I hear that if you take two tokes on the kind of supercharged industrial-strength joint that's the most common kind of grass available (unless you grow your kindlier and milder own), you're tripping for a week. Which was never the point of grass at *all*. And there are so many prescription drugs to abuse that addictive personalities are positively spoilt for choice.

For myself, I don't feel even the tiniest twinge of a wish to indulge in illicit substances again, though many of my friends and colleagues still do so (and then they hypocritically yell at their kids and grandkids for wanting to try a joint)—been there, done it. But neither do I feel the need or the desire to self-flagellate about my past use. It is what it was, and I'm neither sorry nor proud (well, perhaps more proudly amused than sorry...). And certainly not apologetic or ashamed, so anyone who thinks I ought to be either is herewith offered the option of biting me.

I graduated from Harpur in June of 1967, B.A. in hand. It was the height of the Summer of Love, and there was some talk of driving out to San Francisco with friends to join in, but in the end I decided not. So I went back to my parents' house for the summer, got a typical English major's job in the city and started looking for a suitable apartment to move into with two sorority sisters from Bonaventure, which we did in the fall, to West 15th Street (two blocks from hip hangout Max's Kansas City). And also I started looking for a gig in rock and roll.

Get A Job, Sha-Na-Na-Na

In August 1967, I saw my first issue of Jazz & Pop magazine on a newsstand in the building where I then worked, Crowell Collier Macmillan Publishing, over on Third Avenue and 53rd Street. Macmillan was my first straight-world job (go-go dancing didn't make the résumé), and I was working as the editorial assistant to the director of a children's dictionary project, for the princely sum of $65 a week.

The magazine, with its bright sunflower-power cover, caught my eye immediately, and as it turned out, that was the first issue of Jazz & Pop ever; that very month was the month it went over from Jazz to Jazz & Pop. Oooooh, karma! But that proved well for me, because if it had been just Jazz magazine, as it had been only the month before, I would never have looked at it twice and would never in a million years have bought it. But I did. I grabbed it and dashed upstairs to my little cubicle and positively devoured it: it had stories all about the progressive rock I had loved for several years by then, and I fell in love with the magazine on the spot.

In fact, so swooningly enamored was I with it — its terrific stories, its reviews of records I loved, its clean graphics — that I sat down and composed a letter to Pauline Rivelli, the editor and publisher. A *woman* editor and publisher — surely a good sign, I thought hopefully. My basic message, though I managed to phrase it a bit more elegantly, was "Please let me come and work for you oh pleasepleasepleeeeease! You won't be sorry! I'll be terrific! I promise! You'll see!" I sent it off, crossed my fingers, and sat back to await a response.

It took a few months. But it came. And in February 1968, I was hired. It seemed like magic. And perhaps it was.

When I arrived to start my new and thrilling gig as editorial assistant, fully aware that I had landed the job of my and everybody else's dreams and was the envy of absolutely everyone I knew, so excited that I couldn't sleep the night before, the magazine was just three people including me, all of them female—a monthly, slick, hip music magazine produced entirely by women, for a readership about 90% male. The girl I was replacing, who didn't write and who was leaving to get married, stayed on a while to show me the ropes and serve as receptionist until Pauline hired a new one. I was twenty-one.

The new receptionist was eighteen. She was the hip and delightful Laura Roberts, and also served as our subscription manager, though we all turned a hand to whatever needed doing. She'd lived in New Orleans, and her mother, Susan Roberts, wrote books on psychic phenomena. Two years later, Laura married her live-in boyfriend, bass player Stu Woods; he was in a band called Brethren, which played the Fillmore East, and subsequently became a much sought-after session player, which he is to this day, having appeared on many albums and in bands of his own.

Other people would come along over the course of the next three years. Janice Coughlan, several years older than I and a Boston native with a wry sense of humor—and a fellow *Dune* fan—was hired to be publisher's assistant and our staff photographer. Terry Towne, daughter of the publisher of one of the music-biz trades, joined us as our advertising manager and sometime interviewer (she and I went to talk to Elton John and Bernie Taupin together on their first tour here—a very odd, though entertaining, afternoon).

And then, of course, there was Pauline Rivelli. Tallish, with short dark hair and a very New York attitude. She had grown up in Little Italy, so naturally we immediately nicknamed her "Pauline Ravioli"; her occasional writing pseudonym—we all used them from time to time, generally to hide our shameful favoritism, though I doubt anyone was ever fooled—was "Ringo Pasta". Pauline never gave away much of herself: she was born in 1929, only eight years my mother's junior, my youngest aunt's age, seventeen years older than I; but she certainly didn't seem to be their contemporary, and in fact we all put her at least ten years younger. Because she seemed a *lot* younger, from a whole other generation than they. Or at least half generation. Every now and then, she'd share a story of her youth, or her life, and they were always funny, warm ones, so that we'd be curious to hear more; but for the most part she kept her own counsel.

Jazz magazine, and then Jazz & Pop, was her dream accomplished. She was a jazz baby at heart, but was smart enough to see the writing on the wall and change her tune accordingly, falling completely in love with the new rock. She'd loved music her whole life: she was a published songwriter, a member of NARAS (the National Association of Recording Arts & Sciences, the Academy of the music biz), and her acquaintance in the field included giants. Execs and legendary talent discoverers like John Hammond, Clive Davis, Ahmet Ertegun; artists like John and Alice Coltrane, B. B. King, Janis Joplin, Nina Simone…Pauline knew them all, and they knew and respected her.

And so did we. The full force of the feminist movement was still a few years from cresting, but young women of my particular vintage sensed that we were already part of the gathering tsunami. Except for the real radical firebrands, people like the late Shulamith Firestone and others of her ilk, we didn't think about it in feminist terms, not yet; it was just us, just doing what we did, no big deal. Except it was. And women like Pauline were the ones who started it. By example and by policy, she was a role model for me: a mentor, perhaps the strongest one of my life. She showed me that it was possible to get what you wanted, and taught me how to go about it: not by bitching or whining or complaining, but simply by going after it until either you got it or you didn't; and if you didn't, you would just figure out another approach and try again. But you certainly didn't take no for an answer, and surprisingly often the universe responded and said yes.

After Jazz & Pop folded in 1971, not long after I left, Pauline started up another music magazine, Words & Music; then she went to work at WEA, Warner-Elektra-Atlantic, the corporate amalgam of three separate label giants that would, along with the CBS empire, come to dominate the 70's musical scene. I lost track of her after that; then, after *Strange Days* was published, I got a letter from her via my publishers, full of warm praise and affection and reminiscences.

She was in Miami Beach, working as a publicity director first for a hotel chain and then for the Chamber of Commerce, and living with a long-term boyfriend; she seemed happy to be done with music. I instantly phoned her, but she wasn't home; the next day, Hurricane Andrew hit and communications were out for weeks. We finally connected a couple of months later, and kept up casual contact over the intervening years: birthday cards, Christmas cards, the occasional phone call.

Pauline died in 2010. I don't know any details. We didn't always see eye to eye about stuff, and sometimes she drove me crazy with micromanagement, not to mention strange and unaccountable decisions that on occasions superseded my authority as editor or just plain personally pissed me off. But I do know that without her in my life, as boss and mentor and friend, I would never have had the chance to do what I did or have the life I've had. Dear Pauline Ravioli, thank you and rock on forever.

Places I Remember

1841 Broadway was a fun place to work. I could take the RR train from the East Village and be there in twenty minutes on a good morning, and after work I could even afford the occasional cab home on evenings when I was really tired — the fare back then, for a straight-shot trip down Broadway, was about two bucks door to door, plus tip (it's more than twenty now, and thanks to the tiny dictator Mayor Michael Bloomberg you can't even drive straight down Broadway anymore, because of all his stupid little carbon-monoxide-riddled "plazas" that only tourists ever sit in…).

There was a terrific old-school coffee shop on the ground floor (now a Starbucks, of course…), and I ate there pretty much every day. My unvarying takeout breakfast was rye toast well done and a large Coke with ice (hey, caffeine is caffeine, right?, and I detest the taste of coffee) and my usual takeout lunch was a grilled ham and cheese sandwich; they would shout out the short-order lingo as soon as I walked in the side door by the counter — whisky down, scratch one, Dutch combo.

Downstairs on the second floor and several others was Atlantic Records (where I and several other guests were once entertained to a private luncheon with Eric Clapton, Delaney and Bonnie, and Atlantic president Ahmet Ertegun); around the corner at 1855 Broadway, and later in the brand-new Gulf + Western building that we watched going up across the street, between us and the park, was Elektra, label of the Doors, Love and Judy Collins. Other record companies were nearby, there were several public relations outfits within walking distance and the building had other music-biz tenants as well.

There wasn't much else around—you had to walk four or five blocks for any kind of real shopping or dining, though it was pleasant having Central Park so close. Between 60th and 61st on Broadway was a Chock Full O' Nuts, where I sometimes varied my lunch preferences with a great and cheap cheeseburger, and next door to it in the Elektra building was a Capezio boutique, where I bought shoes and dresses (there was another downtown on Macdougal Street that also saw my custom). Two blocks down Broadway was the delightfully wacky Huntington Hartford Gallery of Modern Art—a white-marble structure with no windows, Venetian/Mayan detailing and a top-story loggia with portholes, by the architect Edward Durrell Stone, who was apparently on drugs, and good ones too, when he designed it.

Our own building was nothing like so posh or pedigreed: a classic Manhattan office structure of 1920s vintage, though it did have, pleasingly, nice trim and actual crenelations up top. J&P's offices consisted of a suite of three largish, interconnecting, dingy rooms on the top floor, the twelfth, with those pebble-glass-windowed doors. They had the feeling of some rather seedy private eye's offices from a Thirties noir film, probably because they hadn't been redecorated since then. The ladies' room was on the next floor down, and to get there you had to go out on the outside fire stairs, which was more horrible than you can imagine. It wasn't a fire escape, which would have been totally terrifying, but bad enough: an open staircase, so you went out onto an exposed wind-tunnel section that was protected from a twelve-story plunge only by some iron railings, then back inside to the stair part. I soon learned not to pee at work unless I really, really had to (which iron-bladder discipline would later serve me well at Woodstock).

Despite our altitude, we didn't have much of a view — those cool crenelations and the Coliseum across the street got in the way — though we did have a fine expanse of northern sky to contemplate. My office was cozy and private, with its own door out to the hall. I had a really nice old oak desk and an oldish Royal upright manual typewriter on a metal stand; the wall behind me had a corkboard and rock posters all over it, while shelves with magazine back stock, shipping materials and other detritus took up the facing wall, along with two filing cabinets full of photos. Pauline had the end office, the biggest of the three rooms. The middle room was Laura's domain: besides her desk, it contained the big tables from which we shipped out the magazines every month, as up until almost the end of my three years there we did all our own subscription fulfillment — though the building super was the one who actually lugged the heavy mail sacks full of issues downstairs and down the block to the post office. But we ran out labels from little drawers of metal stamps with subscribers' addresses, and stuffed envelopes with the current ish, and sealed and postage-metered and labeled them up, all by hand.

We were modestly successful financially, in repute more so: we had a paying subscription list of considerable size, and we sold about twice as many more copies on newsstands; also we comped almost everybody in the music biz — musicians, managers, publicists, label execs, venue owners, record and music store personnel, anyone with any kind of connection whatsoever to rock or jazz. Our masthead boasted some extremely impressive names as advisors, contributing editors, consultants and such, and most of them did actual writing. Much of it gratis, though we did manage to pay small honorariums to the regulars, among whom were people like Ralph J. Gleason and Nat Hentoff.

And that was it, just the three of us, until Pauline took on Janice, Terry and an art director, Louis Queralt, first guy on staff. Though I still didn't take any chances: I continued to push my input whenever I could, though I failed miserably on two occasions, when Pauline and Lou insisted on using to draw the cover art a certain cartoonist who shall be nameless here. His cover for the October 1970 issue was beyond dreadful; but his drawing of Judy Collins for the December 1970 issue was so unbelievably ghastly that her label president personally called me to ask what the hell had I been thinking and to let me know that Judy was furious, as well she might be.

I confessed my agreement, appallment and shame, and offered humble apologies to Ms. Collins, whom I greatly admired, and to the label chief, whom I liked, but disclaimed all responsibility. I had fought as hard as I could to kill the horrible thing, but ultimately it was Pauline's magazine, she was the publisher—what could I do? She seemed to have some weird idea that this guy was terrific and would not be told differently, as she used his godawful work several more times, though, thankfully, only after I had moved on. Good thing that I had insisted on personally designing Jim's own cover appearance on the September 1970 issue; there might have been bloodshed otherwise.

At the end of 1968, Pauline, wanting to concentrate on the publishing end of things, appointed me as editor. Even with my sumptuous raise ($150 a week! $200 the next year!) and grand new title (which did look so nice on the masthead, a journalism dream achieved), I decided to stay in my own office, initially, rather than shift to Pauline's bigger one. She had moved across the hall to two rooms, one of which was her office and the other of which became our all-purpose room: layout space for the art director, the fulfillment division (a mailing table and storage for issues and mail sacks), and an area for Janice. Eventually I did relocate to the big office vacated by Pauline, and Terry, who had had a desk in Laura's middle room, moved into my old digs. But as it turned out, as fate was working up to it, I wouldn't be there for very much longer.

Well, You've Got Your Diamonds and You've Got Your Pretty Clothes

This is the clothes porn/jewel porn section. Guys might want to skip over…you have been warned.

It being rock and roll, of course, we could dress as we pleased for work. Pauline, not that into clothes, generally wore more business-y attire than the rest of us, mostly neat pantsuits or trousers (never jeans!) with pretty blouses and long vests, and in winter a big, elegant Russian-looking fur hat; Janice emulated her to a lesser degree of formality, Laura and Terry were more casual-hippie.

But I, who had never had much money for really cool threads before, had somehow, and quite surprisingly, turned into something of a clotheshorse, and I was having a ball going all rich-hippie, or at least as rich as I could afford. I didn't have a vast wardrobe in high school, though I always looked nice in my wool pleated skirts and big mohair sweaters, and of course in convent school as a child (Our Lady of Perpetual Help Academy, in Queens) it had been a fetching little navy-blue uniform jumper and white blouse. But once I was in college I dressed quite well and hiply and did my thrifty best, designing and making a lot of my own clothes, like my character Rennie Stride, to compensate for what I coveted and couldn't manage to buy.

As a junior-year boyfriend (who introduced me to the Fugs, taking me to see them at the Café Wha? in the summer of 1966, and I want to say I caught Hendrix there too, when he was still Jimmy James, but I'm not sure of that) told me, you can't keep a creative person down, and whether it was writing or sewing clothes, I very early learned how to make creativity serve my needs. I never did learn to build a closet that worked together, though, the way all the fashion mags tell you that Frenchwomen do: every piece was a star unto itself, and that was how I liked it.

Those were the days of good-quality, ridiculously inexpensive, wildly creative clothing. I rejoiced in owning dresses by Betsey Johnson for Paraphernalia, shoes by Allan Block and Capezio and Olofdaughters, leather thighboots from St. Marks Leather, Young Edwardian/Arpeja Empire-waisted muslin frocks, an embroidered sheepskin Afghan coat (shades of *Almost Famous!*), gray pigskin gaucho pants, a minidress with white peace symbols the size of silver-dollar pancakes printed all over it (every chick in the scene, even Janis Joplin, had that dress), brown leather culottes with a big bronze buckle, gold leather jeans from the Stitching Horse, bellbottoms in various fabrics, a cavalry-buttoned cream maxicoat in heavy cotton and a gray twill one as well, assorted poet shirts and Romanian peasant blouses, some of them see-through and worn braless, big floppy hats, skirts in all lengths — micro and mini and midi and maxi and floor-sweeper.

Most of my rather preppy college attire — madras shifts, Oxford-cloth button-down shirts, corduroy smocks, A-line dresses, tartan kilts worn with kneesocks and loafers and cardies — was completely unsuited to my new line of work, though my last two years at school had seen the stealth arrival in my closet of ruffled-neckline granny dresses and batik-print elephant bells and skin-tight jeans and denim minis (if the hem didn't clear my palm with my arm held at my side, the skirt was too long and must be taken up immediately) worn with skimpy, close-fitting ribbed poor-boy tops.

Clothes from England, too. That was how people dressed in New York, more London than L.A.: hip new designers like Annacat and Ossie Clark and Alice Pollock and Jeff Banks and Biba; later on, as I grew more prosperous, upscaling to Gina Fratini and Annabelinda. My favorite outfit was the one I chose to wear to meet Jim for the first time: a micro-length dark-gold velour tunic with long, loose sleeves, worn over shiny brown leather pants and cocoa suede boots, with a long gold chain and tigereye scarab drop earrings bought at a jeweler's shop in Olean; my favorite dress, which came along a bit later, was the Gina Fratini confection on the jacket of *Strange Days*.

Even though by then I could afford to buy a lot of the clothes I coveted, I still sewed for myself, designing and adapting patterns and then buying the makings at the many fabric, button and trim stores that lined First Avenue in my neighborhood at the time: a brown paisley rayon pantsuit with Mao collar, inspired by Grace Slick's outfit on *Surrealistic Pillow* (I proudly wore it to see the Airplane at the Café Au Go-Go in early 1967); a gold buckskin jacket with silver conchos instead of buttons; a floor-length skirt of maroon crushed velvet worn with a satin shirt and a belted brown leather vest; a dolly-girl minidress of black Liberty cotton, with a print of white flower sprigs and wide white lace embroidery bands at hem and cuffs; the de rigueur Joplinesque tunic and pants made from two lace tablecloths; a brown velvet Cossack shirt and microskirt; a cream leather outfit that consisted of a deeply scoopnecked sleeveless top, fastened across my C-cup bralessness by a single faille frog, and matching hiphugger pants, worn to the Doors party at the Hilton after the Felt Forum shows in January 1970; leather and snakeskin and suede bags with beaded fringe right down to the floor.

I gave a lot of these outfits, both made and store-bought, to Rennie in the various rock mystery novels—my way of memorializing them, since I didn't keep more than a few, tucked away in my old college trunk. But they've held up beautifully, which is more than today's cheapo fashions from H&M and suchlike places will be doing forty years hence.

I didn't have much jewelry in those days—deeply ironic, in light of how *that* was to play out. In addition to my high-school and college class rings and sorority pin and aquamarine birthstone ring, a gold watch that was a graduation gift from my parents and a delicate gold cross my grandma had given me (which, much as I loved her, as a nascent Pagan I just couldn't bring myself to wear), I owned a silver expansion ID bracelet which had been a gift for my seventh birthday, some Celtic knotwork silver pieces, three or four rings, several strands of beads, a couple of pendants.

I'd had my ears pierced in 1964, and by this time I possessed about three dozen pairs of dollar earrings from my favorite earring store on Bleecker Street, near MacDougal: huge delicate silver hoops that reached my collarbone (I was always putting my hand right through them brushing my hair), black wooden circles, small drops set with coral or turquoise. Plus a few pairs of better ones— heavily carved silver crescent hoops, jade beads in a cage of twisted silver wire (a nineteenth-birthday gift from sorority sisters Susie Donoghue and Noreen Shanfelter), plain gold studs, filigree shoulderdusters set with citrines (another gift from Noreen), bellydance earrings of many long gold chains that I'd worn for my go-go gig, the aforementioned tigereye scarabs. I still own just about all this stuff, being of a dragonish nature and tending to hoard, though a lot of the cheap earrings have somehow vanished.

After Jim entered the picture, of course, the carat count zoomed into the stratosphere, in quality and quantity alike. He was incredibly generous and his taste in jewels was superb: an Art Deco engagement ring set with an emerald the size of his thumbnail, a diamond crossover wedding ring, the stunning mid-Victorian aquamarine and diamond suite that was my chief wedding present from him, a gold charm bracelet, an enormous opal heart pendant the size of my palm, engraved on the gold back in his own handwriting *For my wife/My Patricia/I love you/Jim*; a bunch more, some costly, some just sweetly thoughtful—wooden hairsticks bought after dinner in Chinatown, a fancy Spanish comb to hold up my auburn tresses.

Their value to me has nothing to do with price: they are all priceless—treasured gifts of love—and are all safely kept in a bank vault, along with his private edition books and the poems and letters he also gave me.

It was the heyday of vintage, too: every weekend you'd go out scouting the many little thrift and antique shops in both Villages, or even sometimes venture uptown to Yorkville and thereabouts for charity-shop designer stuff you could tart up. I found the lace tablecloths for my Janis-style pantsuit in one such shop—probably not the fate that the original owner had envisioned for them when she consigned them there. One of everybody's favorite places was the Ridge Trading Company warehouse, over on Bond Street, for inexpensive vintage furs in very good condition: I bought my first fur there, a glossy black French lapin coat (bunny fur!). I put a big fancy single button at the standup collar and wore it until it fell apart—Jimi Hendrix, encountering me swathed in it at a press party one night, called me Venus in Furs. (Many years later, I'm happy to say, I was able to replace it in black mink—thanks to Oliver Stone. But that's another story…)

Five O'Clock (A.M.) World

A typical day would involve some work on my Pop Talk column, proofreading the long galleys when they arrived from the printer, jotting down ideas and a wish list for the next few issues, phoning up publicists at labels or agencies for photos to go with the articles they'd persuaded us to run on acts of theirs, wrangling Fillmore East tickets for the upcoming weekend, helping Pauline paste up mechanicals or crop photos, helping Laura and Janice do the subscription run if the magazines were due to go out, assigning records to our assorted freelancers to review, trying to score a big interview with a big group (the horse-trading was incredible: you'd get the superstar you wanted to talk to, but you had to agree to do a couple of stories on unknowns to pay for it). Being the editor of the magazine precluded me from freelancing in other magazines or newspapers, which was sad, as I would have liked to maybe branch out a bit, but on the whole I was quite content to be where I was, and to stay there.

Often we'd have visitors: writer and friend Ellen Sander would pop in regularly to deliver her column "Rapport"; Linda Eastman (pre-McCartney) came up several times in my early days to drop off photos—I have a vivid memory of her in my office, handing Brian Jones pics to me across my desk and chatting amiably for an hour or so; Jim, of course, once we started up together; other writers and musicians and family and friends as well.

After work, there was invariably something to do every night of the week, often well into the wee small hours: a press party at a club or restaurant, which might or might not include a performance, or some act would be playing at Carnegie Hall or the Fillmore East or Lincoln Center, or there was a screening for a movie, or maybe a band would be recording and there would be an invitation to hang out with them in the studio (considerably less exciting than it sounds, trust me).

There was always something happening that would oblige me to keep rocknroll hours, albeit modest ones, and Pauline understood the need to sleep in after the occasional five a.m. revel, but Friday and Saturday nights were sacred to the Fillmore East; I was there just about every weekend, except if I really didn't like any of the bands on tap. And sometimes it was nice to just go home and read quietly and eat takeout Chinese food by myself, from the cheapo Chinese restaurant of choice on Second Avenue and Seventh Street, Sing Wu, with five-inch-high chocolate cream pie for dessert, from Ratner's right next door to the Fillmore East.

But all in all, I was a very lucky girl and I knew it, and was profoundly grateful.

I decorated my office (and my new East Village apartment) with the colorful music posters I bought in Village shops, or that record companies sent me. I still have many of them: among my prize possessions are two original Jim Morrison Film Festival posters that the Canadian rock magazine Poppin printed up to publicize the festival, which it had sponsored and which featured a showing of Jim's personally produced 16mm film *HWY* — one signed to me by Jim, when he saw it on my office wall, with a little drawing appended.

There's also a wonderful Jefferson Airplane poster for a Fillmore East gig — Egyptian-style graphics, with the group standing on the top wing of a biplane, dressed as Pharaonic royalty holding guitars and tambourines and hash pipes. One of my other favorites is a poster for a New Year's Eve concert at the Avalon, with a fantastic galleon labeled 1967 sailing off into the sunset through Hokusai-style waves, but I only bought that one for the gorgeous artwork; I mainly stuck to Doors and Airplane posters. I also have a rather bittersweet trophy: an original poster from the closing of the Fillmore East, a very simple listing, in chronological order, of all the acts that ever played there, in typical Thirties-style graphics — though someone got the order wrong for the Doors' supporting acts. Now, of course, the posters are all wildly collectible.

Strangely, we didn't have a stereo in the office, which seems odd now that I think of it but didn't bother me or any of the rest of us at the time. I did all my music listening at home, on a component system I'd selected with advice from the owner of Manny's Music, who was a friend of the magazine, and I wired it up myself: Dual turntable, Fisher tuner, huge wood-encased KLH 17 speakers which weighed a ton apiece (and which I still have — the sound is superb), souped-up cartridge and headshell, Sennheiser 'phones. At over $500, it was the most expensive thing I'd ever bought, apart from my college education; but it was a professional necessity. On one solo New York stay at the Navarro Hotel two blocks east of the J&P office, Jim had bought himself a little record player at Sam Goody's just to have something to listen to while here — label execs had given him about twenty albums, including his favorite of the bunch, the soundtrack to the film Z — and he very sweetly offered the stereo to us on his departure, so that finally we could have some music while we worked…

Since absolute power corrupts, absolutely!, I enjoyed exercising it by getting people I knew into the magazine to review and interview. So my sorority sisters and close friends from Bonaventure j-school, Noreen Shanfelter and my roommate Susan Donoghue, were drafted first; later, my then-boyfriend and very shortly thereafter ex-boyfriend David Walley, who also wrote for the East Village Other and assorted other undergrounds, and was by far the most politically minded person I knew (and generally the most stoned as well).

But our big score was when David brought us *his* roommate, from Rutgers University, the gifted and musically knowledgeable Lenny Kaye, who looked like a very cute, very tall and very longhaired saluki and who became one of our best writers—and later, of course, a rock star himself. Lenny wrote tons of stuff for us, including a cover-story interview with Arthur Lee of Love, but his crowning effort was a long, brilliant, beautifully done piece on a cappella doo-wop music that a young New York poet named Patti Smith happened to read and flip over. (The idea of an unknown Patti Smith reading Jazz & Pop is still, even at this late date, mind-boggling…) She contacted Lenny at his day job in an oldies record store, and the rest is history. So I'm responsible for the Patti Smith Group, sort of. What *are* First Causes, anyway?

But Patti had this intellectual (and perhaps not entirely so) crush on Jim, though she was never to meet him in person, and so I fought shy of going to see the PSG play in the early days, because…well, you know, because. I finally saw them in concert for the first time, at the Wiltern Theater in L.A. a few years back, and I was knocked out (and moved to tears by "Ghost Dance" and "Gone Again").

When I went backstage after, with my hosts Steve Hochman, then a rock critic at the Los Angeles Times, and his wife, my dearest friend ever the late Mary Herczog (author of several Frommer's guides and a wonderful novel called *Figures of Echo*), Lenny, that sweet man, welcomed me with open arms, a big hug and "There's the woman who gave me my start in rock and roll!" Right there in front of Patti and Michael Stipe and God and everybody. I was so proud.

Absolute power also corrupts in that it lets you play favorites. And did we ever. Not being a weekly or biweekly newspaper like the Village Voice or the East Village Other or Rolling Stone—more timely and ostensibly more hard news-oriented, by virtue of their more frequent appearance—we could allow ourselves the luxury of mostly just writing about people we liked, or that our readership liked, or that we wanted them to like, and we each had our own favorites. The Doors and the Airplane for me, of course, while Pauline was devoted to the Mothers of Invention and her friend Frank Zappa (whose work, apart from "Trouble Comin' Every Day", which I really liked, I could not stand at any price), and we all adored Janis and Big Brother.

We had writers who were big Beatles fans, but not so much the Stones, for some unknown reason; in my entire tenure there was only one cover story on the unmossy ones, in April of 1968, featuring one of Linda Eastman's Brian Jones photographs, taken on that notorious cruise around Manhattan Island that she'd bluffed her way onto. For all my devotion, Jim graced only one cover (the most beautiful one we ever had, and no, not just because it was him), and the Doors as a group never had one; the Airplane got one group cover, in 1950's lounge-act gear, while Grace Slick and Paul Kantner later each got separate solo covers; Janis and Jimi got one apiece, while the Beatles had one of all four of them, John and Paul shared one, and Paul had one to himself. (I don't have permission to publish the covers here, unfortunately, but they can all be seen on my Facebook and MySpace pages…URLs on copyright page.)

Besides the usual suspects, we covered lots of bands and artists who didn't get much press elsewhere, or at least not yet: Randy Newman; Amboy Dukes; Alvin Lee; Elvin Jones; Van Morrison (a great interview by Danny Goldberg, later Kurt Cobain's manager and president of Atlantic Records, in which Van wonders pessimistically if his new single is really any good after all—a little thing he just tossed off called "Brown-Eyed Girl"!); Ian Anderson; Roberta Flack. Contributing editor Jay Ruby did a brilliant one with Donovan; David Walley ditto with Iggy Stooge, as he then was, and another with the entire MC5, which last piece I consider a classic of Sixties rock journalism (you can find it online). Jazzmen and bluesmen too: T-Bone Walker, Muddy Waters, B.B. King, Larry Coryell, Tony Williams, Pharaoh Sanders, Jean-Luc Ponty, Gary Burton.

Anyway, we gave our pet sounds as much ink as we felt we could get away with. Thankfully, our audience was as enamored of those bands as we were ourselves, so apart from the odd cranky letter to the editor, we never got flak for it.

Besides all the usual articles and interviews and reviews, Jazz & Pop ran two polls every year, and a colossal amount of work they were, too: the Critics' Poll results ran in the February issue, and the Readers' Poll ones in the May issue. Just about every critic around participated, from Vince Aletti to Ritchie Yorke; in fact, Robert Christgau, who every year offered suggestions for tweaking the voting procedures, usually in hopes of benefiting his own favorite bands, finally instituted his own poll in the Village Voice, his chief vehicle at the time, where he could make his own voting rules, and called it the Pazz & Jop Poll in commemoration. I voted for rock people in jazz categories, and vice versa, just to make some kind of quixotic point about how categories were all bogus anyway.

We had a very loyal readership that was much engaged in what we were doing. Especially for a magazine created and published entirely by chicks for an audience that was mostly guys: clearly we were doing something right. The people who wrote for us were mostly guys as well, so perhaps that had a lot to do with it. I was the chief female writer, and for a while, till Ellen Sander came on board, the only female columnist, though Pauline would occasionally kick in a review, interview or editorial. When Janice and Terry joined the staff, they too did reviews, and Susie and Noreen, and later three or four more, but that was about it. For some reason, the few other female rock writers around never appeared in our pages, perhaps because they had regular gigs that prevented it. It seems strange now that they didn't, but I don't remember really thinking it weird at the time, so there it was.

Our other reviewers and writers came from all over the musical lot. Pauline had a cadre of old jazz guys who stayed on once she'd made the switch to "& Pop", though some purists huffed off in high dudgeon rather than betray their noble jazz principles to this horrible new devil music and the talentless yetis who played it—which was fine with me (and the talentless yetis as well). All of the remaining dudes were older than I and my cohort: many of them were college academics of one stripe or another; most were delightful and loved rock with a passion; several were sour, sexist, over-politicized grouches only interested in their stale political agendas and how to torture the music into backing those up.

More of my own connections signed up for the trip: enthusiastic, good writers, well-informed musically; also cheap. We didn't pay reviewers much, if anything, though the gig came with free records, concert tickets and byline glory, though sometimes big, long reviews were worth ten dollars or more a shot. Of course, they could always take the vast quantities of records down to Sam Goody's or local record stores and sell them—a favorite source of supplemental income for undergrounders. I dumped a lot of stuff there myself: you wouldn't believe how many albums were tossed out on an unsuspecting world, in hopes that something, anything, would catch the public's fickle ear—though you always got more for a record if it didn't have PROMOTIONAL COPY stamped on it, even if your friends thought that was really really cool.

Then we started hearing from young rock critics beginning to make reputations elsewhere. I had a memorable phone call (collect!) from someone by the name of Lester Bangs, asking if he could review for us, but by the time he got around to asking I was just about ready to move on from the magazine, so I don't know if he ever phoned back or wrote anything for it. But others did: a twenty-year-old kid named Dave Marsh, for one, just getting started on his rock-writing career, and of course our good friend the ever-radical head of the White Panther Party, John Sinclair, who reviewed for us from his prison cell, where he was draconically incarcerated for ten years for having been found in possession of two (2) joints, and for whom Lennon and Ono played benefits.

We loved John, and he loved us. I never touched a word of his copy, not because I'd been told not to (which I hadn't) but because I knew it didn't need it, and I wouldn't have dreamed of it anyway. His stuff was great just as it was.

❖

Which couldn't always be said for all of the carryovers from the Jazz days. There were a few hissy fits, and as I said a few 'graphs up, some of the hissers flounced away never to return. But others came along, attracted by the format and the easy-going style: we didn't have the Byzantine power struggles that went on at other publications, and the only politics on tap was the liberal variety that we all espoused. We worked for Senator Robert Kennedy's 1968 Presidential run—hooking the campaign up with supportive artists, labels and promoters—and were devastated at his assassination. Pauline always claimed we were on Nixon's media enemies list, but I don't know if that was true, though of course I'd love to think so. Still, perhaps we were on an enemies list of some sort, as there were several strange little episodes apparently caused by our political slant (including my sister being delayed in getting security clearance for a government job, by a gimlet-eyed inquisitor who wanted to know what her sibling was up to these days), which made us very proud indeed.

Hound Dogs

Which brings us to the issue of sexism in rock, which I later address in the Pop Talk column "Rock Around the Cock". Well…I have to say that major sexism certainly existed in rock, as it did in the world at large at that time, and it certainly annoyed me whenever I encountered it up close and personal. It grew fatiguing having to prove your intellectual cred with some rock guy when all he was trying to do was find out, like any other guy, if he could possibly maybe interest you at some point into letting him get into your pants; but I also have to say in all honesty that I really didn't run into anywhere near as much of it as many other young women did who weren't in my line of work, and the guys weren't anywhere near as obnoxious as you might have expected.

Paradoxically, and contradictorily, rock was both a freeing environment for women and an oppressive one, sometimes both at the same time. Sure, you ran into leering, groping sleazebags in the music biz, just as you would in any other male-dominated industry. And sure, it was pretty insulting to hear Robert Plant command me, like some arrogant young sultan to a promising new harem consignment, "Hey, you in the lace nightie, get over here and sit on my face!", backstage at the Fillmore East one night, when I wore my lace-tablecloth pantsuit to a Led Zeppelin show (and yes, I turned down the Golden God's ever so suave invitation, in no uncertain terms…besides, I very soon thereafter had an infinitely superior rock star's face to sit on anytime we wanted). And why shouldn't I have been able to wear whatever the hell I felt like to a concert and not get hit on for it? (Adding insult to injury, some bonehead was shooting an independent film about groupies that night—the Zep boys must have been surrounded in the dressing room by a dozen apiece—and actually asked me to sign a release to be in it. Yeah, like *that* was gonna happen…)

But because of the peculiar feeling in the air, the nature of the colossal societal shifts taking place, it was also the easiest thing in the world to simply be accepted as a reporter, a journalist, a person regardless of gender. You just had to go in with that attitude and stick to it. Not all the guys were pigs by any means; in fact, most were not, and I was treated with professionalism, respect and courtesy, even chivalry. If at bottom it was because I was "press" before I was "chick", and they were afraid to behave badly to me lest I retaliate in print, well, I could live with that, and I did. In all modesty, I'd always been far too smart (Mensa, baby! My IQ was considerably higher than my weight!) for people not to feel extremely stupid telling me I couldn't do anything just because I was female.

Still, apart from artists (who had their own set of problems), neither were there a lot of women around in rock, at least women who *weren't* groupies, or publicists, or secretaries at labels—the Vinyl Ceiling—and I always thought they didn't have it anywhere near as good as I did. Pretty much no women rock record executives or studio personnel—no female engineers or producers. A few radio personalities. As for journalists, maybe a dozen in New York, a handful more scattered across the country. Pauline was the only woman publisher, and I was the only editor-in-chief (though there was a managing editor or two of my own age around). Sadly, the boys' club would stay that way for quite a while, and by the time it started to really change I'd left the journalistic field and the rock-reportage field as well.

But though the sexism was not quite universal, it was pretty pervasive, often masquerading under all sorts of guises (it was legal in those days for companies to put M or F on their help-wanted ads, and, funny thing, all the M ads were for interesting, promotable, well-paying jobs and all the F ads required typing, offered no room for promotion and paid a lot less). Such attitudes turned up in the most unexpected places—the political activists of the counterculture, despite their self-proclaimed liberalism, were notoriously guilty of this sort of thing. Black activist Stokely Carmichael even famously said that the only place for women in the Movement was prone. He meant supine, of course, the moron. As for women on the white side of activism, well, they were basically limited to fetching coffee and, yes, typing. Some liberation. So I, and my few colleagues, began to think of ourselves as rather lucky, and even a bit spoiled.

We had writers *on my own magazine*—not the guys of my own vintage, who were all pretty cool, but those older, old-line jazzbos I mentioned above, the knickers-in-a-twist failed academics—who didn't like one little bit being edited by someone half their age with twice their brains (and way better legs) who they nevertheless willfully perceived as not being up to their lofty intellectual standards (again, *MENSA*??), and who thought women were genetically unfit to write about rock or any other kind of music because women were nothing but uneducated, untalented gossipmongering lightweights who only wanted to write about how music made them feeeeel, or else just blether endlessly about rock stars' crotches. And sure, there were some female writers who were like that (some men writers too), though none of them worked for me, or would have been allowed to; I and the other serious women critics around looked upon them with as much disdain as these guys did.

But the male Jazz & Pop writers most guilty of this offense were the same writers who, frankly, positively groveled and abased themselves (sometimes quite literally: there are even photographs) at the feet of black jazz musicians; so racist no, but sexist yes. Also notably Marxist, a few of them, the tiresome little Commie vermin, wanting only to advance their own moth-eaten Red agenda into the new day that was dawning, which they were too dumb to see wanted none of it. Perhaps it all tied into problems with a paucity of testosterone, as it so often does. It apparently never occurred to these blockheads that by opining so about women, in their own columns *that women let them have* in a magazine *that women published*, they were actually trashing their own management and staff: Pauline, and me, and all the rest of us. Kind of a logic gap there, right? I let their columns run as they wrote them, because I wanted them to look like the condescending jackasses they were, and the readers always gave them hell for it so I guess it all worked out.

Still, I'd have to say that I encountered more sexist aggro from some of the men on my own staff than I did from any rock star I ever met...including that little blond charmer Robert Plant.

Love Hides in Familiar Faces

There was also a mysterious personal issue that ran around the office: Pauline's long-term relationship with noted record producer Bob Thiele. We never knew for sure whether they were officially married or not (on the whole, we thought not); some years later he did marry singer Teresa Brewer, who had been one of the acts on his label, and when he died in 1996 Pauline was not mentioned in his obit (then again, neither was I when Jim died).

But in the years I was at Jazz & Pop, Thiele was the power behind the throne; indeed, not even so much behind it as serving as secret minister of the exchequer—he'd helped bankroll operations to one extent or another ever since its founding as Jazz in 1962, though Pauline never openly discussed it and I only found out about it decades later. And of course he was a brilliant blues and jazz producer: everyone from John Coltrane and Dizzy Gillespie to T-Bone Walker and B.B. King.

Quite honestly, I didn't care for him very much, though we were on cordial terms and he even asked me to write liner notes for him so I could qualify for NARAS membership. I resented the way Pauline was always pushing his label, Flying Dutchman Records (which I named, actually, when Thiele asked me to come up with something; he liked aviation and was of Dutch descent, so it was a no-brainer) and its rather dull artist roster—then again, since he was helping to subsidize the magazine, I could see the pro quo for the quid.

And then of course there was Jim and me, which started when we met in January 1969, in a private interview at the Plaza Hotel (see "When the Music's Over: An Audience with the Doors"), *nothing* like the way it was depicted in the appalling Oliver Stone movie. If getting the magazine job had been magic, or the result of extremely powerful directed thinking—which is really the definition of magic, come to think of it—coming together with Jim was all that to the nth degree, a fairytale playing out in real life. And ingenuous as it sounds, that is how I've always thought of it: I desperately wanted it to happen, I couldn't imagine it *not* happening, I couldn't bear that it *shouldn't* happen, I knew as soon as I laid eyes on him that it was *going* to happen. And, as so often is the case when you're very clear about what you want, the universe will so arrange itself as to give it to you.

If the universe didn't disappoint us, we didn't disappoint it: there were actual literal fairytale sparks when we touched hands for the first time, the prince and princess of instant karma. We worked our way through acquaintanceship to friendship (he sent letters and books, asked me to comment on poems); got romantic in September 1969, though we kept it a secret for a few months more; and lasted all the way through to his death in Paris in July 1971—encompassing our Celtic wedding on June 24, 1970. Except for unavoidable references in context, I don't go into the relationship much here, having written a 400-page book about it, *Strange Days: My Life With and Without Jim Morrison*, which appeared in 1992, chiefly to set the record straight after the execrable movie of the previous year. You can check it out if you require more details. Be warned, though: not all fairytales have happy endings, and the universe always exacts a price for what it hands out…

❖

Nevertheless, there did seem to be an undeniable pattern of the ladies of Jazz & Pop getting involved with music men: Jim and me, Pauline and Bob, Laura and Stu, Janice and a writer for Billboard, Terry and a member of I believe it was Grand Funk Railroad. (Though I do like to think I made the best score…)

Which, I suppose, doesn't say a whole lot for our journalistic integrity. But in those days nobody thought twice about it: it wasn't as if we were sleeping with White House sources or Soviet spies…and we were hardly the only ones doing so, male and female alike. You had critics with musicians, label execs with writers, photographers with rock stars, critics with groupies, musicians with groupies, execs with groupies…just about any combination you could think of, we were putting into play.

Still, yeah, we did tend to cosset our men in print. Thiele had a whole special insert for the newly founded Flying Dutchman in one issue; Jim got a solo cover and his poem "Anatomy of Rock" published for the first time (and a very perceptive piece in the same issue called "*Morrison Hotel* Revisited", which I did *not* write and which appears here), plus many reviews and references; Stu Woods' band, Brethren, had a big feature interview plus a nice review, though I don't recall Grand Funk, if that was indeed the band, getting similar favors. Perhaps we had to draw the line somewhere.

Did that make us groupies? Some people probably thought so; some probably still do, or will do. I'm not among them, though, then or now; I considered it dating in the workplace, as did everyone else I knew. We lived in the rockerverse all day long, we never met anyone *not* in the business; who else were we going to get romantic with? I had a lot more going for me than just sleeping with a rock star (Jim was the only one, ever), and I fiercely rejected anyone who dared presume to call me a groupie.

The favoritism was a more serious charge: though in fairness, how many male rock critics had fanboyish public crushes on artists, not even sublimated ones — invariably Dylan or the Beatles or the Stones, later Springsteen — and how many of them would have done something about it if only they could have, and how many of them gushed on about their man-crushes worse than any groupies going, and how many of them were dissed for it with the groupie label? Yeah, right, I rest my case. If anything, my romance with Jim made me go *harder* on him and the band, not easier, which is inverted favoritism and just as unfair as the straight-up sort; when you love something, you hold it to a higher standard, not a lesser one. But when Jim remarked, laughing, that he could always tell when I was mad at him because all he had to do was read my latest review, I knew it was time to hang up my Doors-reviewing spurs.

But It's All Over Now

By then it really didn't matter, though. When Jim and I had that teasing conversation in his car in L.A., I had already resigned from Jazz & Pop and was about to start a job as senior copywriter at RCA Records' in-house agency, as soon as I returned from California, in February of 1971. I ended up staying at the label for almost three years, learning quite a bit about the business side of the music business, with Jim reassuring me several times that I wasn't selling out. But I had never thought I was.

At RCA, I created David Bowie's first American ad campaigns (for *Hunky Dory*, *Ziggy Stardust*, *Aladdin Sane* and *Pin Ups*), and was lucky enough to get to work with him personally — he was a smart and charming collaborator, and we came up with some very nice stuff, for his print ads and radio spots both.

At that time, it was unusual for an artist to take a personal interest in his own advertising, even more unusual to be allowed to have an active hand in it (especially a newly signed artist without much sales history yet in the U.S.; of course, Bowie absolutely supernova'd mere months later, with the release of *Ziggy* — my tagline: "Space music for the spaced and sane" — and then he could have pretty much anything he wanted). With good reason: most of them didn't have a clue as to what was suitable or effective; even if they had, they would have had even less clue as to how to make it happen, and it was rare that the creative teams ever met with the artists they were creating campaigns for.

But David, who'd studied design at school in England, including layout and typography, really wanted to be involved. After all, it was for his benefit, going out in *his* name to sell *his* work, and he was informed, knowledgeable and inspired, with a clear vision in all things concerning his art. Our then creative director, Kurt Brokaw:

> "I remember a first 'positioning' meeting with him, telling him on the basis of the *Hunky Dory* listenings that I felt his prime markets were the downtown gay crowd and Upper East Side fashion plates. He smiled and said he was aiming for a mass teen audience, and I thought, 'You haven't got enough tricks in your Marcel Marceau mime bag to make that happen'. As usual, I was on another planet and hadn't a clue of his potential. Wish I could remember more, but he was much more your artist than mine."

As Bowie went on to show for the rest of his career, he wasn't just being an egotistical control freak, either, like some other artists I could name; he had the chops and he had a Plan. He knew all about making a personal brand for himself, long before it was even being thought of by his fellows; he accomplished it brilliantly, as we've seen, becoming arguably the most innovative solo rock artist of his generation, and it was an absolute delight working with him.

For his print ads, both consumer (publications like Rolling Stone, Circus, the Village Voice) and trade (Billboard, Cash Box, Record World), we kept it simple. The albums had such incredibly beautiful jacket graphics that we didn't need to do anything but showcase them, and I kept the copy concepts as lean as I could to help create the mystique David wanted. We recorded the radio spots in the fancy new RCA rock studio in our building at 1133 Sixth Avenue, all Tiffany lamps and paisley and exotic woods—I remember being invited there a year later to listen, enthralled, as David laid down tracks for "Jean Genie" (I'd been to a lot of sessions, but the only other major vocalist I'd been lucky enough to hear record like that, up close and personal, was Jim, for "The WASP: Texas Radio and the Big Beat", recorded in the Doors' office building on Santa Monica Boulevard, with Jim using the downstairs bathroom for a vocal booth).

Anyway, after we'd done all the scripts I'd worked up for *Hunky Dory*, David asked if he could just try something. I said of course, whatever you want, and he came up with the most engaging spot of all: no copy, my music bed track, approved by him and using all the best hooks, for which he recorded a tag in a rapid-fire delivery, with laughter in his voice, "My name is David Bowie, my NAME is David Bowie, my name IS David Bowie, my name is DAVID Bowie, my name is David BOWIE. My new album is *Hunky Dory*, and it's on RCA Records and Tapes." Perfect. Probably the most felicitous interaction with an artist I was to have in my entire record-advertising career, and I've thought fondly of

David ever since.

I managed to land some of the plummier artist assignments, not just Bowie, and was quite possessive about them all; I was the go-to writer for the Kinks and Lou Reed, among others, and had probably waaaay too much fun. For the Kinks' RCA debut, *Muswell Hillbillies*, my art director, John Kelley, and I cooked up a memorable spec ad: "RCA Records welcomes the Kinks to its warm corporate bosom", with a lovely full-page pen-and-ink rendering of the iconic RCA dog Nipper with, um, nipp*les*. Which landed us in corporate hot water with the mighty General Sarnoff himself, head of RCA, who took grave exception to the gender reassignment we gave his late beloved pooch. Still, in the long-copy ad that actually ended up running, for which the Nipples ad was merely a stalking-horse ploy so we could get what we really wanted, I got to use the phrase "épater le bourgeoisie", which you don't get to use in ads very often, or pretty much ever, so it wasn't a total loss. (And I still have a two-foot-high plastic Nipper for a souvenir.)

Kelley and I also got in trouble for a Lou Reed ad where we fake-graffiti'd a subway car for that nice urban-decay gritty feel: that caper made the New York Times ad news page when the Metropolitan Transit Authority vigorously complained to the State Attorney General's office, going so far in its outrage as to track down, by its serial number, the car we'd shot in. They then carefully compared it to the ad to make sure the heinous vandalism was all genuine retouching and we hadn't actually spray-painted the goddamn train, so convincing was our work and so well did it blend in with the *real* graffiti with which the car was plastered. Yeah, guys, don't bother cleaning up your disgustingly filthy trains, but by all means waste time, energy and taxpayer money CHECKING THE DAMN GRAFFITI and giving us aggro, you token pinheads.

So we were publicly scolded by the MTA for glorifying vandalism and presenting civic defacement as cool and bringing shame upon a distinguished corporation, and Kurt, a hip, smart and personable adman who was almost sacked over the thing (sorry, boss!), was quoted in the Times piece as having sniffed, "We used to be autonomous."

Well, I mean, *really*! We'd been *hired* to be hip and outrageous and get attention, so the suits shouldn't have been complaining. But for the most part we were far less dramatic: my tagline for that Lou Reed album, his first for the label, was "Songs and secrets from the phantom of rock", and the line for Bowie's third was "David Bowie is enough to drive *Aladdin Sane*." I also worked on Reed's campaigns for *Transformer* and *Berlin*, the Airplane's releases for their new label, Grunt, and many, many ads for classical, country and Elvis, all of which were mainstays of the catalogue.

And I was at RCA when Jim died.

In late 1973 I moved over to CBS Records' in-house ad agency, which was considered the music business's gold-standard top-of-the-line creative department—everyone wanted to work there, and as a rule the ads were spectacularly creative and classy. Well, except of course for that obnoxious, or just plain noxious, one with the much-mocked headline "The Man Can't Bust Our Music"—oy. But before my time, so I can't be blamed for that one.

Over the next seven years I rose from senior writer to copy-director rank. My personal artist roster—we did hundreds of radio spots a year, and probably thousands of print ads—included Barbra Streisand (another artist keenly concerned with her advertising, though not nearly so cool about it as Bowie had been, just diva-ish), Wings (ditto on the concern, but Paul and Linda were a lot easier to deal with than Babs), Bruce Springsteen, Boston, James Taylor, Billy Joel, Aerosmith, Blue Öyster Cult, Toto, Mike Oldfield, Tangerine Dream, Mott the Hoople ("When you're Mott, you're hot") and just about every other Columbia or Epic artist of the time, again including country and classical. For Billy Joel's *The Stranger* campaign, I was nominated for two Clios, including the prestigious National Campaign one — five finalist nominees out of more than 9,000 entries from forty-two countries. I know scorn has been cast on the Clios of late, and perhaps rightly, but back then I felt as though I'd been nominated for an Oscar.

Readers might not be familiar with how it works, writing ads for records, and undoubtedly it is very different these days, so perhaps it's worth explaining a bit.

As rock really began to heat up, after the Monterey Pop Festival of June 1967, CBS, RCA, Atlantic and other major labels, to counterprogram their staid employee ranks, had started hiring "house hippies" for their in-house ad agencies and publicity and a&r departments: people who understood and loved the music — fellow critics drawn from the ranks of alternative publications like Circus, Creem and Rock, musicians and songwriters. Authors Ed Naha and Thomas McNamee were at CBS through the mid-70's, when I was, and I hired former Captain Beefheart accomplice, guitar god Gary Lucas, as a copywriter. One of our radio producers, Stefan Bright (a friend to this day), had been a producer for Jimi Hendrix in the Alan Douglas days, and young product managers who were fans as well had come on board.

On the Olympian end of the scale, talent-spotters like Ahmet Ertegun at Atlantic and Columbia's Bruce Lundvall (and before him the legendary John Hammond, discoverer of Dylan and so many more), were into the music as deeply as we were, and had been for decades. But we didn't deal with deities like those on a regular basis: instead, we had to go up against the mid-level management suits, day in, day out, trying to get what we wanted and what we felt the artist deserved and needed, in the teeth of their gray-flannel opposition. They didn't see the music as art, those sales guys; they saw it as product, and that's what they called it.

As far as ad creation itself went, it wasn't like writing copy for cornflakes or detergent or cars; you couldn't really say, "Hey, kids, here's the new improved Aerosmith album! Now twice as effective! Cleans your ears out like a power tool and gets your laundry even brighter!" Much as you might *want* to say that, which could have made for a very amusing ad, actually. It was a lot more intangible than that: almost like writing a very quick, very tiny album review. Back then, long-copy ads, a whole pageful of words usually artily set in grayed-out heavily leaded Futura Thin, were pretty popular, and thanks to the greatly talented designers, CBS Records ads had a totally distinctive and recognizable Look to them—you could always tell it was one of ours. But generally, and especially for trade ads, you had three or four paragraphs to work with at most, which taught you how to really cut things down to the bone. It's maybe not so strange that I, who can't write a book without taking five chapters just to clear my narrative throat, had a surprising knack for ad writing, which I treated more like haiku.

So, the process. The writer, designer and radio producer would get the assignment for a new album campaign from the creative director: each of us was more or less recognized as specializing in or being partial to a particular artist, so we all had a slate of our own "clients", so to speak, and got huffy if one of our pet acts was assigned elsewhere. We also generally had creative partners with whom we worked more often than not, though the teams weren't set in stone and everybody worked with everybody else. As the writer, you were point man: before you even set fingers to keyboard, you would first off consult with the product managers as to how they wanted to handle the artist—what they wanted emphasized (or ignored), which cuts were going to be pushed as singles, sales or airplay history if any. Sometimes the artists themselves, or their managers, would want in on the process, which could go either way. Then you sat down with your designer or radio producer to brainstorm, developing different ads, though related ones, for print and radio, and different ones still for consumer and trade.

Consumer let you be more creatively off-the-wall and have more fun, to catch the attention of your target audience, which, basically, was yourself—musically sophisticated, college-educated twentysomethings, probably stoned, poring obsessively through music magazines or lolling about listening to FM. Trade required a more nuts-and-bolts approach, being geared to the business types that formed the bulk of music-biz employees: older men, suburban-straight family guys who could just as easily have been selling shoes or office equipment, and approached selling records in the same manner—not hip, not heads, often not even liking the music and knowing very little about it or its antecedents. I recall having a pre-*Pepper* Beatles album playing in my CBS office one day and this bigwig marketing dude, hearing it, actually asked me what band was that and did I think they were worth trying to sign to us…

In the music business, there was business and there was music, and I knew from the first which side I was always going to come down on.

Radio was different, and a whole lot of fun. For radio spots, invariably one minute in length, we had more flexibility, because the music would be right there speaking for itself.

(Record companies did very, very little TV advertising back then, and when they did it was almost always ten- or fifteen-second spots, barely enough to get the album's name and the artist's name and the label's name out there—though I do remember a striking ten-second one we did at RCA for Bowie's *Pin Ups* album, using the stunning jacket-art photo of David and supermodel Twiggy, these two unspeakably beautiful creatures from some other planet, for which we animated a single sparkling tear running down her cheek and back up again, all that we had time for.) Invariably, rock radio commercials in those days employed local dj's from the local FM stations: their voices were very recognizable to hip listeners, and their sensibilities and understanding of the music were equal to our own.

The procedure was for the copywriter to write the script independently, again checking with product management as to which cuts they wanted included, usually the current single to be featured, especially if it was charting, and maybe hooks from FM hits they hoped to have cross over to AM. The scripts generally didn't have anything to do with the print ads, though sometimes they did if the concept worked, especially the tagline if we'd developed one for all across the board, and often we made little playlets out of the things, especially if we had certain talent in mind to do the voiceovers. Then the writer (who as director was required to be in the studio for the recording) and producer would get together and decide how the music would fall—when it should be up, when it needed to be under the voiceover, which hooks worked best in which order—and choose the appropriate actor or actors to read the script. The spots were almost entirely sixty-second ones: generally we had twenty-five or thirty seconds at most for the voiceover; the rest was for the music and the tagline.

After we had script approval from half a dozen people,

we'd book time at our studio of choice. No choice at all when I was at RCA: we had to use the in-house union facilities, which apart from the rock studio were sadly outdated. But for CBS, it was always and forever Clack Studios on West 45th Street, run by a dear friend and colleague who rejoiced in the name of Thomas Courtenay-Clack, a descendant of the Courtenay earls of Devon, medieval power brokers and allies of the Plantagenet kings.

Tom, since retired and still a dear friend (and always just "Clack" to us), was an affable Brit who'd made a name for himself doing sound effects at the BBC in London, as well as all kinds of live radio (dramas, newsreels, housewife request shows, children's hour—you name it), and his extensive sound-effects library (available online, at The Hollywood Edge) was famous in studio circles. He was a genius engineer, and his domain was the best place in the city to make radio spots; the premises consisted of three separate studios, all equipped with the best tech available, and there were two other engineers besides Tom. They were all terrific, but he was the star, and we all vied with one another to book him for our own spots, not just CBS but other record companies as well. He was known for mixing "in the red"—sound-level needles slammed way over into the red or danger decibel zone, nobody else recorded like that—to get the best possible sound contrast. His tape splicing was legendary—we called him the Golden Razorblade, and while working he invariably held one in his teeth like a rose, for ease of access.

He was also the quintessential Englishman: a former public-school boy (Wellington College, one of the Top Schools and by repute a more than usually hard-line place) and traditional London clubman, complete with magnificent Victorian-style muttonchop sideburns, Clack had the studio manager serve formal tea at four every afternoon, in quintessentially English style: on a proper tea trolley, with china and silver, cream and sugar, lemon if you preferred, usually some kind of scones or biscuits (in the English sense) as well. Everything stopped for tea time, and it was served to whoever was working: clients, studio personnel, any talent there recording. So civilized.

RCA had been pretty fuddy-duddy where radio was concerned: the work with Bowie had been about as adventurous as it ever got, and because of those union rules we still had to do all the work in-house, at the RCA studios, with mostly elderly engineers who were more used to recording symphonies or Perry Como than Lou Reed, and who didn't have a clue as to how to do spots any differently.

But Tom has been good enough to explain the secret of his success, which, again, might be interesting for you digital babies to read about, since it hasn't been done like this for decades and probably never will be again:

> "First, I would record the voice on quarter-inch tape. They [*the voiceover actor*] could hear some of the music from the album beforehand, but I never let them listen while they were recording even if they wanted to: it was always best to get them clean and have them concentrate on getting the message clear and clean. Having edited together a good voice take, we [*Tom, the producer and the writer*] would then assemble the spot onto a multitrack tape machine—in the 70's an 8-track, later a 16-track.
>
> My particular skill, which I had learned doing live radio at the BBC, was the ability to cue up a piece of music on the vinyl LP and fly it into the multitrack on cue, by starting the turntable and whipping open the fader to make a clean entry.

I worked standing up, operating the multitrack by remote and dashing back and forth between turntable, mono tape machine (with the voice on it) and the mixing console, razor blade clenched in my teeth for editing. We would pick the hooks that we wanted to use, which could often be found on the disc by seeing where the grooves were most dense. I would dot the needle around till we found the right bit, then scrub the record back and forth by hand to find the exact groove, wind it back a quarter-turn, put the multitrack into 'record' and at the exact moment start the turntable and open the fader.

This process was so fast that one time we built a 60-second spot in twelve minutes. The basic theory was, if possible, to get bits of instrumental under the lines of the voiceover, so that there would not be a clash of voices, then pop up with the hook on the beat so that it would be musically stylish. Sometimes there would be elegant cross-fades, but all in all it was an exercise in making the spot nice to listen to and to show off the best bits of the album. The winning part for me was being able to make spots far faster than the big music studios at CBS and RCA etc., where they would have to copy off the bits they wanted from the album, then edit them, then play them onto the multi."

See? Genius. He was right, too, about how fast he could make them: it took me freakin' *days* with the RCA engineers, employing their dinosaur-era technique of three-machine mixing and endless tedious back-timing, to make *one* spot, which is why, my first session with Clack, when we did four in one afternoon, I thought I'd died and gone to studio heaven.

Also unlike RCA, CBS let us really cut loose and have some fun: we gave work to legitimate actors, great ones even like renowned Shakespearean John Wood, famed documentary announcers like Peter Thomas, even novelty talent like NFL player Larry Csonka and a boys' choir from a noted Manhattan church. But our biggest source of voiceover talent was the cast of "Saturday Night Live".

We did innumerable spots with founding Not Ready for Prime Time Players Dan Aykroyd, John Belushi, Jane Curtin, Bill Murray, Laraine Newman and Gilda Radner (Chevy Chase was gone by then, and Garrett Morris let it be known that he was above doing radio spots). It worked out great for all concerned: we got excellent and quirky spots, not to mention the benefit of their hip cred and bragging rights, and they made a bit of extra money for an hour's easy work and got served afternoon tea. They weren't making a lot from SNL at that stage; in fact, one of them told me that we earned more than they did, which hardly seemed possible. But he might have been putting me on.

Tom again:

> "There was a memorable session with Bill Murray, Jane Curtin, Belushi and Laraine (I think). You had about three different scripts for them which they took and flew with in directions that no one could have imagined. Murray, in particular, was so creative and funny it blew my mind. They were all on a level of wit and talent that was above anything I'd encountered. We pretty much let them go crazy and then we had to put it all together later with what we had on tape."

Another day, not the one Clack mentions, we had all three studios filled up, with Jane in one and Belushi in another, working on two spots for this hot new act called Boston, and Laraine and Murray with me in the third doing a *Star Wars* spoof I'd written. They were all amused to see the others up so early and working—Bill, coming into the control booth to say hi and get the script before we started recording, said that it looked like a rehearsal for the show out there. He then proceeded to riff off the script, telling outrageous Polish jokes and then shouting "The Polish jokes are having no effect, Your Highness!" Though he did compliment me on the writing, which was very kind of him and embarrassed me no end. But we loved working with them: they were all terrific and charming, each quirky in their own way, and so hilarious that it was real work to keep to the damn scripts— their improvising was so much funnier that we'd just sit there and helplessly listen, laughing so hard we cried.

Pretty much what you saw on TV was what you got in person: Jane was very responsible, just as you'd expect, always there early, no-nonsense, ready to work; Belushi was, well, Belushi, also pretty much just as you'd expect; Gilda was endearingly vague, often apologetically returning our calls a day too late and the spot would be already recorded. Laraine would absently, and flexibly, stand there at the mike with her knee beside her ear and her foot up over her head, doing ballet stretches, or folded up into a chair like a paper clip; Bill didn't even own an alarm clock the first time we booked him, and rather sheepishly requested that producer Janice Scott, with whom I most often teamed and who became a close friend, give him a wakeup call so he'd be on time for the session. But they were all tremendous fun, and very professional indeed, and now I can boast that I directed Bill Murray and John Belushi. Good times, good times; thanks, guys!

One of the most enjoyable parts of my copy-directorial

duties was to work up the twice-yearly product presentations for the CBS Records conventions, to be shown to the whole officer class of the company. Held in places like London, New Orleans, Atlanta or Los Angeles, in January and July — with the summer installments being the bigger, more important deal held in the bigger, more important cities — these things were huge, and took enormous amounts of time and energy to bring off, like planning an invasion. The hotels and performing spaces were booked at least a year in advance, lodging and transport for hundreds of people as well; there were folks employed just to handle the conventions, since as soon as one was over it was time to start planning the next.

Even for us in the creative group, logistics were incredibly complicated: we'd start two or three months ahead — I'd have the product managers get me information on the upcoming releases for the next six months, as well as music requirements, and write a script for each act. Then Janice Scott and I would head over to Clack's to record the voiceover actors for each segment and bounce together a voice-and-music track, until we had what amounted to a mini music video with sales pitch attached. It took weeks of long, long working days in the studio — sometimes we'd be recording and mixing all day and never see our offices until eight at night. Meanwhile, we would also be working with the designers on the visual component of the program, mostly slides but some live footage — these were pre-MTV days, so there wasn't usually much of that available — and go to yet another studio to put the whole thing together. Besides the product segments, there would be some kind of razzle-dazzle thematic opening and close, and each day would have brief introductory and concluding framing pieces.

Janice and I did the lion's share of the convention work,

but there were other teams involved too—it wasn't just us. Once the production was finished—usually right down to the wire, and it precluded the two of us from most other work—we'd have to fly out early to the venue to hand-deliver the tapes (safeties were shipped) and make sure everything was okay. When the convention started, the presentations, which were each several hours long, took up most of the mornings and afternoons, interspersed with small sales and marketing meetings that, thankfully, we creatives didn't have to bother with; the evenings were devoted to all-hands-on-deck banquets, after which we were entertained by big-name company artists performing. The rest of the time, or when we snuck out, we were free to sightsee and do as we pleased, and one of the nights—these things went on for a week—was always devoted to a special, off-site treat for everybody: a barbecue at the Warner Bros. Western backlot during the L.A. convention, a formal reception at the Royal Academy of Arts during the London one.

So it came to pass that I was present, excitingly, at the notorious summer 1977 convention in London, when one Declan Patrick McManus, better known as Elvis Costello, began to play for us as we all emerged, exhausted, from that day's product presentation show at the London Hilton, to stagger back up Park Lane to our crash pad, the Grosvenor House. It was quite a landmark moment in busking history, there in the Hilton lobby, with young Mr. Costello auditioning his heart out ten feet away, and we were all very impressed with him, to say the least—obviously so, considering that he was signed to a Columbia contract shortly thereafter by some of the very people who'd heard him play. Even the cops who dragged him away (and fined him five pounds for being an annoyance) thought it was a brilliant idea. Insane, but brilliant. Six months later, he was playing the January convention as a label headliner himself, at the Fairmont Hotel in New Orleans. It doesn't get much more rocknroll than that.

Once I left J&P, I didn't keep up with writing about rock. I couldn't admit it in so many words even in *Strange Days*, but I was so absolutely shattered by Jim's death that even the mere thought of writing as a rock critic again froze my entire being into splintered ice. I just wasn't interested anymore, and I very seldom even attended concerts: a couple of Airplane gigs, for auld lang syne; my friends the British folk-rock group Steeleye Span; anything dictated by work at RCA or CBS, like Presley or Springsteen or Billy Joel, that I was required to attend—but it hurt too much to write, and there wasn't anything I cared to write about anyway.

I broke out of it only three times: once when I interviewed Carly Simon in 1972, doing a feature on her for the New York Herald, one of her first bits of coverage ever, and she was a delight to talk to (I even got to sit next to her mother, who looked like Eleanor of Aquitaine in a rose jersey wimple, at the Carnegie Hall debut concert, and we had a lovely chat; and later with Carly herself, backstage and at the Carnegie Deli); and again when Sue Donoghue, who had become managing editor of Rock magazine, coaxed me to do two pieces. One was on women in rock, and I disliked it so much when it was done that I requested my byline be taken off it. The second, "The Decline and Fall of Intelligent Rock Criticism", pretty much said it all about how I felt, and was my last piece of critical rock writing ever.

For some reason, though, I couldn't quit music altogether, even though it held so many painful reminders of Jim clobbering me out of nowhere on a daily basis, making me feel like a princess in exile, a rock Cinderella reduced to sweeping out the ashes and grieving for her dead Prince Charming. I had one picture of Jim on my office wall, the one that was the cover of the September issue of Jazz & Pop, my favorite photo of him ever (see my Facebook page) — for defiance and validation, reminder and consolation both. I never explained to anyone but Janice Scott why it was there, figuring it was none of their business and I really didn't care for them to know anyway, because there would only be prying personal questions that would feel like red-hot knives; but another CBS friend told me later, after I'd left, "Everybody knew about it — you and Jim. But nobody *knew* about it."

Still, writing record ads seemed the perfect balance of distance and involvement, not to mention paying handsomely, providing free concert tickets and free records — we could order ten a month, even the big expensive boxed classical sets — offering convenient access to drugs and hardly seeming like work at all. I did well at it, winning a bunch of awards from the Art Directors Club and other places, besides the two Clio nods. Those were the halcyon days of the record ad, which never will come again; but for me, the music got steadily less involving and more irksome, and by the time I was let go from CBS in one of the great label purges of the early 1980's, I was very glad to be gone.

Paperback (and Hardcover) Writer

Out of the music biz for good after a dozen years — a rather unexpected career that I hadn't planned at all but that I had totally loved — I left with enough money to stay home and start to write my own books, as I had always wanted to. That's when The Keltiad first emerged from hyperspace, even though the idea had been around since college in one shape or another — in fact, Jim had been the first person to hear about it — Irish, Welsh and Scottish legends set in a futuristic interstellar space empire called Keltia. *Star Wars* meets King Arthur. The first of the series, *The Copper Crown*, appeared in 1984; seven more novels came after, and I'll get around presently to writing and publishing two more that will finish off the series, probably in e-books first, given today's publishing parameters.

In 1990, I got involved with Oliver Stone's Doors movie, which appeared the following year and from which I came away with a new appreciation for the hard work moviemaking really is and a new friend in the gifted and gracious actress who played me, Kathleen Quinlan. In 1992, my response to the movie and what it had said about Jim was published by Dutton—*Strange Days: My Life With and Without Jim Morrison*. I'd never wanted to write a book about Jim and me, but there was no way in hell I would have let that movie stand as the unchallenged truth about him, or about us together. The book was born in fury and written in blood—not all of it my own. I am very proud of it indeed, and I think Jim would be proud of me for writing it.

The last Keltiad book to appear (though the chronological first in the series), *The Deer's Cry*, came out in 1998, but my publishing company, HarperCollins, unceremoniously declined the next book. Midlist authors like me were being dropped all over the industry; as for the Kelts, no one else wanted to pick up a long, intricate series that had already been at three other houses (Bluejay, NAL/Signet and Roc, before the switch to HarperCollins, following my longtime editor), however well received critically (which it was) or however beloved of its fans (which it also was), so that was effectively the end of it.

But now, through the miracle that is indie/online publishing, at last I'll be able to eventually send my Kelts off in a blaze of glory, to the satisfaction of their readers and myself. And yah-boo-sucks to traditional publishers: even though it means no advance, it also means not having to deal with half-educated morons half my age; I prefer having complete control in any case, as what writer wouldn't. Not to mention a far greater royalty share. But even if I never make a penny off my current books through online publishing, it would still be worth it to me in integrity and honor, to have them the way I want them. So I guess I'm a hippie of sorts after all.

And there's another series now: *The Rock & Roll Murders: The Rennie Stride Mysteries.* Murders at famous rock venues — Woodstock, the Fillmores East and West, Monterey Pop, Abbey Road studios, the Royal Albert Hall, the Whisky A Go-Go. There's a protagonist newspaper reporter, Rennie Stride, who is definitely not me, though she's certainly mouthy enough (perhaps, marginally, me as I might have been, had I chosen a different journalistic path — I've never worked for a newspaper and never had any desire to) and a superstar English lead guitarist co-protagonist, Turk Wayland, who is definitely not Jim (not even close). There are six to date, and I'm simultaneously closing in on at least four more. It's nice to be able to put your past to work for you...and to settle old grudges in good clean homicidal fashion without ending up on death row.

Other projects: out later this year or early next, a historical novel I've been working on for years, set in the time of Alfred the Great, only my heroes are the Vikings — *Son of the Northern Star.* Some short stories, which I'm finally learning how to write, set in the Keltiverse. A fairytale novella: *The Gates of Overwave.* Maybe, one day, a book I wrote two decades ago: *The Crystal Ship: The Shaman and the Priestess,* a spiritual memoir using Jim and me as the vehicles for getting into some serious metaphysical stuff — who says archetypes no longer exist in the real world? And, perhaps, another day, though thanks EVER so much to the Sonny Bono/Walt Disney copyright laws (extending the laws to seventy-five years from fifty, to protect Mickey goddamn Mouse) I won't live to see it, even the publication of Jim's private poetry and letters and songs and drawings, all of which he made for me, and for us: *Fireheart: The True Lost Writings of Jim Morrison*.

We'll see.

Well, that's about it. I won't keep you any longer. Hopefully, this has been enough background for you to go on with; hopefully also, not so much that it bored you stupid. But I wanted to give everyone who wasn't there an idea of the sublimely intense and different feel of the time, a time that is no more, and to give everyone who *was* there a bit of a jog to the old memory banks. I trust a pleasant one, either way.

Now. Let's *ROCK*.

September 1968

My first proper Pop Talk column. Before I came on the scene, Pop Talk, a monthly featured column, had been written by Pauline, and was merely a collection of snippets that she gleaned from press releases and the occasional bit of gossip—which format morphed into "I Heard the News Today Oh Boy", a small section tacked onto the end of most of my own columns.

When I first came on board, she started me off doing the same, for the initial few months of my employment—she had a lot else to do, and she'd never particularly enjoyed assembling the column anyway, preferring to interview people like John and Alice Coltrane and others she knew from the jazz scene. As who wouldn't?

Fine with me: I had been hired as an editorial assistant and this was my first real journalism job. I was learning the ropes, learning how to edit this very specific vehicle for an equally specific and demanding audience, making contacts, trying to find my way through the musical dazzle and the terrific excitement of The Best Job In The World. Which I was even getting paid for! And free records! And free concert tickets! And meeting artists! What a great gig!

Putting together Pop Talk those first few months wasn't really writing, of course, not right off the bat—just cut and paste and proof and retype, and occasionally rewrite where it needed it. But I didn't mind in the slightest: it was still writing for a rock magazine. Then, as both Pauline and I became more confident in my writing ability and musical sensibilities, she started to give me more rein...and I grabbed the bit and ran.

"Give Spencer an amphetamine!" yelled a sympathetic freak as Bill Graham piggybacked Jefferson Airplane's exhausted drummer back onstage for the third set of encores.

"Spencer who?" said Grace Slick, and danced around the stage. The Airplane was at the Fillmore East, July 19-20, and now it was 3:05 Sunday morning, the last set, with a packed house, and balloons, and a twelve-foot wood and canvas Day-Glo biplane sitting outside in Second Avenue. There was H. P. Lovecraft, who earlier had given a tight, interesting, brilliant and happy performance. And then there was Jefferson Airplane.

I have seen the Airplane more times than I have fingers and toes, and despite all the flak about [*After Bathing at*] *Baxter's* being a colossal down and they're not together and they fight all the time, I have never had such a good time listening to them as I did at the Fillmore that night. Starting out with "Saturday Afternoon/Won't You Try", and finishing up with "The Ballad of You and Me and Pooneil", in between they were into some beautiful things: old, new and some of their best live stuff. Musically, the Airplane is without question the finest band around. The Grateful Dead will make you happier, perhaps, in an acid-beaming-Buddha-smile kind of way, but for sheer staggering technical brilliance and virtuosity, the Airplane cuts everybody. Perhaps it's because they have just about everything a group could possibly want: Jorma [*Kaukonen*], Jack [*Casady*] and Spencer [*Dryden*] function as the core, with Cream-style interactions that lift off the top of your head; vocalists Marty [*Balin*], Grace and Paul [*Kantner*], with this kind of a base to work on, can pretty much do whatever they please, and it all comes out together. Nice.

Two things drug me about recent Airplane operational procedure, though, and the second far more than the first: one, magnificent guitarist that he is, Jorma is possibly the worst blues singer I have ever heard. On his own material ("The Last Wall of the Castle", etc.), he does a fine vocal job, and on blues *guitar* he gets off some powerful riffs, but blues singing is another thing entirely, and it's just not his.

The second complaint is of a more serious nature, and it is that I am more than a little tired of having to watch Marty Balin walk offstage during shows because he has nothing to do. After *Surrealistic Pillow,* and especially since about ten months ago, Marty seems to have been edged more and more into the background: he almost never plays anything more than tambourine in concert (except for very occasional bass), and on many of the songs he is held to second- or third-voice harmonies. This is truly a waste: Marty has an incredibly beautiful and expressive voice, in many respects far finer than Grace's, and he certainly deserves better things to do. Toward the end of the set at the Fillmore the group got into older material ("Today", "It's No Secret", "3/5 of a Mile"), and it was an absolute stone joy to watch Marty tear into the songs. Would that it happened more often.

Other Airplane scenes: there is still some vague talk of a film to be directed by Conrad Rooks (he of *Chappaqua* renown), which would star the Airplane as a 1980's rock group. More definite: a fourth LP (perhaps to be called *Greasy Heart,* perhaps not), which should be more of a mind-blower than even their last. Outside songwriters featured on the record will include former Byrd David Crosby with a number called "Triad", and Airplane associate/manager Gary Blackman (whose hysterical laughter is heard at the close of Spencer Dryden's opus "A Small Package of Value

Will Come to You Shortly", on the *Baxter's* LP.

I HEARD THE NEWS TODAY, OH BOY: Bill Graham on Cream: "If you believe some of the rumors you hear, they're all probably pregnant." Eric Clapton on Cream: "There's been a big change of attitudes among ourselves." And so Cream will be separating come fall, Jack Bruce to go into production, Ginger Baker to start up another group and Clapton himself to first take "a big holiday", then to probably put together a group where he can define the music but not have to be the leader. Thinking along the same lines is Buddy Miles, whose idea of Supergroup is Clapton, himself, Stephen Stills and Stevie Winwood, and who now is in London to discuss the project … First Jeff Beck LP on Epic, entitled *Truth*, just released … Tenor saxophonist Albert Ayler brought his sound to New York's Café Au Go-Go for two weeks in July. Playing opposite Sea Train (a revived and metamorphosed Blues Project), the Ayler quartet proved once again (as did Charles Lloyd and Cecil Taylor at San Francisco's Fillmore Auditorium) that rock audiences and jazz audiences need not be mutually exclusive. Are you listening, Bill Graham? … Folk-funk duo Bunky and Jake have been playing various New York caves (The Scene, The Bitter End, Café Au Go-Go, among others), and have a second album in the works for Mercury … Benefit showing of *Magical Mystery Tour* at the Fillmore East August 11, with Liberation News Services receiving the proceeds … Bill Graham has moved the San Francisco Fillmore (not so much a building, more a state of mind) from its old location at 1805 Geary to what was formerly the Carousel Ballroom, owned and operated with amiable inefficiency by the Grateful Dead, Jefferson Airplane and assorted friends. Reason for the move: the new building is bigger, more conveniently located (Market and Van Ness, in case you were wondering) and away from the harassment patrons occasionally received from black Fillmore District residents, more and more frequent since the King assassination. Graham's lease on the old Fillmore runs to 1973; he plans to donate the building to interested black community groups and black militants (who, Graham states positively, have never been involved in the harassment incidents). The new ballroom, after some slight remodeling, will be known as Fillmore West ... Word has it that Moby Grape has broken up for good and aye ... Ars Nova is alive and quite well in Fun City. The various hassles of the Elektra group were recorded in Life magazine's celebrated rock issue (which could have been a whole lot better than it was); anyway, things appear to have straightened themselves out for the group and a second album will be forthcoming ... Gross Note of the Month: Dobie Gray ("In Crowd") has a new red, white & blue single, "God Bless America", top-40 radio should just love it ... And FINALLY: any interest in a union for rock entertainers? A. F. of M. seems to forget where their money is. Which is, I suppose, no surprise at all...

October 1968

POP TALK:
STREET FIGHTING MAN (AND WOMAN)

Having some fun with politics and music: my first theme piece. My general attitudes were as flaming-liberal as those of most of my contemporaries, but I was never as deeply into hardcore Sixties politics and radical activism as a lot of other people were; or, if I was, I was into it from a different place, some strange other viewpoint, probably skewed and certainly jaundiced. It's hard to quantify: I wouldn't, and didn't ever, describe myself as a political person—certainly not an activist, though I did attend demonstrations from time to time, more as an observer than a participant, in fact almost as a judge—but I did feel that I saw things in terms of politics. Not party politics. Human politics.

"Where have all the flowers gone?" has been a question posed by just about every major journalism-Establishment rag you could think of, all too ready with vulture eagerness to celebrate the death of a movement they never could understand, much less accept to any significant degree. In recent months, however, many of us have been asking the same question (with, needless to say, a different emphasis), and if the kind of thing now being laid down for us by people like the Stones, the Airplane, the Doors, etc., etc., is a reliable indication (and it is), well may we ask.

Call it the New Protest Movement, if you like labels: whatever it is, in energy, scope, awareness, commitment and ultimate power, it is far beyond its work-shirted brother of the first half of the decade. Things have come full circle: we have unstrung our ethnically battered guitars, wheeled through a spectrum of love and pot and beads and pretty colors, realized that beautiful as that trip was, it would never accomplish anything absolute; and the thing to do now is take what we learned and use it. Waiting has filled.

Which is, of course, what the music is all about. There has never been anything like it before: there couldn't be. All the developments of the   past, say, three years have suddenly coalesced into a purposive, fearsomely inevitable whole, and if you care to, you can trace it all back without a single snag. There's politics: I write this on the eve of the Democratic Convention; they've arrested the pig [*the Yippie Party was running an actual pig as a Presidential candidate – PKM*] and a goodly number of his loyal constituents, and right now it looks like Humph [*Vice President Hubert Humphrey*], and those concentration camps in Pennsylvania are still there, brothers. And Czechoslovakia…and Biafra… and the black people in our cities…it all fits together.

Then there is the music. The folk movement gave it a voice of militancy and outrage; Dylan gave it words; the drug scene gave it insight and perception (yes, it really did). Plug in an amplifier and there you are. An extra added dividend is the tremendous number of people the music has picked up along the way: ex-folkniks and aging teenyboppers and jazz aficionados and college professors and just about everyone over the age of reason. They all come to it from different directions and different backgrounds, and it speaks to all of them alike. Rock has truly earned itself its audience: a universal audience in that everybody *has* to listen to it whether they like it or not. It is omnipresent: it reaches people in a way that classical music or jazz or folk music could never do. It has taken over the function of social criticism for this generation that used to be found on editorial pages of newspapers or in esoteric periodicals—and you can dance to it. What more could you want?

A lot more, say the Stones, Airplane, Doors and all the rest. Things have progressed to such a point that the cause (world consciousness) and the result (us) are just about evenly balanced. Perhaps it may be naïve to suggest that music—specifically, today's music—may help to alter the balance of power; but consider the fact that within the span of the next four years, substantially more than half the American population will be under thirty years of age. What will be the chief influence on this majority? Rock music: Mick Jagger cuts Hedley Donovan any day. And what does Mick Jagger have to say that you won't find in Time magazine, look you never so carefully? This.

> *Hey, think the time is right*
> *for a palace revolution*
> [...]
> *But what can a poor boy do*
> *except sing for a rock and roll band?*

What do the Doors have to say? "They've got the guns, but we've got the numbers/Gonna win, yeah, we're taking over." Jefferson Airplane intones: "In loyalty to their kind/ They cannot tolerate our minds/In loyalty to our kind/We cannot tolerate their obstruction." [*A word-for-word, and at the time uncredited, Paul Kantner lift from the classic John Wyndham science-fiction novel* Rebirth; *apparently sampling got started earlier than we thought.—PKM*] The Beatles have a new single entitled "Revolution". It all seems to be pretty well polarized by now, set in its path; but where is it going?

One place it *isn't* going is into the trap of earlier protest music, which began promisingly and then fell into a pattern of general aimless ranting, no solutions offered. This isn't really protest music, it's more like threat music. It presents the dual situation (them/us), outlines the alternatives, definite courses to follow: and then it warns of the consequences of the wrong choice. It isn't just electric saber-rattling, either; this music reflects the ideas, feelings and generic makeup of its followers far more accurately than any other media competitor. If it says "Revolt", it means it; better be ready.

So the flowers are gone, then; or maybe they've just been transformed. There's a [*Jules*] Feiffer cartoon that shows various freaky-looking people running up to a straight with an attaché case, all shouting "I give you this flower out of love", and pelting him with daffodils; in short order the straight succumbs to flower allergy, and one of the freaks, standing over the body, says wonderingly, "Flowers kill"; then, "Let's escalate." Perhaps music will work just as well.

I HEARD THE NEWS TODAY OH BOY: Well, maybe now you'll listen next time mother tells you to turn-down-the-stereo-you'll-go-deaf-before-you're-twenty. A researcher at the University of Tennessee has conducted tests involving a black-and-white guinea pig (chosen because the guinea pig's ear structure and biochemical processes are very similar to those of man) and rock music, and has reached the conclusion that rock music played at extremely loud levels (such as in discotheques, where the decibel count frequently hits 125) is potentially harmful to cells of the inner ear. Anyone who's ever walked out of the Fillmore with bleeding eardrums is aware of the occupational hazard involved, and probably cares even less than the guinea pig. Pillar of the rock community Steve Paul [*owner and operator of the primo New York music club The Scene*] commented, "Should a major increase in guinea pig attendance occur at The Scene, we'll certainly bear their comfort in mind." ... Apple Corps Ltd. released its first records under the

Apple logo (a green apple for the A side, the core on the B side). The August 26 releases included a Beatles single, "Revolution" b/w "Hey Jude"; "Thingumybob", a Paul McCartney composition done by the Black Dyke Mills Band; "Sour Milk Sea" by Jackie Lomax; and "Turn Turn" by 18-year-old Twiggy-discovered Mary Hopkin. An LP of soundtrack music for the film *Wonderwall* (composed by George Harrison) will be released shortly, and the long-awaited follow-up album to *Sgt. Pepper* will probably come out in late October. In other Beatle action, McGraw-Hill is rushing *The Beatles: The Authorized Biography* into September 30 publication; the book is written by Hunter Davies, who enjoyed the full cooperation of his subjects. Meanwhile, over at Putnam, another Beatles biography (*The Beatles: The Real Story*), this one done by Julius Fast, appeared August 29, and did not have *any* cooperation from the Beatles … Labor Day weekend in San Francisco was highlighted by the four-day Palace of Fine Arts Festival, held as a benefit for the Haight-Ashbury Medical Clinic and the Atheneum Arts Foundation. The festival, which began on Friday night, August 30, and ran through Monday afternoon, September 2, featured such performers as the Grateful Dead, Big Brother and the Holding Company (who will reportedly lose Janis Joplin in November, Janis splitting to form another group and Big Brother continuing on its own), the Youngbloods, San Francisco Mime Troupe, Initial Shock, and many others … Record Industry Association of America certified 33 albums and 23 singles as Gold Records in the first six months of 1968. Albums included *Bob Dylan's Greatest Hits*, the Doors' *Strange Days*, *Are You Experienced* by the Jimi Hendrix Experience, Dylan's *John Wesley Harding*, Cream's *Disraeli Gears* … Al Kooper's first single production for Columbia has been released: "Long-Haired Boy", an original composition by Tim Rose … Canned Heat left for London September 3 for two weeks of concerts and television appearances; a third album is forthcoming ... And finally, something to look forward to with eagerness, anticipation and skepticism: next year's New York Rock Festival (yes, that same Festival that this year saw the Doors, and Jimi Hendrix and Janis Joplin upon the very same stage) will boast as star people the Rolling Stones and Bob Dylan; whether together or separately nobody seems to know. Does it really matter?

REVIEW:
CHEAP THRILLS, Big Brother & The Holding Company

My first big feature piece, a two-page spread with a great picture of Janis, taken by Pauline, at the Newport Folk Festival that summer. The prominence of such a feature spread for a record, instead of just a review, illustrated how major Big Brother had become by that time and how eagerly this LP had been anticipated. Perhaps my review was not as musicologically serious or correct as it could have been, or as some other writer might have made it, but I wanted to get the thing as close in feel as I could, in journalistic prose, to the album itself. And I adored the band. Nobody could have possibly imagined then that this, their second album, would also be their last...

BIG BROTHER & THE HOLDING COMPANY ◆ Cheap Thrills (Columbia KCS 9700). Janis Joplin (vo); James Gurley (g, vo); Sam Andrew (g, b, vo); Peter Albin (b, vo); David Getz (d, vo). *Combination of the Two; I Need A Man To Love; Summertime; Piece of My Heart; Turtle Blues; Oh Sweet Mary; Ball and Chain.*

You can almost see it: the Fillmore on a Saturday night, you're sitting maybe in the front row with your feet up on the stage or maybe you're on the floor or standing in the back by yourself. People are moving around you, talking, laughing; the light show is bubbling aimlessly on the screen. One by one, the group straggles out across the stage, picks up instruments, starts to tune up. Then Bill Graham materializes out of the wings, blinks once in the spotlight glare as he steps to the microphone, smiles, looks at the floor and says allinoneword: "Four gentlemen and one great, great broad—Big Brother!" His introduction is half lost in the applause and the roar as the band crashes into "Combination of the Two", and then Janis Joplin steps out front, grins, and starts to flail away at a gourd, and you know that everything's all right.

That's the nicest thing about *Cheap Thrills*: everything *is* all right, more than all right. It's got the incredible electricity of the best Big Brother live performances and it presents the group in a way that everybody can dig. If you've never seen the group live, the record will lay down for you exactly why people go away from their sets shaking their heads, incoherent and glassy-eyed. If you have, it brings everything back to you, in the comfort of your own living room even, and you can jump up and dance around the house whenever you please.

So that's how *Cheap Thrills* begins, then: "Combination of the Two" (exactly which two is never made quite clear; at least it escapes *me*) is a good opening choice. Sam is featured on lead vocal, though he's regrettably hard to hear, with Janis wailing in the background and James and Sam doing mostly chorded guitar work. The nice thing about Big Brother (almost unique in this respect among the major groups) is that all its members do vocals. This results in a solid sound and a certain degree of independence from Janis' lead voice; magnificent as she is, there are nevertheless times when she does not belong up front, and "Combination of the Two" is one of them. Happily, the band carries itself, and by contrast, Janis' gleeful "Gonna knock ya, rock ya, gonna sock it to ya now!" solo challenge is appropriately effective.

Three of the tracks on *Cheap Thrills*—"I Need A Man to Love", and "Turtle Blues" and "Oh Sweet Mary" on the second side—although by no means inferior songs, nevertheless strike me as being a cut below the general level of the album. On "I Need A Man to Love" and "Turtle Blues", Janis sings lead in a fine tough blues style; the arrangements are good though unobtrusive, (except for John Simon's knockout piano on "Turtle"), and the songs are anything but boring — they're just all one color, and hard to get into, and as of this writing I still haven't succeeded. "Oh Sweet Mary", on the other hand, is a fast-moving number, with lead vocal by Sam, and the only complaint I have about it is that the long singing guitar line is lifted from the group's concert performances of "The Cuckoo" [or " Coo Coo", as *they spelled it — PKM*] (they do a beautiful hard-rock version of this, by the way, that I wish they had included on the album).

However, they did include what are probably everybody's all-time Big Brother favorites: "Summertime", "Piece of My Heart" and "Ball and Chain", and any one of these tracks justifies getting the album.

The first time I ever heard Janis do "Summertime", she just stood there, swaying in time to the lead-in, and then somebody handed her up a knot of flowers from the front row. She looked really pleased, like "Flowers for *me*?", and walked over to the side of the stage, poured some water into her Southern Comfort glass, stuffed the flowers in it and set it down on the front of the stage. Then she stepped back, surveyed the effect, decided it fit the mood of the song, closed her eyes and soared right into it.

She starts it high, soft, her voice near cracking but never going over; toward the end of each verse she brings harder things into it, and the resolution at the song's end is superb. The really good thing about the recorded version is that the interplay between guitars and drums is finally audible: in concert it's much too delicate to be heard clearly, and anyway on this song you're usually too busy concentrating on Janis' spectacular slides to pay much mind to the accompaniment. Sam does some classic fill-ins here that are intricate and lovely and clash nicely with the lead guitar's wandering riff: the overall sound is hollow, almost—you can hear exactly how and where everybody fits into what everybody else is doing. Nice.

"Piece of My Heart" is something else entirely. What it more or less amounts to is everybody doing his thing as hard as he possibly can, and Janis doing hers harder than that. The song (famous also as done by Erma Franklin, Aretha's sister) alternates between screaming sledgehammer choruses and verses phrased like a cat walking over broken glass, and it usually winds up with Janis down on her knees on the stage. It has to be seen to be believed; and then you think that nothing could possibly be more exciting than this.

Until Big Brother does "Ball and Chain."

There have been so many words flung around on the subject of "Ball and Chain" that it seems almost superfluous and/ or presumptuous to add to them. And besides, what can you say? Really.

"Ball and Chain", though, isn't a song; it's musical assault and battery. Joplin cuts everybody in sight (including, emphatically, Big Mama Thornton, whose song this is): she whispers, builds, shouts, screams, soars and falls, and she pulls you right along with her, every inch. The band is equal to her, relying on beautifully understated guitar and drum punctuation, some skittering feedback and fuzz and karate-abrupt rhythm chops. There's a good feedback break that goes on a little too long and is a shade too uncontrolled, but it fits well, and then Janis begins the final unaccompanied swoops that end in the spectacular vocal acrobatics for which she is justly celebrated. And that's it: Bill Graham wishes everybody a happy Sunday, and a few bars of what sounds like a Bach Mass closes the album.

Cheap Thrills is a nice warm comfortable record. No tricks. Nothing superfluous. Nothing fancy. Just straightforward ballsy music and honest emotion: good clean raunch. And the band contributes just much as Janis. In the stampede of people falling all over themselves to acclaim Joplin (and she certainly deserves it, every word), the band is either overlooked entirely or dismissed with one or two sentences, and this is a lamentable thing. Granted, they're not the Airplane or the Dead, but they're not meant to be; neither are they merely a backup band for their star lady. They are fine musicians, every one, who work together well and merit more than the cavalier treatment they've been getting. Sam and David were both at one time or another practicing jazz musicians, James and Peter into country, blues and old-line rock: and it all comes out in their present freewheeling style. It's an amalgam with the purpose of interaction: the band bounces the music off Janis, and Janis draws upon the energies of the band to fuel her vocals, and this is just as noticeable on the album as it is in concert performances.

Which brings us to Janis herself. Words fail. The way she tells it (in Columbia's official bio) is like this: "I don't know what happened. I just exploded. I'd never sung like that before. I'd been into a Bessie Smith-type thing, you know, big open notes. I stood still and I sang simple. But you *can't* sing like that in front of a rock band, all that rhythm and volume going. You have to sing loud and move wild with all that in back of you. It happened the first time, but then I got turned on to Otis Redding, and I got into it more than ever. Now I don't know how to perform any other way. I've tried cooling myself and not screaming, and I've walked off feeling like nothing."

Which underlines the only inherent flaw in any Big Brother recording: you can't watch. Joplin onstage is truly awesome: she scowls, she chortles, she thrashes her hair and pounds her thigh and points her finger and waves her fists and swings the microphone like a scythe, and she plainly and obviously loves every minute of it, and a wondrous amount of this comes through on the recording.

Which is, ultimately, why *Cheap Thrills* is going to be a monster album. Sure, it's erratically engineered in places, and some of the songs aren't the greatest (where's "Roadblock"?), but it's wild and it's exciting and it's exuberant as hell, and it loves you. Cheap thrills indeed.

REVIEW:
CROWN OF CREATION, Jefferson Airplane

This was a HUGE deal for me, getting to review a Jefferson Airplane album. They had been my favorite group for a couple of years by this point, and the most senior J&P reviewers had always written up the preceding albums. But this was my shot, and I was thrilled.

Oh, full disclosure: that "friend" with the atomic Airplane poster configuration on her wall? Me. I was too embarrassed to cop to it in the review, because I thought I would look like some hippie wacko and it might have freaked out the band. But I really did have it there in the West Fifteenth Street apartment I shared with Sue Donoghue and another SBU sorority sister, in late 1967, before my move to the East Village in 1968. I don't know why I was impelled to construct it; it just felt...right. Or maybe I was just psychic.

Also my official, self-composed (natch!) J&P bio. **In addition to our regular pop record reviewers, this month we introduce Patricia Kennely, no stranger to JAZZ & POP. Editorial Assistant and POP TALK columnist, Patricia offered the following biographical data:**
      Irish ancient spell Cinnfhaolidh but KennEEEly say, Pisceswaterdaughter, kilodecade old (=2.2), Middle-earth native by way of Perelandra and points west, currently NYC resident due to pineapple timewarp and California geology.

JEFFERSON AIRPLANE ✦ *Crown of Creation* **(RCA LSP 4058). Marty Balin (vo, g); Grace Slick (vo, p, or); Paul Kantner (vo, rhythm g); Jorma Kaukonen (lead g, vo); Jack Casady (b); Spencer Dryden**

(d, p, or, vo). *Lather; In Time; Triad; Star Track; Share A Little Joke; Chushingura; If You Feel; Crown of Creation; Ice Cream Phoenix; Greasy Heart; The House at Pooneil Corners.*

A friend of mine has had on her wall for over a year now a poster collage, and right in the middle of it is the Hiroshima mushroom cloud billowing up behind the familiar, smiling *Surrealistic Pillow* Jefferson Airplane; and nobody liked the idea, and nobody could see why, and all my friend would say was, "Wait." So now here is *Crown of Creation,* Jefferson Airplane's fourth album, with a poisonous gold cover fireball embracing a haggard, unsmiling, very much older Airplane, and you see that Alice has discovered there are all sorts of mushrooms, and I see what my friend was getting at.

One thing you learn after three years of Airplane presence is to expect only what happens; that way you're never surprised at anything they may do. Nobody could have expected *Crown of Creation,* maybe not even the group themselves, and especially not as the successor to *After Bathing at Baxter's;* but it has the right kind of inevitably logical feeling about it, and it's magnificent music, and nobody is surprised.

This is wizards' music, apocalypse-rock, a reverse mirror image of *Baxter's:* none of the love sounds of their first three records, but rather a cosmic love-hate, a violence of anger and frustration that is born of love. It had to happen: there is a lot of blood in this album, blood and bitterness and murders in the Haight and Nixon and Humphrey and Mordor and a Newfoundland dog whose master was assassinated and cracked dust over the guitar strings and the killer cloud boiling up over it all.

A deceptive Peter-Paul-and-Mary guitar leads into

"Lather", one of the two Grace Slick compositions on the album. It's a wistful, folky-sounding song about what's going to happen to us all if we're not careful ("Lather was thirty years old today/They took away all of his toys"), a San Francisco Childe ballad, with some absolutely brilliant sound effects under the lyrics, a water-clear Slick vocal, and Jorma's guitar whining like a stray puppy.

By comparison, the next two tracks, a Balin-Kantner collaboration, "In Time", and ex-Byrd David Crosby's "Triad", strike me as arid and uncomfortable. "In Time" especially is fragmented, full of false starts and lumpy as an old couch. Just as it begins to move somewhere definite, it breaks off and swings someplace else; the melody seems reminiscent of scraps from "Wild Tyme (h)" and "Watch Her Ride", and the lyrics are undistinguished, though Paul turns in an excellent lead vocal. Balin-Kantner have done far better things. As for "Triad", outside of a good jazz vocal by Grace, there is not much there. The arrangement is repetitious and static, and the whole idea ("What can we do now that we both love you … I don't really see/why can't we go on as three"), although intriguing in its possibilities, doesn't quite come off, and the opening of "Star Track" comes as an immediate relief, clearing your head like a snort of ammonia.

"Star Track" is a tough Kaukonen screamer on the order of "The Last Wall of the Castle", something you can pound your fist to on a table or a friend. Besides, it's good advice:

You can fool your friends about the way it ends
But you can't fool yourself
Take your head in hand and make your own demands
Or you'll crystallize on the shelf
[…]

Jorma's vocal is gritty and tight and beautiful, the music is solid. A near-perfect cut.

A Marty Balin original, "Share A Little Joke", and

"Chushingura", a Spencer Dryden instrumental, finish out the side. "Joke" goes in for sophisticated phrasing and Balin mystic melancholy, and is held up by some of Jack Casady's most effective bass playing ("Yggdrasil bass", so say the notes, which presumably makes him the Midgard serpent). The cut trails off into the *2001* [*A Space Odyssey*] metal-monolith buzz of "Chushingura", which features Spencer with a nifty steel ball solo that sounds at first like a short in your speakers.

This first side is highly personal, individual: you can *become* these songs very automatically, with almost no effort whatever. But with the second side, the mood is set, things really begin to move and all you can do is watch and try to grok. The songs grow together in the way of *Baxter's*, or *Sgt. Pepper*, or one or two other albums: positioning, stasis and tension and flow, and everything becomes more or less a lead-in to the final cut.

"If You Feel" opens it up, an uptempo dance on the edge of the grave; Marty's lead vocal is filled with desperate exuberance, and it spills right over into "Crown of Creation", which can only be described as a Paul Kantner protest song. Think of it. A defiant *recitative* credo punctuates the center: "In loyalty to their kind/They cannot tolerate our minds/In loyalty to our kind/We cannot tolerate their obstruction." This is not the Airplane we used to know: what is going down?

And it doesn't let up, either: "Ice Cream Phoenix", co-authored by Jorma and Airplane associate Charles Cockey, sounds like Wallace Stevens set to music. "Phoenix" poses some extremely uncharacteristic Airplane questions. Can the group who use to shout joyfully "It's a time for growing and time for knowing love" really ask in seriousness "Tell me why if you think you know/why people love if there's no tomorrow/and still not cry when it's time to go?" Of course they can: there have been some strange changes, all round.Last stop before the end is "Greasy Heart", the other Slick original on this album, which was released as a single some months back (the Airplane thumbing their collective nose at the top-40). This is a wormwood song: it cuts like a flensing knife at all the tricked-up chicks who keep their beauty-magazine faces in jars by the door and have minds and men to match. As a single, "Greasy Heart" was undirected and aimless; here it fits into place perfectly. Grace does a snaketongue vocal, closely doubletracked in parts, with what sounds like Spencer or Paul on the chorus lines in nice free-form stylings.

All of this, however, becomes mere prelude as the feedback bath that opened "The Ballad of You and Me and Pooneil" [on *Baxter's*] screams into "The House at Pooneil Corners". This is quite possibly as close as anyone will come to a rock blasphemy: Paul and Marty take "Pooneil" and turn it ninety degrees from everything else. "Pooneil Corners" is covered with fallout and filled with probability: the armadillo of "Pooneil" has become a rhinoceros, and you may "do what you can to get balled and high", but it won't help much. (Neither will the printed lyric sheet: RCA, for some incredible reason, has put "bulsht around us" for a most clearly enunciated "bullshit around us", and "bald and hi" for the above-mentioned "balled and high." Honest.)

The song opens out into a heavy, ominous organ and guitar figure, with a Götterdämmerung bass and the lead guitar shrieking like an air-raid siren. Marty, Paul and Grace trade off the vocals with Greek-chorus dispassion: there's not much emotion in "Pooneil Corners", there doesn't have to be. The words speak for themselves:

Everything someday will be gone except silence
Earth will be quiet again

Seas from clouds will wash off the ashes of violence
Left as the memory of men
There will be no survivors, my friend
[...]

And that's how it ends — how it will all end.

Crown of Creation is not a happy album; in fact, it's a down, in the non-pejorative sense, the way good Greek tragedy is a down. Even more so, because it is so excruciatingly immediate — it's you yourself, and the Airplane along with you, and everybody you know, who will wind up as jelly and juice and bubbles on the floor. *Crown of Creation* smiles like love and chants like death; and faced with this, "you know I'm still gonna need you around", Jefferson Airplane; more than ever, now…

Probably my best album review; certainly my favorite Airplane album. And thanks to Airplane manager Bill Thompson, for all those backstage passes.

November 1968

This was my editorial in response to the events of the Democratic Presidential convention of August 1968 in Chicago.

The cover of this particularly political issue, mentioned below, featured a full-color photo of Bill Graham, Stevie Winwood of Traffic and jazzman Ornette Coleman, on an orange-tone background collage of photos of scenes from police riots, Robert Kennedy, Dr. Martin Luther King, Jr., Janis Joplin, Paul McCartney, John Lennon, Lyndon Johnson, John Coltrane, and others both black and white.

JAZZ & POP usually features a cover story in each issue: this month the cover itself is the story.

The color photograph was taken September 24 at the Fillmore East in New York; the surrounding photographs were taken at different times in different places. Even though times have changed and the old order has truly begun to fade, there is a thing that has not changed nor faded, and that is music. Whether the music be pop and Stevie Winwood, or jazz and Ornette Coleman, or blues or folk or whatever, it is still the bond that holds us all together, and it will continue to be so: through our own efforts, through the efforts of artists like Ornette and Stevie, and through the efforts of administrators like Bill Graham, we shall overcome.

If developments in the wake of the Battle of Chicago are any indication, it looks as though the new domestic policy of the United States of America is going to be Beat the Press and Mace the Nation.

And there is very little left to prevent it. True for form, the Democratic and Republican Presidential candidates are applying soothing inanities to the legitimately aroused public, treating, as usual, effect instead of cause, putting political Band-aids of a social cancer. "Law and order," they mouth, "must be maintained"; and never stop to see (nor would they recognize if they saw) that "law" is not always "justice" and "order" has never meant "rigidity".

What they really mean, of course, by their dream of a nation run by the forces of law and order is a nation where there are no bearded protestors, no dissenting men and women "betraying" their country by daring to criticize, no hippies and Yippies and McCarthyites and young people willing to put their bodies on the line to expose the fraud and injustice upon which this country operates: this is what they really want, and another, uglier name for a country run by this kind of law and order is "police state."

They are frightened, these people, badly frightened of a changing world in which they see no place for themselves, and as long as they hold to their dead and rotting ideas, they *will* not see a place, and there will never *be* a place. These are the people who right now are literally fighting for their survival, who cling to the kind of insular reality that is no reality at all ("The Chicago police were protecting themselves," says The Pigpen's Mayor Richard J. Daley, and believes it); who would rather die than lend a hand and refuse point-blank to get out of the road. These are the people who have transformed legitimately constituted police forces into the functioning shock troops of reaction and conservatism, and the Chicago police are in the van.

What happened in Chicago was a watershed for what is to come. Not the sum total of all His Honor's rationalizations can hide the plain fact that in August in Chicago Mayor Daley's cops went berserk, with his sanction, and there is nothing to prevent it happening again. If, as the Mayor claims, it was a cut-and-dried case of the police protecting themselves (with clubs, Mace, tear gas, clubs, fists and clubs) against terrorists and assassins (with lethal flowers, folk songs and long hair), why were badges carefully removed from all police lapels? Why were McCarthyites, photographers, the press, peace delegates and television crews singled out for special viciousness? Why were medical personnel attacked as they tried to assist the injured? And why the hell did Hubert Humphrey not open the mind and heart he once had, but choose instead to raise his voice above the screams and the sound of clubs hitting skulls and pontificate nervously on the "politics of joy"?

Politics of joy? Politics of death. The patriots who were beaten at Chicago, and those who will be beaten at other places in time to come, are the conscience of this country, and they will not kill themselves off to gratify the deathwish of Hubert Humphrey and Richard Nixon and George Wallace and the constituencies they so truly represent.

No, the police of Chicago were not afraid of the possible physical force the demonstrators might muster: they were afraid of the ideas they could not share, the philosophies they could never understand, the lifestyles they could never be part of. Like primitives, they distrusted and hated the new, the unknown; like primitives, they reacted in the only way they knew—with their clubs. They will learn, perhaps, someday, that you cannot club an idea, nor can you spray it with Mace or push it through a plate-glass window. They will learn too that you cannot kill an idea with bullets; when they learn it all, they will remember.

What place has all this in a music magazine?, some readers have asked, and criticized us for being "political". Any publication that claims to treat today's music with any degree of seriousness must concern itself not only with form, but with content. The music of today does not merely contain social comment, it is itself social comment. It is medium and message: and as long as the music finds within itself the responsibility to be "political" so must this magazine, and any who call themselves critics.

It is marching music for the Armies of the Night, the Second American Revolution. There is a new Continental Army in the land: its soldiers are men and women both, blacks and whites both, hippies and Yippies and students and radicals and war critics and acidheads and housewives. It is just as raggedly uniformed and ill-disciplined as its ancestor, just as vital, just as true: and after its baptism of blood at Chicago, it has become just willing to fight to the death so that its country may live.

Two hundred years, there is a new Revolution at hand. Pray God it is not two hundred years, or two years, too late.

––––––––––––––––––––

My personal note, in an adjacent multipage feature wherein many of our writers and associate editors commented on the topic of Chicago:

It's nice to know that the Chicagestapo had the blessing and approval of Mayor Daley: imagine what would have happened if they had merely acted irresponsibly on their own.

I did not go to Pig City, for a number of reasons, but mostly because street fighting has never been my thing, and there are better ways to reach the desired ends. Oh, I've been to all the demonstrations, have campaign buttons from the various Mobilizations, been blooded and gassed at the nastier scenes; my credentials are all in order, and if my wild-eyed revolutionary friends prove right, I suppose I could play underground games as well as anybody.

I felt it watching the convention coverage: bloodlust. Righteous wrath. Take the pigs apart with my bare hands. But what good is that, meeting them on their own terms and their own ground? Perhaps violence is truly the only language they understand, but if we start to speak it, we become fascists ourselves. Besides, they'd stomp us good: they're far better at that sort of thing than we could ever be. God knows they've practiced enough.

What then? I wish I knew. But I do know this: they say, Do it our way or we'll beat you bloody, shut your mouths and get off the streets or we'll crack your heads. This is how people talk who are desperately afraid: they are the ones who are up against the wall, not we.

And who are we? "Our children," says the national press, jolted into awareness at last by Mace in its own eyes and a club on its skull, "our children, beaten up by the police." "Your sons and your daughters, beyond your command," Dylan answers. He is right. We're nobody's children now, nobody's sons and daughters. We're orphans.

Reading this, I am struck almost senseless by how close the parallels are to what we're still seeing today: changing names here and there, I could have written this last week about the Occupy movement. How far we've come in some respects, yet in others we have been frozen in our tracks.

I'm not going into any deep exegesis of Chicago '68 and its lasting imprint, or lack thereof, on our national psyche. If you are too young to remember, go look it up and read about it. If you are old enough and don't remember, go look it up and shame on you for having forgotten. Either way, learn.

POP TALK:
A NIGHT AT THE WHITNEY

The Whitney Museum of American Art in New York is some seventy blocks from the Village, and it is a great place for an acid trip. It looks like a demented staircase ("inverted ziggurat" is what they call it); it has light-flashing junk sculptures and black-light elevators and it is probably the freakiest building ever constructed. Nevertheless, the Whitney is the kind of place where the curators are probably listed in the Social Register, and no matter how hard you try to ignore it, the Very Beautiful very pores of the Very Beautiful walls quietly insinuate in your ears, "MONEY..."

So it's that kind of a place, right? So naturally we had trouble getting in on the rainy night of October 3, because we — well, we looked *weird*. You know. Not *Right*. In fact, we looked like dirty degenerate dope fiend HIPPIES (even though we were wearing our very best party clothes), but after all, it wasn't *our* museum... We were there by invitation to witness what may win my vote as the Scene of the Year, something to tell my grandchildren about: "An Evening with Glenn McKay's Head Lights", accompanied by the mighty Jefferson Airplane — all this, you dig, in the Whitney, as contemporary American Art. Or at least I suppose that's how the trustees must have explained it to their wives.

At any rate, it was an Event for the "Friends of the Museum", with invited press and a pre-show cocktail crush (among the Franz Kline paintings) like what you read about. There was not too much hair in sight: freaks were definitely in the minority. Thirty is a generous count, and that includes the Airplane, McKay's crew and representatives of the hip press. But we had pure hearts, and the strength of ten, you know, and by then we were invisible as well, so we were ambling innocently around the cocktail party, gobbling cookies to ease the great hunger and sampling such exotic drugs as gin and Scotch. But we get very bored very quickly, and we did, so we decided to go upstairs to watch the Airplane set up. As we were splitting, a large fat man in a Nehru suit leered at us, "Would you please save me the seeds?", and his blue-haired wife trilled an orchestrated laugh that must have spanned three octaves. That was just the beginning: these people may be socially prominent (in their hearts, they know they're Right), and all the rest of that bullshit shuck, but I think even the Chicago police have better manners.

Revenge came swiftly. Up on the third floor, then, the lights were off, people were milling around, and we were standing with our elbows planted on the stage right in front of Jorma's amplifier. Head Lights started to spin, the Airplane was tuning up, and we were stone rapping to each other in the dark. Then this unmistakable voice snaked out of a corner of the stage, in massively amplified bell-clear tones: "I'VE ...just...stepped...on a socialite's TOE." Yes, folks, Grace Slick was sockin' it to 'em. She riffed on for about ten minutes on socialites and their strange habits and quaint attire and "Your lover, madam...YOUR LOVER... thinks you have sophisticated little TITS, and your HUSBAND, well, he thinks you're just a drag," and then she stalked onstage in a long silky striped dress, the light show exploded and so did the band.

The Airplane just keeps getting better and better and tighter and louder and better and weirder and better, every time, all the time. They did a spectacular first set ("It's No Secret", "Plastic Fantastic Lover", "In Time", "Star Track", "Watch Her Ride, "White Rabbit", "Crown of Creation" and a few others), all of which was most totally wasted on about ninety per cent of this particular audience. Then McKay's people did a brilliant exhibition to accompany classical pianist Raymond Lewenthal (no, I've never heard of him either) in a program of preludes by Scriabin and the *Dante Sonata* of Franz Liszt; I found Lewenthal condescending and pretentious enough to make me want to kick him, but Head Lights outdid themselves. Any one of their masterpieces of slides, transparencies or liquid diffusions cuts everything the Whitney has hanging on its walls.

By the time the Airplane was sober enough to walk back down the stairs (I asked why juice is the current hip high; answer: "It's legal, people will buy it for you, and if you have a good head, you'll have a good head no matter what you're on, so why not?"), all the Beautiful People had left, apparently unwilling to ruin their oh-such-a-lovely-event-darling-and-weren't-those–hippies-precious evening with a case of guinea pig ear. (One man, indeed, insisted for some reason on sitting on the stage in front of Jack's amp—but with his fingers securely in his ears; I don't know why). It was nice of them to leave, though: everybody was much happier for the second act, but those who left missed one of the legendary Kaukonen-Casady jams. This one was particularly good: just Jack and Jorma in a freestyle modal electric raga. Grace sauntered around the stage, announced them as Ravi Kaukonen and Ali Akbar Casady, then sat down on the side; what she was snorting then, brother, was *not* the best licks in town.

After about twenty minutes, Spencer joined the jam, then Paul; Marty was thrashing away in the corner on tambourine, and Grace came over to sit next to us on the stage.

"What song is this gonna be, Paul? 'China breaking'?"

"Guess again, baby."

"Well, I don't know your songs…"

"Yeah, but this one's yours. "

And so it was: "Somebody to Love". After that I don't remember much of what they did because I had gone into the kind of trance generally associated with mystic visions. But I do recall "Won't You Try/Saturday Afternoon", "Greasy Heart" (Grace: "This song...is dedicated...to 66 East 78th Street...which means...ABSOLUTELY NOTHING!") [*Actually, that was the address of Grace's own alma mater, Finch College, located not too many blocks away from the Whitney — PKM*], one of Jorma's interminable blues numbers and "Fat Angel." The very last number was a back-to-back nonstop cosmic mindfuck: "The Ballad of You and Me and Pooneil" linked by a feedback shudder to "The House at Pooneil Corners", and I remember thinking that now I had heard this and I could die happy.

It was over at 2 a.m. Clouds were scudding over the full moon when we came out of the museum. I don't know how we got home.

I HEARD THE NEWS TODAY OH BOY: Congratulations to Bill and Bonnie Graham on the birth of their first: David Wolodia Graham, born September 20, in San Francisco ... Frank Zappa, head Mother of Invention, has joined with manager Herb Cohen to form Bizarre, Inc., which will be responsible for all Mother activity as well as functioning as a "total entertainment organization", with branches in television, motion pictures, records, publishing, radio programming and management ... Steve Paul's The Scene had its name changed to Biafra from August 26 to September 5. The New York rock showcase was the headquarters for a contemporary music benefit marathon that raised many thousands of dollars for the American Committee to Keep Biafra Alive; all proceeds went towards the purchase of air transport and food stockpiles for the

African nation. Performers who contributed their services included Joan Baez, Peter Walker, Richie Havens, The Jimi Hendrix Experience, the Chambers Brothers, the entire cast of *Hair*, Eric Andersen and many others … Jeff Beck has added pianist Nicky Hopkins to his Group. Hopkins, probably England's top rock pianist, is responsible for the solo work on the Beatle single "Revolution", as well as piano on all the Rolling Stones LPs and Beck's own first album … Elektra group David Peel and the Lower East Side have their first release out: Have A Marijuana … Heavy fall schedule at Fillmore East includes Steppenwolf, Buddy Rich and His Orchestra, The Move (November 15-16), Iron Butterfly paired with Canned Heat (November 22-23), and Jefferson Airplane in a possible three-day Thanksgiving gig (November 28, 29, 30) … John Sebastian has split The Lovin' Spoonful to go off on his own. Sebastian has signed with MGM and is presently recording his first solo album for the label (LP produced by Paul Rothchild); he has also written six songs for a Broadway "play with music", *Jimmy Shine*, which will star Dustin Hoffman. As *Jimmy Shine* will not have an original cast LP, Sebastian is recording the songs on his own album, using different musicians for each track. So far, he has worked with Stephen Stills (guitarist for the now-defunct Buffalo Springfield, and one-third of the personnel on the *Supersession* LP), Harvey Brooks (formerly of the Electric Flag), Ike and Tina Turner's backing group the Ikettes, and pianist Paul Harris. Release date will be sometime in November … Joan Baez booked five sessions in Nashville to record her next album; this will be her first venture into country music … Donovan is touring the U.S. and Canada during October and November, including a gig at New York's Carnegie Hall. Epic has released Don's sixth album to coincide with the tour; LP is entitled *Hurdy-Gurdy Man*, and includes both that tune and "Jennifer Juniper", both recent hit singles … Apparently still unresolved is the colossal Rolling Stones vs. London Records hassle over the cover of the *Beggars Banquet* LP. Jagger has been quoted to the effect that "It looks like a Christmas release now." The cover that is causing so much trouble is a great wraparound photo of the graffiti-covered wall of a really raunchy-looking bathroom: credits, song titles and clever sayings ("God rolls His own") are scribbled all over the cracked plaster. Alternative plan is to package the record in brown paper bags stamped "Unfit for Children" … All record company presidents should make the nighttime scene as often as Columbia chief Clive Davis. At Tim Hardin's Café Au Go Go opening September 27, Davis was on hand with Columbia publicity head Bob Altschuler to cheer on their newly signed artist. On the bill with Hardin were Elektra's new group Rhinoceros and vocalist Van Morrison; in the audience were Papa John Phillips with Mama Michelle … According to The Hammond World Atlas we got in the mail, there is a Linn County in Iowa, Kansas, Missouri and Oregon. The real Linn County was in Manhattan, though, at Steve Paul's The Scene, where they opened in October for a four-day gig. Personnel were Larry Easter, tenor and soprano saxophone, who when asked about influences answers Archie Shepp, Pharaoh Sanders and John Coltrane; Stephen Miller, organist and vocalist; Fred Walk, guitar; Snake McAndrew, drums; and Dino Long, bass. The group is into a funky avant-garde jazz/blues/pop bag, doing mostly original material; first Mercury LP *Proud Flesh Soothseer* has just been released … Musical score for a film version of Evergreen Review's own *Barbarella* done by Bob Crewe and Charlie Fox. Two Crewe groups, the Glitterhouse and the Bob Crewe Generation Orchestra, perform on the soundtrack … Auditions continue for Janis Joplin's new band; so far nobody has been signed. If and when she gets things together, the first album will be produced by Eddie Kramer (tentatively set for January) … Jim Morrison cut his hair. Al Kooper cut his hair. Jerry Garcia cut his hair. Jack Casady did not cut his hair. You are all free. This is a recorded announcement.

That Whitney thing was a strange and strained evening, to be sure. I had only contempt for the Social Register Hippies of the day, the self-described "Beautiful People" trying to ape their juniors and perceived inferiors, people like—well, like utterly forgettable, utterly unbeautiful people whose names are pretty much forgotten by now, so I won't even bother; the sort who got themselves all tricked out in Guccipucciooochiecoochie (which no real head would ever have been caught dead in; that was the kind of gear our parents would wear, if we had rich pretentious totally unhip parents) and madly pranced around places like Club El Morocco and the Peppermint Lounge (again, which no real head would ever have been caught dead in) trying to dance, puffing away on cigarettes and sloshing back Scotch because they were too pissant scared to actually try joints.

Funny, too, because Grace Wing Slick herself came from a background not altogether unlike theirs: posh Palo Alto antecedents, finishing-school college at Finch here in NYC, a fellow alumna of presidential daughter Tricia Nixon. Only, at least she had the brains to see it all for the sham it was, and for the goof the band played it as.

BOOK REVIEWS:

THE BEATLES: The Authorized Biography,
Hunter Davies. (McGraw-Hill, 358 pages, $6.95)

THE BEATLES: The Real Story,
Julius Fast. (Putnam, 252 pages, $5.95)

Contemporary pop psychology has it that there are two kinds of people in the world: those who are Beatles and those who are not. Of the two Beatle biographies published recently, Julius Fast's appears dedicated to affirming this proposition, while Hunter Davies' strives to assure the reader that the Beatles are just folks, you know, boys from humble origins who happened to make good, just plain people — just like us.

Fast's work is subtitled *The Real Story*, which it is not. Handicapped by the non-cooperation of the Beatles (he never spoke to them), further handicapped by the necessity of beating out the Davies book to publication, Fast nevertheless rose to the occasion like flotsam in New York harbor.

The brother of historical novelist Howard Fast, Julius Fast's apparent literary forte is zapping out spinoffs from other people's books. When *Human Sexual Response* was published, Fast was pressed into service to pump out *What You Should Know About Human Sexual Response*; and when Putnam got wind of the impending McGraw-Hill Beatle coup, Fast again did yeoman's service. Denied access to his subjects, he turned to the mountains of existing material — articles, studies, clippings, reviews, quotable quotes — on or by the Beatles, changed the tenses here and there, and added a few connecting clauses; somebody did a quickie pseudo-baroque dust jacket, and there you are: instant book.

Davies' work is subtitled *The Authorized Biography*, which it is. The author was granted fullest cooperation and a number of private audiences by his subjects, as well as a tremendous amount of help from miscellaneous friends, enemies, wives, parents, step-parents, aunts, business associates, teenyboppers and even an ex-Beatle. The book cannot but benefit from such a wealth of personal data, but after a while it does get tedious having to mentally splice the various days in the life of each Beatle into some kind of order.

The merits of the Davis biography are chiefly the Beatles' own: candor, irreverence, honesty, unpretentiousness. The best chapters are those in which the Beatles themselves do most of the talking, explaining their history, their lives, their work. (John on Beatle music: "We're a con. We know we're conning them, because we know people want to be conned. They've given us the freedom to con them. Let's stick in that there, we say, that'll start them puzzling. I'm sure all artists do, when they realize it's a con. I bet Picasso sticks things in. I bet he's been laughing his balls off for the last eighty years.")

The Davies chronology is particularly fearsome: each Beatle is traced separately from birth (with brief accounts of the ancestry of parents and grandparents as well), through schooldays up to the formation of the first pre-Beatle group, the Quarrymen skiffle band. From then on, John, Paul and George (Ringo not coming in sight until 1962) are treated as a cohesive unit; early Beatles Pete Best and the late Stuart Sutcliffe are handled with compassion and care.

Davies documents the days of Beatlemania, the constant touring, the screaming, the strain; later he recounts the ennui and isolation that led in the end to *Sgt. Pepper*, drugs, the Maharishi, Apple, Yoko Ono and the biggest metamorphosis in the history of pop music. What Davies does best, though, is the directness of personal contact he gives to the book, something few biographers modern or ancient have managed to do: there is a scene in a narrow attic room in Paul's London house one afternoon; John and Paul are writing "With A Little Help from My Friends." Lines are tossed around (Cynthia Lennon suggests "I just feel fine"; they do not use it), backings worked out, and the song is finished by nightfall, ready to record. The bulk of Lennon-McCartney songwriting is done in similar pastiche fashion, even such pop epics as "A Day in the Life" and "I Am the Walrus" ("Or I was when I sat down to write the song," Lennon equivocates.)

The overall impression of the Beatles according to Davies is one of high complexity: just four of your ordinary garden-variety geniuses, you know who have received such adulation as only a handful of others in all history have ever received, but who are still individuals under it all. "We're not the four moptops anymore," Paul McCartney cautions; they are not. They have been molded by their experiences into four realistic, hard-headed, amoral iconoclasts; one can only wonder where they will go from here.

December 1968

"Nothing Is Real", says the subtitle of *Yellow Submarine*, but after seeing the incredibly beautiful King Features–United Artists animated Beatle cartoon, I am not so sure.

The whole thing, of course, is based vaguely on the song of the same name and the Concept of the *Sgt. Pepper* album; but only vaguely. There is a plot, for those of you who are made happy by such things, and a happy ending, and even a Message; there is also a lot of trippiness and insane visual effects, if that is what pleases you most. The best thing of all is that you cannot separate *Yellow Submarine* into arbitrary and convenient sections; it is one splendid, shining, uniformly brilliant piece of genius, and I grinned all the way home after seeing it. [*Of course, the contact high I got at the screening may have contributed just the teensiest bit to my merry mood… — PKM*]

The story, in its barest outlines, is this: Under the sea is a land called Pepperland, where everybody is happy and musical and warm. On the borders of Pepperland, the Blue Meanies, who hate happiness and music and warmth (but music especially: it causes them to shrink and self-destruct), have launched an invasion that eventually conquers all the land and all its inhabitants but one. That one is Old Fred, the Sea Captain, who makes his escape in the Yellow Submarine and reaches Liverpool, where he obtains the help of the Beatles. They go with him in the Submarine back under the sea to Pepperland, sailing through many sore trials and desperate straits; they rout the Blue Meanies, restore life and joy to Pepperland and finally convert the Meanies into happy creatures, all through the power of music.

A narration does nothing to convey the true impact of the film: it must be seen. Heinz Edelmann's animations are superb: 1920's-style cartoon Beatles in psychedelic drag and Liverpool accents; marvelous monsters (the Chief Blue Meanie, the Deadly Flying Glove and the Snapping Turtle Turks and the Giant Stomping Boots and the Apple Bonkers); a genuine Nowhere Man (Jeremy Hilary Boob); the Seas of Consumer Products, Time, Music, Monsters, Phrenology (also known as The Headlands), Holes and Green.

But the real strength of *Yellow Submarine* (it saved Pepperland, didn't it?) is the music. Four new songs ("All Together Now", "Hey Bulldog", "All Too Much", and George Harrison's "Northern Song") are added to the tracks from *Sgt. Pepper*; all are fitted beautifully into the framework of the film, some as whole sequences ("Lucy in the Sky with Diamonds"), some as fragments (the 40-second buildup from "A Day in the Life" is illustrated by dazzling landscapes flashing past at almost subliminal speed, too quick to remember or even quite see: at the very peak of the musical rush, London Bridge yawns open and you fall through into real and screamingly sudden blackness). Incidental music abounds throughout the film, but it is so tastefully done that you are never aware of it.

Yellow Submarine will be seen equally, I think, by adults and children. It is a contemporary classic on a level with *The Lord of the Rings*. There is nothing childish about either, yet both retain a sense of childlike wonder and love of beauty that other classics, such as *Alice in Wonderland* or *Winnie the Pooh*, for all their good qualities, miss by miles. There is wickedness in *Yellow Submarine*, to be sure; but somehow it's all there to be laughed at, and that's the *real* way to win.

At the conclusion of *Yellow Submarine*, all four real-life Beatles come on-camera, John busy with a telescope. "Newer and bluer Meanies have been sighted in the vicinity of this theatre," he reports seriously. "There's only one way to go out…SINGING!" The seriousness is real; perhaps all we really *do* need is love, maybe singing really *can* do in Blue Meanies. Perhaps the Beatles are right, and *Yellow Submarine* is both their revolution and their opening gun. If that is true, as I suspect it may well be, then *Yellow Submarine* is the most subversive thing I have ever seen or imagined, and you can't see it fast enough.

I HEARD THE NEWS TODAY OH BOY: First it was guinea pigs, now it's termites. According to preliminary studies made by a California entomologist, Group A termites were exposed to blues band music and were spurred to increased activity, neglecting family life in favor of foraging and eating for themselves, instead of caring for their larvae and queen as they should have been doing. Group B termites were subjected to a British rock band's music and were even more bugged, stimulated to even greater activity and "in danger of eating themselves out of house and home." Any conclusions you care to make are your own business … Phil Spector, the grand old man of rock producers, is back in the studios again after two years of retirement … Bill Graham has been up against the wall lately in New York and San Francisco both. Street radicals in both places have been demanding free use of the Fillmores at least one night a week for ostensibly community-oriented purposes; in New York, the demands were accompanied by threats that "If we don't get it, we'll burn the place down." Hopefully things are resolved by now: at any rate, Bill has done more good for the community than all the radical groups put together;

maybe that's what they're really pissed off about ... The Who's next album, set for December release on Decca, is a pop opera composed by Peter Townshend, lead guitarist for the group. Entitled *Deaf, Dumb and Blind Boy*, the opera depicts the world as experienced by the child, including a sequence in which he is seduced by his uncle. According to vocalist Roger Daltrey, "The storyline is centered on a deaf, dumb and blind boy and his reactions to things that are repugnant to most people. Being seduced by his uncle is merely a new experience to the boy. The message, if it can be called that, is that nothing is totally evil." ... Acute tonsillitis forced the cancellation of Mama Cass Elliott's $40,000 a week engagement at Las Vegas' Caesar's Palace. Still, Cass is not doing too badly: ABC has scheduled her for a one-hour special in January, a European tour and appearances at Carnegie and Philharmonic Halls in New York ... In other Mamas and Papas action, ABC Records' million-dollar suit is still pending against John and Michelle Phillips and Denny Doherty, for alleged non-fulfillment of contractual obligations. Cass is not being sued because she made her LP *Dream A Little Dream* for Dunhill, which satisfied her contract. In their turn, the Ms and the Ps are reportedly suing ABC after a very highly-placed ABC official called the group "four animals" in print ... Canned Heat cut a single called "Refried Christmas" with David Seville and the Chipmunks ... Rock groups have been running into more than their fair share of hassles lately in New York City. Cream, in town for their American farewell concert November 2 (for which they made $104,000), was denied accommodations by just about every hotel in the city; the Jimi Hendrix Experience was refused a booking by Carnegie Hal, on the grounds that "in his other appearances, in other places, the audience got very much out of hand. They destroyed furniture and draperies. We cannot afford to take the chance." Offered a posted surety bond by the concert promoter, Carnegie informed him that Hendrix would not be allowed to play there under *any* circumstances. Jimi's appearance was rescheduled for Lincoln Center's Philharmonic Hall, a few blocks to the north ... The latest in the seemingly unending trail of neo-Monterey pop festivals is the 1968 Miami Pop Festival, to be held at Gulfstream Park December 28-30. The lineup includes the Grateful Dead, Steppenwolf, Canned Heat, H. P. Lovecraft, Buffy Sainte-Marie, Iron Butterfly and numerous others ... Apple Productions releases its first albums on the American market during the month of November, the first and foremost of course being the Beatles' double album *The Beatles* [*which would come to be universally known as the "White Album"*], which should be out by the time you read this. The other LPs to come are the controversial *Two Virgins*, the John Lennon–Yoko Ono album to be released in the U.S. by Tetragrammaton Records; George Harrison's soundtrack album *Wonderwall*; an LP by the Modern Jazz Quartet, *Under the Jasmine Tree* (recorded in New York); and the first record produced by Apple a&r manager Peter Asher, featuring James Taylor and entitled *James Taylor and Son*. Scheduled for December release are the soundtrack from *Yellow Submarine* and the first LP by Mary Hopkin ... Mick Jagger and Marianne Faithfull are expecting their first child momentarily; John Lennon and Yoko Ono's first is due in March.

REVIEW:
ELECTRIC LADYLAND, Jimi Hendrix Experience

Deeply embarrassing, but here's how it sounded when I didn't much care for the subject. Which was why, after this effort, I tried to only ever write about bands I really, really liked...

JIMI HENDRIX EXPERIENCE ◆ *Electric Ladyland* (Reprise 2R56307). Jimi Hendrix (vo, g); Noel Redding (b, vo); Mitch Mitchell (d). *...And the Gods Made Love; Have You Ever Been (To Electric Ladyland); Crosstown Traffic; Voodoo Child; Little Miss Strange; Long Hot Summer Night; Come On (Part 1); Gypsy Eyes; Burning of the Midnight Lamp; Rainy Day Dream Away; 1983...; Moon, Turn the Tides; Still Raining Still Dreaming; House Burning Down; All Along the Watchtower; Voodoo Child (Slight Return).*

Jimi Hendrix, born the night the moon turned fire red, carried on eagles' backs across magic mountains, raised by mountain lions in mystic landscapes, has made a third album, and somehow it manages to simultaneously sound like nothing, and everything, you've ever heard from him before.

Electric Ladyland is a two-LP stretch of essential Hendrix, mystical, musical, psychic, elemental. I admit to misgivings before I listened to it (which can be summed up: How the hell is he going to make it through four sides?). But he does, and it works, and although in places the album scrapes woefully thin, it never breaks and it never once sounds mangy.

Musically, *Electric Ladyland* is not all that different from its predecessor, *Axis: Bold As Love*, though *Axis* was very different indeed from *Are You Experienced?*. On *Ladyland* we get what amounts to a further distillation of the Hendrix sound: not much new. After a while all his riffs begin to sound alike; he is not the most inventive guitarist around, though certainly one of the most capable, and when compared to people like Jorma Kaukonen or Jeff Beck, Hendrix tends to sound unnecessarily cluttered and blurred around the edges. As for sidemen Noel Redding and Mitch Mitchell, they do what they are supposed to do, generally well (despite the talk of colossal differences between Hendrix and Redding supposedly leading to the trio's imminent breakup).

All the songs are Jimi's on *Ladyland*, except three: one of these, "Little Miss Strange", was composed by Redding and is my personal favorite. The songs cycle through air and water and fire, Hendrix being a creature in whom earth (common clay, that is) is not a major component. On "House Burning Down", there is some rather inept moralizing (a social statement?); on "Moon, Turn the Tides" and "Voodoo Child" we get science fiction. (The really fine thing, of course, about "Voodoo Child" is the presence of Jack Casady and Stevie Winwood: Jack's bass playing is always a joy, and Stevie, to my mind, is one of the very best rock keyboard men around. Jimi's treatment of the Dylan song "All Along the Watchtower" is particularly interesting: he keeps the bare bones of the song, and then carefully drapes it in his own colors, giving it a texture and an emotional quality of despair and anxiety that the original did not have. This is not necessarily *better*, mind: just different, and I like the two versions equally.

One unusual feature about *Ladyland* is the rather large number of guest stars Hendrix presents: besides Casady and Winwood, appearances are put in by Al Kooper, Buddy Miles, Chris Wood and several others, though nobody is let loose enough to really knock anybody out; Jimi is totally in command all the way through. Technically, the album is superb; stereo separation, mixing, multitracking are all done to perfection by engineer Eddie Kramer.

Electric Ladyland is a good album. I think you need it.

See? I wasn't even impressed enough to work up a decent go-out line. And yet I stand by the review for being honestly how I considered the album at the time. I really didn't think Jimi was the best guitarist on the planet, though most of the musicians I've ever spoken to, and just about all the guitarists, did. My opinion has since altered so far in that I acknowledge his technical brilliance and honor his innovations: if all those great musicians think he's greater than they are, well, they should know, and it is not for me to say them nay.

Still, to my ear, Jimi's music doesn't do anything for me: it's not melody-driven as I prefer, nor does it speak to my soul, nor give me any joy or delight or exaltation of spirit, and I would much rather listen to Jorma Kaukonen or John Cipollina or Robby Krieger or Eric Clapton or Nokie Edwards of the Ventures, who do all those things for me any day of the week and six times on Sunday. Hendrix is for me the Emperor's New Clothes—no matter how hard I try, no matter how many people tell me how great he is, I just don't see it. Very nice guy, though.

Then again, I don't see the supposed great genius of Frank Sinatra either—I think he's off-pitch, flat and boring. But even Jim thought Sinatra was brilliant. Maybe it's me.

January 1969

Ten years ago [*We're talking 1958 here, when I was twelve —
PKM*] the world was young and rock and roll was king and
I was listening to J. S. Bach and not very much else (except
for some Beethoven in lighter moments). I never owned an
AM radio, I went to school dances only rarely, at parties I
sat in a corner with a few like-minded soulmates and talked
of many things: Jack Kerouac, Ayn Rand, cabbages, kings.
I therefore managed to avoid just about every available
opportunity to hear, in their time and context, people like
Elvis, Chuck Berry, Little Richard; while Ritchie Valens and
Buddy Holly and Danny and the Juniors were totally out of
my ken (though I could distinguish blindfolded between
the New York Philharmonic and the Cleveland).

Now this kind of educational gap, though by no means
unique or "special", was nevertheless an oddity among my
sociological peer group, and I never thought the day would
come when I would sorely rue my lack of knowledge, much
actually seek out what I had been at such pains to avoid.

So when I first discovered that rock was worth
discovering (post-Dismal Dick Clark and the South Philly
cretin scene, at the time of the Great Beatle Advent), I also
found that I had a lot of rooting to do. And where did I have
to root? Right: good old mid-fifties rock and roll.

So I listened to "Teen Angel" and "Donna" and
"Chantilly Lace" and "Heartbreak Hotel" and "Bird Dog"

[*though I liked the Everly Brothers and even owned a few of their 45's, and in truth had heard all these songs many times before – PKM*] and any other middle-aged greasy-hearted group I could find. And I don't think I missed all that much. No doubt it was different then, but fifties rock and roll shows up now as a very odd blend of country-crass-commercial, bleached blues, soap-opera sentiment and some rather astonishing necrophilia. The only major component that comes out right is the sexuality, and that, I think, intrigues me more than the music itself.

Nobody should ever forget that rock music is about fucking and that's all it's about. Is not sexual energy the basis of all human action, and is not music a primary expression of energy?

The first premise is sound, at any rate. Elvis' thrashings may seem pretty pallid (judging by his recent television special) compared to Joplin, Jagger, or even Morrison, but he was far away the most outrageous thing around back then; and besides, he had Religion, so he couldn't have been all bad. What else was there? Pat Boone?

At any rate, the Presley-Boone standoff, then the South Philly super grease job (remember Franny? Bob and Justine?), all eventually crumpled under the weight of their own respectability: circumstances beyond their own control, if you will. How could a basically nice Catholic kid like Fabian compete with Mick Jagger, that dirty British baddie? Things began to open up around then; the Eisenhower prissiness years had all gone by and when the Stones sang "King Bee" in the early Sixties, the kids listened, and wondered why nobody had ever done it before.

It *had* all been done before, of course; by backcountry bluesmen who were never considered at all "respectable" or the sort of thing "nice" people might ever listen to. It took a long while to get up front: but everything had started changing by that time, and "I want to hold your hand" eventually did manage to become "Let's spend the night together", and now even "Why don't we do it in the road?"

There was a great deal to overcome: parents, record companies, evangelists, self-righteous disc jockeys and advertising-scared radio stations. Sex, of course has always been profitable: or rather, the exploitation of sex has always been profitable. The businessmen who objected to Mick Jagger probably whiled away their commuting time with *The Carpetbaggers*, on the theory that if it sells it must be all right, and if it's sordid, it will sell. Jagger, on the other hand, was merely honest.

So chicks stopped being smashed up by trains while trying to save their boyfriends' high school rings and started to get (musically) balled. The Puritan ethic was vestigial by now, but still strong in its dying gasps. Which meant we got sanctimonious Lou Christie ("And in this car/Our love went—MUCH too far"); and the Beatles had progressed from handholding to seduction ("We talked until two/And then she said it's time for bed"). For four clean-cut lads from Liverpool (the Image again; actually, they'd put in a year or so of black-leather gigs on Hamburg's gross Reeperbahn, the 42nd Street of the World), that was pretty strong stuff.

But by 1966, sex was here to stay, according to the button on Brian Jones' lapel. San Francisco was preaching love; Airplane Grace was quoted in Time magazine: "Be free! Free in love, free in sex!" Even glossy women's magazines were debating what they termed the New Morality. Morality, new or otherwise, had not very much to do with it; what was really involved was not New Morality but Old Hypocrisy. (Ralph J. Gleason had a classic line about this: something to the effect that two long-haired kids in a sleeping bag is fornication, two short-haired kids in a car is sexual experience, and their parents swacked out on juice in a motel is making love.)

Just as the music around now has polarized itself around violent changes (revolution, if you insist; but it's not gonna happen, friends, not for a good long while), music in '66-'67 was breaking out on the subject on the subject it had had to sing around (rather than about) for lo these ten long years. Censorship proved rather astounding: there was one radio station that wouldn't play anything unless it was accompanied by printed lyrics for both sides; [*Frank*] Zappa ran afoul of a very strange legality (peculiar to MGM Records, apparently) that it's only obscene if it's printed: sung on the record, it's a work of art. "Let's spend the night together" was an outrage to decent people everywhere, but "Strangers in the night, lovers at first sight, shooby dooby doo" was just easily forgivable impetuousness. (My personal favorite line of this period is Jefferson Airplane's, in "Martha" on the *After Bathing at Baxter's* LP: "She does as she pleases/her heels rise for me." RCA must not have been listening.)

And now nobody really cares. "No one will be watching us; why don't we do it in the road?" the Beatles suggest. "Bet your mama don't know you can bite like that/Bet she never saw you scratch my back," Jagger grins, in "Stray Cat Blues" on *Beggars Banquet*, and Grace Slick invites us to a *ménage à trois*, via David Crosby's "Triad". John and Yoko [*Two Virgins*]: "And they were both naked, the man and his wife, and they were not ashamed." Morrison in Vogue: skin, leather and long hair — cock rock. Things are out in the open, right up front, pun intended. ("But Mother wouldn't approve!" "Nonsense, your mother loved it!")

Getting back to the original hypothesis (you remember: rock is about balling and that's all it about), it comes to my mind that the second half is not quite so valid as the first. Rock is now, always has been, and always will be, chiefly concerned with fucking, but what has happened now, I think, is that the musicians have taken the sexual energy transmitted automatically by the music and superimposed on it mind ideas. "Crown of Creation" (the song) or "The Fool on the Hill" or even Judy Collins' new-directed material, though not outwardly governed by physicality, nevertheless are solidly grounded in the tradition, and use its familiarity to push their ideas through.

Combining the newly liberated music with the newly liberated visuals of its artists is just one more manifestation of the new open society that is taking shape. So, if you want to do it in the road…go right ahead.

I HEARD THE NEWS TODAY OH BOY: Kind of late to be talking about Bill Graham's Thanksgiving dinner at the Fillmore East, but it was a nice thing. Pop equivalents of the Pilgrims were too numerous to mention; sitting with Bill Thompson (J. Airplane's manager) and M. Schmidt (same's producer) was nice too … The great Bill Graham/ Up Against the Wall Motherfuckers dispute was resolved recently when Bill agreed to allow the New York street group a series of four Wednesday nights' use of the rock theatre: artists appearing for the free community benefits included the Fugs, David Peel and the Lower East Side, and the Group Image (who are probably the only people in Manhattan who understand what communality is all about) … Both Marianne Faithfull (Mick Jagger) and Yoko Ono (John Lennon) suffered miscarriages in London recently, within twenty-four hours of each other … A huge "homecoming" is planned for Christmas Day in New York's Central Park Sheep Meadow: at this writing promised attendances include Dylan, some Beatles and a list of pop scenemakers that reads like the partridge in a pear tree. If it all comes off, I had a good time and maybe I even saw you there … Two chicks in Chicago who call themselves The Plaster Casters practice a somewhat unusual avocation: that of making casts of pop stars' rigs. Jimi Hendrix and Buddy Miles are but two of the many who, so far, have been preserved for posterity. The implications of this are of course staggering: there is talk of a museum, a Hall of Fame type thing, perhaps; Herb Cohen, Mothers of Invention manager, is rumored to be up (so to speak) for the casts to be reproduced in lollipop form—All-Day Suckers, what else? It could all even replace blowup posters in the dreams of teenyboppers: now you too can have your very own Jim Morrison—no, no, I can't go on. Ellen Sander reports in full in the current Realist, go read it there … Sander also reports that Janis Joplin's new fur coat is a token of esteem from the very grateful Southern Comfort people … Amazing Grace Slick's blackface makeup on a recent Smothers Brothers show drew widespread approval from militant black groups. She also gave a black-leather-gloved clenched-fist salute at the end of "Crown of Creation" ("I see their ways too often for my liking…"). Asked about the makeup, Grace replied, "All women wear makeup, why not black? Next time I might wear green. Besides, there were no blacks on the show and I thought the quota needed adjusting." … Tim Hardin completed his first LP for Columbia and had a solid month of club and college dates through December … British group Gun is scheduled to debut on the West Coast sometime in February. Race with the Devil, their first album, is on Epic … Hendrix drummer Mitch Mitchell and jazz flutist Jeremy Steig jammed with Jack and Jorma Airplane during the Plane's Fillmore East Thanksgiving gig … The young man pictured with Michael Lessac on the liner of Lessac's Columbia album Sleep Faster We Need the Pillow is David Zimmerman, brother of another Columbia artist, the former Bob Zimmerman, now, of course, Dylan. Columbia has been getting into good things lately: they had a happening in early December at their 30th Street recording studio to help celebrate their Bach to Rock promotion campaign, which began in August (the promotion, not the party, although at times it seemed that way). The three albums involved, Switched-On Bach, (which I heard late one night on a generally stuffy FM classical station), Terry Riley's "In C" and Rock and Other Four-Letter Words, break on through conventional classical forms and out into a truly incredible field of sound; Bach to Rock (it really doesn't rhyme) pulls in people like John Cage, David Tudor, Steven Reich, J. Marks and Shipen Lebzelter, Morton Subotnick and a cast of thousands … One more shear job to add to the list we ran a couple of issues back: Joan Baez. On her it looks good.

Actually, I was greatly and disingenuously exaggerating for effect in this, and was nowhere near as ignorant of the pop music of the day as I made myself out to be. It just didn't mean all that much in my life yet. I vividly recall being at a cafeteria sock hop in the sixth grade at Belmont Elementary School and hearing something over the loudspeakers that sounded nothing like my parents' dance music. "Who is THAT?" I asked one of the older greaser girls in her pink angora sweater and tight kickpleated skirt. She looked at me in my little plaid shirtwaist dress and saddle shoes, and either pityingly or scornfully informed me, "Bo Diddly-o, kid."

Which wasn't exactly informative. But it was enough to get me interested, even at that tender age. Though I still preferred Pat Boone to Elvis, I was very much aware that I shouldn't. So I started buying 45's with my limited pocket money, just things I liked, and some of my choices wouldn't disgrace me even today: the Ventures, Sam Cooke, the Everly Brothers, Johnny Mathis, Frankie Lymon and the Teenagers, the Silhouettes, Gene Vincent. It didn't take more than a few years for folk to come my way:

Peter, Paul & Mary, who were my gateway drug to Dylan; Buffy Sainte-Marie; Judy Collins; more obscure faves like Mimi and Richard Fariña, Sandy Bull, Patrick Sky.

There would follow many "Who is THAT?" moments, of course; but that was the first.

As for the rock=sex aspect: well, for someone who at the time of writing this had been to bed with exactly two guys (the first of whom I had had to be engaged to before I'd give it up, the second of whom I lived with stormily for a whole four months, which is probably waaaaay too much information so we'll just forge right ahead then shall we yes we shall), for a sum total of perhaps two score of, well, scores, I certainly did seem to think I knew what the hell I was talking about.

It's difficult to convey, at a distance of almost five decades, just how new and amazing all this was to nice young middle-class college-educated white-bread kids—girls especially—who'd never before considered doing anything of the sort until they got married. And I certainly wouldn't dream of denying that it was pretty gosh-darn fun: living with your boyfriend, and all the various freedoms that that implied, was suddenly stylish. Though you still tried not to let your parents know about it, it was really more to protect them than to protect you and your beau. Some things never change.

REVIEW:
THE BEATLES (the "White Album")

THE BEATLES ◆ (Apple SWBO 101). John Lennon (vo, g); Paul McCartney (vo, b, p); George Harrison (vo, g); Ringo Starr (vo, d). *Back in the USSR; Dear Prudence; Glass Onion; Ob-La-Di, Ob-La-Da; Wild Honey Pie; The Continuing Story of Bungalow Bill; While My Guitar Gently Weeps; Happiness Is A Warm Gun; Martha My Dear; I'm So Tired; Blackbird; Piggies; Rocky Raccoon; Don't Pass Me By; Why Don't We Do It in the Road?; I Will; Julia; Birthday; Yer Blues; Mother Nature's Son; Everybody's Got Something to Hide Except Me and My Monkey; Sexy Sadie; Helter Skelter; Long Long Long; Revolution 1; Honey Pie; Savoy Truffle; Cry Baby Cry; Revolution 9; Good night.*

Beatles albums, like children and dragons, have to be taken on their own terms. They simply *are*, and it is up to the listener to approach all of them with requisite caution and grace.

This particular Beatles album, packaged like the White Knight in a beautiful non-jacket, plumped out by wonderful glossy photos and a lyric sheet, is no exception to the rule.

In the year and a half since *Sgt. Pepper* first burst upon our collective consciousness, there has been a massive *élan mystique* built up around, and belonging to, the Beatles: partly, it is lamentable but true, by the ecstatic orgasmic press (both under- and aboveground), but also in large part by the mythic behavior of the former Fab Foursome themselves. They were supergroup transcendent (and transcendental), the love ethic incarnate. For a while. Then came *Magical Mystery Tour*, and it was not what had been expected, and everybody seized with glee the opportunity to jump with cleated boots right down the Beatlethroats; some people just can't abide clayfooted gods.

Roughly, the same analogy can be drawn to this new double album. It is not, emphatically not, what everybody expected; it may be what some people dearly wanted (for various reasons: some because they like the way it sounds, others because they longed for another *Magical Mystery Tour* handle, another chance to have a go at Lennon and Co.).

At any rate, *The Beatles* is an album about which any preconception you may have is probably true, because everything is there. Like the Rolling Stones (to a lesser extent) on *their* new album, the Beatles do everybody: we hear Bob Dylan, Rudy Vallee, Harry Belafonte, Chuck Berry, Jefferson Airplane, much Beach Boys, Elvis, office-building elevator Muzak, Bach, Purcell and even, yes, Mick Jagger their good friend. What all this does is rather uncertain: often it works out to "Oh wow, here's the Beatles doing a mock on X." Or Y, or Z.

If it is a put-on, it's an elaborate and sophisticated one. Never crude enough to do straight riffs, the Beatles simply take essences, catchword riffs or phrasing, and parody them to the point of transmutation. Everything that is on these two records cannot be mistaken for anything but Beatles music: one of the hallmarks of a truly good group is that they do not sound like everybody else, and the Beatles never sound like *anybody* else. They never even sound, say, on "Rocky Raccoon", like the Beatles doing a patent Dylan; they simply sound like the Beatles.

The first time I heard this album I thought it was spectacular; then I thought it was dismal. Now I think I won't think about it, but just dig it, because more than anything it is a happy album. "Back in the USSR" is better for you than any amount of magic weed, and who wants to live "A Day in the Life" every time out?

The music pleases me mightily. Most of it is well structured and well executed; the Beatles are back to their own playing. Here, too, there are pieces of everybody: some Jamaica ska shuffling on "Ob-La-Di, Ob-La-Da", Beach Boys falsetto on "Back in the USSR", Dylan guitar and nasals on "Rocky Raccoon", classical pompous harpsichord on "Piggies", clear and clean linear guitar on "Blackbird".

The most sophisticated track on the album is "Revolution No. 9", a blend of noise, music, vocal bits and pieces and a tape-looped male voice that repeats "Num-bah Ni-yun" to the point of near-insanity. Beautifully engineered, the whole thing goes in a circle through stereo earphones and leads right into "Good Night", the logical emotional follow-up to "We'd love to take you home with us." There's not much profound on this: a great deal, like "Why Don't We Do It in the Road?", is nothing else than a cosmic Lennon grin. But the Beatles aren't shucking: they never did, and if *Sgt. Pepper* maybe showed us how to see, then *The Beatles* can perhaps remind us how to laugh.

This particular issue bears a bit of historical annotation, since it was the first time where I knew for a fact that Jim Morrison had noticed me, and, just as importantly, had noticed my work. Mostly because I was sitting in his hotel room interviewing him and watching him actually read the issue. On the cover was a studio photo we'd arranged of Jefferson Airplane ("Hey, how come they're on the cover and we're not?") all dressed up like a lounge act straight out of the greasy heart of the 1950's: Grace in a tarty red satin dress and gold lamé stilettos (which I was given after the shoot, and several years back sold to a collector on eBay for a rather pleasant price), the guys in sleazy tuxes and slicked-back hair. All except for Paul Kantner, who refused point-blank to alter his admittedly lovely blond locks; we later learned he had been reluctant to do so on account of having a steel plate in his head, result of a terrifying high-speed motorcycle crash into a tree in the early Sixties, and then we felt horrible that we'd been annoyed at what we'd perceived as merely his rock diva-ness.

That January '69 cover story was a November '68 interview with the Airplane that I had been scheduled to do, but found myself in the hospital that week with some bizarre neurological symptoms that thankfully amounted to nothing—apparently I'd actually managed to make myself ill with excitement. So Pauline did it instead with one of our contributing editors, Tom Phillips. But I really wasn't up to interviewing, and Pauline and Tom did a terrific job, I have to honestly say a better one than I would have. Besides, I was to have plenty of other reportorial and social encounters with the band thereafter, so I really didn't miss out on much.

Anyway, we had managed to get the review for the recently released White Album into this issue, and Jim, reading the review as we talked that fateful January afternoon at the Plaza, took smiling exception to my position: "No, I'm just glad for them, that they've gotten to that place..." Kind of a gentle swat at me as well as at the Beatles; but that was the last time he ever made fun of my writing, gently or otherwise.

I personally met half the Beatles in the course of my rock life, John and Paul. I had run into John at assorted Yoko art events in the East Village; he was always friendly, as was she. Then later, when I was working for J&P, I was asked to be in their home movie, "Up Your Legs Forever"—a typically strange project in which, by invitation and identified only by number, the bare legs of several hundred people were filmed one person at a time, in an office space in the Elektra building at 1855 Broadway, just up the block from us. All in the interests of world peace, as I recall. And I still *have good legs...*

Paul I didn't meet until several years later at CBS, when I and my art director teammate, Steve Ohler, were tapped to create campaigns for Wings. We were introduced to Paul and Linda, though I forbore to remind her of our past acquaintance or, indeed, of my relationship with Jim, with whom she'd had a one-night stand, and we had a pleasant chat with them and Columbia then-president Bruce Lundvall. During which Paulie, sitting beside me on a rather nice Barcelona sofa, did his level best to embarrass me, in a good-humored sort of way; in fact, he did everything but shake his hair and go "Woooooo". Then, apparently surprised by my resistance to his boyish charm, he leaned over and whispered with the trademark smirk, "I'm just trying to embarrass you, you know." I smiled back, hopefully with equal charm, and said, "Why, Paul, whyever would you want to embarrass a perfect stranger? Besides, it takes a lot more than that to embarrass me..." Which actually made him blush. Linda just rolled her eyes...

March 1969

FEATURE:
WHEN THE MUSIC'S OVER—AN AUDIENCE WITH THE DOORS

This is the original account of my first meeting with Jim, in a private (initially, at least) interview at the Plaza Hotel in January 1969, the day after the Madison Square Garden concert. The dialogue and commentational context here differ quite a bit from the much more detailed two-chapter version of that incredible and wondrous afternoon that I wrote for Strange Days, *because I didn't want to give away so much of our immediate connection in the magazine, wanted to keep it private for ourselves, so this journalistic version was highly edited for our own, indeed, protection. Plus I didn't have the space for more than four pages. But by the time I wrote* Days *I felt more comfortable sharing—in fact, I was eager to share, even to boast, if you like. So if anyone is keeping score, the book version, gathered from my diaries and expanded from this account, is the true and complete one.*

Oddly, I wasn't at all nervous meeting him; perhaps I had resigned myself to karma and fate and all that stuff, and was just letting myself go with the flow. By the time we shook hands as we met and blue sparks shot all over the place as we touched— literal sparks, one of the things I did not mention in this story, because I wanted to keep it private for us, and Jim smiled down at me and said, "Portent," and I could barely manage to look up at him, and OMG OMG OMG, and if you want the complete, much more impossibly fairytale-romantic and intimate version of what happened next, you'll just have to read Days—*by that time things seemed utterly predestined, and both Jim and I were just watching them unfold.*

My subsequent interval with John Densmore and Robby Krieger was jarringly anticlimactic and, though I'd been looking forward to speaking with them, rather disappointing by comparison. Perhaps it was my fault; perhaps they were tired and didn't feel like doing another damn interview; perhaps I was still with Jim in my mind and just wasn't into talking to them.

For the article, I divided the time spent with Jim, solo and in company, into two blocks, but it was really all of a piece, four hours or so, and the talk with John and Robby took place immediately after. I constructed it like this in the magazine because I wanted to close with the Jim scene.

Sometimes it is better to go at the right time...

The interview is set for 2:30. [*I'm early. – PKM*] I am to meet Diane [*Gardiner*], the publicity girl, in the lobby of the Plaza. There are a few random groupies milling aimlessly around. They check out my notebook and tape recorder, nod to each other and move in. I split for the house phone, ask for Bill Siddons, the Doors' manager .

"Hi, I'm from Jazz & Pop, may I speak to Bill or Diane?"

Sleepy soft California voice. "What kind of an *accent* have you got?"

"Who, me, accent? No accent."

"Ah, sure y'do. I'm very hung up on accents, what kind is it.:

"None, really. Can I talk to Diane?"

"Sure. What kind of accent is it?"

"New York."

"That's no New York accent."

"Now it is."

"Now it is. My name's Jim."

"Hello, Jim, my name's Patricia. Is Diane there?'

"Yeah, she's here. Are you coming up? Why don't you come up and talk to me?"

I hold out for Diane and she tells me to come up right away. The suite is way up at the top of the hotel, staring out over the park and the skating rink. Diane meets me at the door and we go into the living room.

He rises to be introduced, wearing the same clothes — unbleached linen peasant shirt, black jeans, black leather boots — that he wore for the previous night's sell-out concert at Madison Square Garden. I am offered a choice of bourbon or cognac; I take the cognac.

"You can say I'm an actor-musician-dancer-politician — there were five of them, what's the other? — writer, yeah, that's it."

" 'Erotic' politician?" I ask, remembering a familiar quote.

"No, just a politician." He smiles; sitting in a too-small French Provincial chair, he looks like a slightly tipsy lion, nothing like the demonic Lizard King of his stage incarnations.

Diane and I get into a number about the alligators in the New York City sewer system. Jim is unimpressed.

"Bullshit."

"No, really, Jim, I had this friend used to be lead harpoon in the alligator patrol boat — "

"Bullshit. Alligators like to lie and bask in the sun, where're they gonna find sun in the sewers? Now *I* will tell *you* a story: there is in New York a rat population twice that of the whole city, and they all live under the ground, and they are held in check by an army of 200,000 *cats*."

I am properly silenced, but militant enough to assert that I liked the alligators better and I hope they are all mutating into monsters. Jim likes this; he is very into reptiles, and we talk for a while about a television show he'd seen on reptiles and amphibians, Komodo dragons and the like.

"It was a good concert," he says expansively, in answer to my question. "I had a good time, and I think the other guys did too. The new material we did—when you play someplace like the Garden, you want to do something special, not just the same old stuff. That's why we had the strings and horns. It probably won't be a permanent part of our sound, not live anyway; the logistics of traveling with all those extra people would be a little too much. The new album,. that we're working on now, will have a lot of that sound on it, but not the one after that. We just wanted something different, just expanding a little, that's all."

He picks up the January issue of Jazz & Pop, studies the cover. "Ho, is that—sure it is. How come they're on the cover and we're not? You know, this cover symbolizes the death, the decadence of rock. Decadence is when you become self-conscious and languorous, when you're not doing anything new. I think that the form of music that we now all rock has progressed to the point of no return, where every body is good , every is group that comes out is a great group, and nobody stands above the crowd. That's decadence. The Jefferson Airplane dressed up like 1950's cats, man, you know what that says? That like the 1960's didn't happen."

I disagree.

"Look at it like this, then," he explains, patiently, like a teacher to a nice but somewhat slow child. "Each generation has to have its wild rebellion and its effulgence of energy and we're here. In the past this was called jazz, and blues; in the immediate past it was called rock and roll; and now it's called rock. I personally think that it's being proven everywhere today that rock is now in its declining phase. It's the tail end of things, nothing is really happening, no mass hysteria, no vital movement. I feel sad to have come in on the end; you know, people like to feel they're in on the beginning of things, but it's still fun. But in five or ten years, it's going to be a whole new thing. The new generation will need their own means of expression; I can't say what it will sound like, but they'll make up some sound that's much above rock and rock is above rock and roll, and they'll have some nonsense word name to call it, and that will be the music.

"By then everybody will be into new things: I hope myself to expand into writing, into films and stage in particular. I am primarily a word man: music is great, I love it, and I love performing, but there are some things I have to say that can't be put to put to music, and could best be communicated in a book—I'll be publishing a book of poems pretty soon—or on the stage. We have made this ten-minute 16-mm. color film that in a way is a first step to this. It has stuff from concerts and backstage, as well as other material, but we're only an excuse. The film isn't really us." He looks up. "Got all that?"

"Sure." I have been casually memorizing everything for the past hour, of course I have it. Jim pours me another cognac. Diane has been in and out during all this, talking to callers and screening out the telephonic groupies. The other Doors come and go; some more people come in after a while: David [*Anderle, a producer*] from Elektra in Los Angeles; Fred [*Myrow*] (whose father wrote "You Make Me Feel So Young"), a classical composer who works with the New York Philharmonic; my press colleague Ellen [*Sander, who wrote a column, "Rapport", for Jazz & Pop*]. We all sit around in a circle as though assisting at a séance. Jim calls room service for more bourbon, more cognac, beer, coffee and fruit. Outside it begins to get dark.

The Doors took shape in the doldrum summer of 1965. Ray Manzarek and Jim Morrison, fellow students at the UCLA film school, met by chance on a Venice, California beach and decided to form a rock group and make a million dollars. Ray brought in Robby Krieger and John Densmore, both of whom he knew from the Maharishi Mahesh Yogi's Los Angeles meditation center, and the deed was done.

The new band — named from you have a choice of stories: Aldous Huxley's (ultimately William Blake's) *The Doors of Perception* or Jim Morrison's "There are things known and things unknown; in between are doors" — began its career with bare-survival-paying gigs at small and now expired Sunset Strip clubs. A stint as the Whisky A Go-Go's more or less house band was abruptly terminated one night when they did the Oedipus sequence of "The End" for the first time, the tourists were scared out of their wits, and the band was summarily fired.

They had been signed by then, though, to an Elektra recording contract, and soon there was a song that Robby Krieger wrote, a song called "Light My Fire"…

"A crucifix is the cheapest thing to do," Jim mutters. "All you need, man, all you need is two sticks."

We are talking about the Garden concert and are agreed that the sound was rotten — I've heard better from a flat-bed campaign loudspeaker truck — and now we are bitching about the lighting effects. I mention that from where we were sitting the four red spots on Jim came together in a cross of light with him at the center, and elicit the above response. Diane says that from where she was the spotlights were invisible and only the red light falling over Jim could be seen (blue light for the other Doors), causing the teenies in front of her to marvel at the miracle: "Oooh, he's smoldering! All red — he's burning up!"

Appreciative laughter. Things have gotten far more social than business; I make a few stabs at further questions, then just sit back and drink my cognac. Ellen kicks a discussion of music into life; Jim eyes closed, talks animatedly about his pet Dionysian–Apollonian approach to music and communication. The telephone in the next room has been going constantly; Diane has been running in and out to answer it. The phone next to Jim rings; everybody comes down two degrees.

David frowns. "How'd they get this number?"

Jim picks it up, still expostulating, and holds it in his hand, finishing his paragraph. The operator's shriek can be heard all the way across the room.

"Jim — the phone."

"Oh — hello — yeah, well, this is Mr. Morrison and the, uh, the doctors are here now — they're in the middle of this operation — yes — on my throat — it's a very delicate situation and so I'd appreciate it if you didn't call till it's over — fine."

He hangs up, goes back to his rap without missing a beat. Ellen breaks out the cannabis chocolate-chip cookies.

"Jim says rock is dead," I announce to John Densmore.

John snorts. "Well that's maybe what he thinks today."

"But — but he was so logical…"

"Jim's always logical; he always means what he says, too. He just changes his mind a whole lot, that's all."

John has red-brown Irish setter hair and mustache, and is full of the nervous energy of the drummer. Robby Krieger sits on a chair across the room; he looks like a hip American Gothic.

"It's not as though one thing dies — right *here* — and another starts — right *there*," Robby adds. "There are 20,000 union bands in Los Angeles alone, and about ten times as many non-union. Rock's not gonna die."

Ray, from all reports the most responsible, articulate

and personable Door, has gone somewhere for dinner and no one can locate him. We settle into the interview without him.

Rock as Theatre? "Oh, we haven't had that one for a long time. Well, we started out just doing what we felt like, and then everybody called it 'theatre' and so it naturally got more theatrical. We are audience, too, you know; we're watching just as much has the audience is, they're onstage just as much as we are. Which is why we like to make a concert as much as possible an audience-participation thing: you probably noticed last night Jim left big holes in songs for people to shout things out, and when they've all yelled whatever they felt like yelling, he'll go back and finish the song,. I remember one time in Texas Jim jumped off the state — it had one of those curtains draped across it, hanging from the apron — and he crawled in under the stage with his hand mike and yelled 'Is anybody gonna come under here with me?' Whole bunch of chicks went running, you know. Then we just played along without him and suddenly he came in on the vocal part from underneath and nobody could figure where his voice was coming from. If *that's* not audience participation—"

Break to watch an interesting bit on the unfocused color television set; it beats talking. I am faintly annoyed. I realize they're gone through this same scene hundreds of times, but if interviews really bug them, then they shouldn't say they'll do them. It rapidly becomes a game: I toss out game questions in my playing-at-interviewer, they throw back game answers in their playing-at-Doors. Straight responses become impossible to obtain, and when boredom seems to triumph, I shaft one final query and prepare to leave.

"People have said that all the Doors have ever done is one album under three separate titles; what do you have to say to a charge like that?"

John is slightly stung, it appears; I am not sympathetic, given the circumstances.

"Oh, hey, listen, we've done three records now with just us — you know, voice, guitar, organ and drums — if those people want to say they think it's all the exactly the same, well, okay if they think so. Anyway, our next album, it's going to be orchestrated, horns, strings. Expanded. It's all just filling and changing; it'll still be us, our sound, above it all. It'll be the Doors and oh yeah, some horns too."

End. Mutual groans on both sides of the suite door as I close it behind me, theirs and mine. I head for the elevators.

Jim's room. We are sitting immobile in our chairs, paralyzed by equal parts of juice and cannabis cookies. Fred gazes meaningfully around the room, then down at his glass.

"I suppose you're all wondering just why you've all been gathered here this afternoon…"

Everybody chuckles; nobody moves. What if he's right? I think Panic. Reasons returns. Somebody pours me another drink.

"Knowledge is creation," Ellen says. I can't see her; the room is pitch-dark and nobody will light a lamp; besides, she has a black dress on. "Like this apple—" She slices it in half with one swipe, like a samurai. "You see the word, 'apple', and right away you make it into an apple in your mind." She bites into her illustration.

" 'Ringo' means 'fish' in Japanese [*actually, it means 'apple;'; we were stoned, you can see where the confusion arose — PKM*]" says Fred.

Jim leans forward, eyes closed. "Ohh — where did the *ringing* start?" he whispers. "Rrrinng — what Ellen said, then it went right into 'Ringo'."

Fred nods. Ellen denies she ever said anything that went rrrinng; she indicates the tiny Indian bells on her pigtails as plausible ringers.

"No, no, it was something you said, and Fred just made it right into 'rrr-Rinngo'."

David is flashing on a stoned Japanese going to a Beatle concert and seeing a fish playing the drums. Outside in Central Park they are skating: if one person falls, six others trip over his prostrate form before he can get up. I sit watching red lights fly in small circles over the park, my journalistic objectivity all shot to hell. It seems that I was born sitting here in this chair, and quite likely that I will die here, having spent all my life here as well. 'Diane comes in. "Jim, there's this girl on the telephone—she's really into your thing, not just superficial. She promises that if she can talk to you for two minutes she'll never bother you again. How about it?"

"Well, I don' know—no, only if she'll talk to everybody—"

"Jim, she wants to talk to *you*."

"Uh-uh—she has to talk to me and Patricia and Fred and Ellen an' David—" He points to each of us in turn around the circle, then stands up, a bit unsteadily, and leaves with Diane. He steps into the little hallway that connects the rooms of the suite, reaching for the light switch.

Ellen calls out, "Don't put the light on, love!"

He turns around. "Did you say 'love'?"

"Sure. "

"Oh." He turns again and closes the door, nodding to himself.

Conversation languishes for a while; nobody wants to say the first word. Jim has returned, and is sitting in his chair again, eyes closed. He looks as though he is floating.

Suddenly he opens his eyes and stares at me. "Wait till I finish my drink."

I am, ah, unsettled; is that a threat or a promise? Diane comes back, takes her place in the circle. Nobody wants the lights on.

Somebody needs to know the time, glad that I'm here. I say, very carefully, that in New York you call N-E-R-V-O-U-S to get the time, but in San Francisco the number is P-O-P-C-O-R-N. Jim is intrigued.

"That says a lot, y'know. I mean about the characters of the respective cities; what else would you call in New York but 'Nervous'?" He grabs the phone and thrusts it at me. "Here . Call them. I want to hear it."

I can't read the push buttons in the dark, so try it by touch. It works. I hang up.

"She said 5:48 and 20 seconds," I say. Good; everyone is pleased, it's not late at all. "No — maybe it was 6?" General laughter: chick's too stoned to hear right. "But there *was* a 48 and a 20."

"You sure?"

"Sure."

Years later. Ellen and I make movements preparatory to splitting; Jim is laughing to himself.

"Did you bring your gun?" he asks. "I left mine in L.A."

"Do you have a gun, Jim?"

He closes his eyes and smiles. "No."

There's a lot I left out—which, again, you can read in Strange Days *if you're interested. In all modesty, I'd say it's well worth checking out. One of the more significant omissions is Jim, slightly on the far side of sober, crashing to his knees and making his way, still on his knees, over to Ellen demanding that she sing "Oh Say Can You See" [sic]. It was kind of bullying behavior, even though Ellen was a good sport about it and after a bit even managed to sing a creditable verse of "Hey Jude" instead. I decided not to report the hassling here (for which Ellen thanked me), and Jim sent us both flowers a day or two later, which was a sweet gesture; he also kissed me goodbye, a REAL kiss, our first.*

I did include all that in Strange Days. *But I left the enforced vocalizing out of the magazine so as not to embarrass either of them, really. And I left the rest out so as not to embarrass Jim and myself...*

REVIEW:
BLESS ITS POINTED LITTLE HEAD, Jefferson Airplane

By now—it's good to be queen—I had exercised the privilege which rank hath, and possessively reserved to myself all reviewing rights to the Doors and the Airplane; I loved them, and I didn't trust anyone else to do justice to either of them. Pauline loved them too, so she was happy to let me have my way, as we both knew that barring some ghastly musical egregiousness on their parts, my reviews of both acts would tend to be on the highly favorable side. And usually this was the case; even when I slapped them on the wrist, it was a loving slap. And no matter what, Airplane and Doors music was the music heard most frequently around my house, despite all the other stuff I had to listen to. It just made me...happy.

JEFFERSON AIRPLANE ✦ *Bless Its Pointed Little Head* (RCA Victor LSP 4133). Marty Balin (vo); Grace Slick (vo, or); Paul Kantner (vo, g); Jorma Kaukonen (lead g, vo); Jack Casady (b); Spencer Dryden (d). *Clergy; 3/5 of A Mile in 10 Seconds; Somebody to Love; Fat Angel; Rock Me Baby; The Other Side of This Life; It's No Secret; Plastic Fantastic Lover; Turn Out the Lights; Bear Melt.* (Recorded live, Fillmores East and West.)

First, swatches of good old 1930's movie dialogue: King Kong, airplane motor noises around the Empire State building, a rock group tuning up underneath it. Then, loud and clear: "The airplane's done it!" King Kong has met his doom. Audience boos. "Ah no, it wasn't the airplane, it was beauty killed the beast!" And the Airplane (Jefferson, that is) has done it again.

One of the nicer things about live albums in general is nobody has to think overmuch about them, neither performers nor audience. They're non-cohesive, non-structured, non-thematic, often sloppy as hell and quite often not much more than a glorified theatre program — but one that you listen to, not read. This is not by any means a put-down, mind, of the concept of live albums; they're also a lot of fun, but of all the live albums I 've heard, I have yet to enjoy one by a group that I have not seen perform at one time or another. This is all probably McLuhanistic in the extreme: a visual experiential memory is always a help (a "mental movie", as Annie Fisher of the Village Voice puts it), and besides being musical in the extreme, JA is very definitely into visuals. Why do you think they all look so weird?

Still, a live album results from taking the live electricity of a concert performance and putting it down onto dead acetate. The "remove" of the studio atmosphere is gone, but another, perhaps more forced attitude is set up in its place. Live is live, after all, and a record is a record.

In the first few weeks of its release, *Bless Its Pointed Little Head* has been characterized as being "full of astonishing power:" and "their best by far;" Now I claim second to no one in my admiration for Jefferson Airplane, but *BIPLH* is going to be characterized by me as filler. Very good filler, to be sure, better than the regular releases of 90% of anyone else around, but filler all the same.

The Airplane has by now accumulated far too much musical savoir faire to do anything really dismal or half-witted; thus, even their worst stuff (*Surrealistic Pillow*) gets gold records. *BIPLH*'s major virtue is that it gets down on record a very fair representation of concert Airplane sound; of course, nothing this side of living protoplasmic actuality will ever duplicate the group's tsunami approach to music, but this record comes creditably close.

Everybody gets a chance up front, which is not always the case on the other albums. Thus there is Marty Balin flinging his voice all over the stage, Grace's vocal ballistics (on "Bear Melt" especially, and a "Somebody To Love", oh joy, that sounds *different)*, Paul relaxed on "Fat Angel", Jorma gritty on "Rock Me Baby". And callooh callay you can actually *hear* Spencer, and Jack's brontosaur bass stomps through your ribcage just like at the Fillmore.

There's really nothing at all wrong with *Bless Its Pointed Little Head*. I'm just spoiled.

By their nature, live LPs are an entire stableful of horses of a different color. You get the chart hits and the album favorites, as a rule, no matter how weary you are of hearing them, because that's what bands have to play live no matter how weary they are of playing them; you get the B-sides or the album secondary songs, which can be quite refreshing when heard live, since the band can stretch out and fool around with them; and very often you get stuff that doesn't come off any album and that maybe the band only ever does live, which can be brilliant (here, for instance, "The Other Side of This Life", a Fred Neil composition and Airplane standby that I'd been hearing live since early 1967. And about time too...).

But live albums are notoriously difficult to review, and maybe they shouldn't be reviewed at all, or at least only selectively. The problem I had with BIPLH is that the stunning clarity the Airplane offers on vinyl, and even in live performance, especially in small clubs, just didn't seem to come through to my ear, much as I was willing it to. The energy did, but not the rest. Still, it was a great selection of songs, and the jacket art—a great black-and-white shot of bassist Jack Casady wrapped unconsciously around a wine bottle, at the end of a line of wine bottles set out on the longest dining table there ever was—was delightful.

April / May 1969

The Beach Boys are announced at the Fillmore: jeers and unkind words. Somebody yells from the balcony, Hey, Bill, how about the Doors? Let 'em play the Garden, somebody else bellows: laughter. The Iron Butterfly sets up: audience, still reeling from Led Zeppelin's magic onslaught, titters and demands "Play 'Wipe-out'!" Janis Joplin had them dancing in the aisles back last summer (yeah, me too; it's hard sometimes to stay objective in this business), but she didn't get anybody up off their rear ends in her February debut with the new band.

What the hell *is* all this? you ask. Well you may.

Pop is exploding like a nova, with a speed that fair boggles the mind. New groups (if I can judge by the tides of press releases that wash across my desk from day to day) are springing up like paisley mushrooms after rain, new records are being zapped out by literally hundreds each week. Like just about everything else, all this is a decidedly mixed blessing.

Rock, as we all know by now, is In. It's a big-money business, and money can do a lot of things. Rock money is responsible for a staggering amount of meretriciousness and sheer glut of musical garbage, but it also is responsible for Bob Dylan and Van Dyke Parks and the Grateful Dead, and the resultant hike in musical standards that artists such as these bring with them. The pop-buying public has become nicely selective and reasonably cool about what they purchase and what they leave in the racks, so much so as to be able to discriminate without a second thought, by and large, between the obviously valuable and the blatantly chickenshit. Face it, there'll always be somebody who will make groups like the Monkees into million-sellers, but the fact remains that quality pop is definitely on the upswing, and who is responsible? Yes, Virginia, the good old capitalistic record companies, with their policies of if-it-has-long-hair-and-enough-coordination-to-learn-three-chords-record-it. If there were nothing at the bottom of the barrel, who then would be at the top?

And who then is responsible for this enlightenment of the general audience? Right again: it's almost fiendishly ironic that the record companies, indirectly and most likely unknowingly for the most part, should have educated the rock public to such a point that 90% or so of their product goes unsold or neglected because it is so godawful, but that's life. What do they really expect: they find a group somewhere groping to be heard, slap them into a double LP, foldout color sleeve, and then sing them p.r. hosannas (in two-part harmony with, yes, rock periodicals that ought to know better) until all collapses in a flurry of nothing, and people blame each other and the group just sits in the ruins wondering where they went wrong.

There is too much of this kind of thing going on: groups *know* if they are good or bad, ready or not; usually they don't have to be told if they need practice or ought to woodshed or fire the bass player. But when a rich, monolithic, father-figure corporation starts force-feeding them seven different sorts of sweet nothings all connected with what a GREAT band they are…well, you know how it is, and I'm absolutely certain I would do exactly the same in a similar situation.

At any rate, far from being more easily pleased as a result

of this catering, the current pop audience is becoming more and more discriminating. Every one of the scenes I quoted at the beginning of this column actually happened: the old idols are flabby around the middle now, and it's shape up or take gas. A shuck group just can't expect to get by anymore; if nothing worse, they'll simply be embarrassed to death by overt audience action comparable to the Tet offensive.

The percentage of good groups to great groups is rapidly rising; though, paradoxically, the "great" groups are dwindling away. One would expect a parallel upsurge of "good" bands breaking on through to the other side of the ranks of greatness, but it just hasn't happened, and the attrition that goes on among the greats is pretty fierce. (In San Francisco alone, the only groundswell bands that have made it through more less intact are Jefferson Airplane and the Grateful Dead; everybody else has had some kind or other of casualty. Elsewhere, the situation is little different.) Sure, the audiences can afford to be discriminating; there is so much around that is good. Some people see in this decadence, self-satisfaction: Jim Morrison for one. What Jim apparently has missed is the mutual stimulation and interaction derived from such a situation, an outside influence providing a needed creative kick in the pants (which is very possibly what the Doors themselves could use, but I am making no suggestions right now).

So on we move, then; but to what? Leonard Cohen and the big-band sound? Who can say?

Bill Graham believes, legitimately enough, that the rock audience of, say, 16-25 years of age is by now musically sophisticated enough, after prolonged mainlined doses of quality pop, to move into other musical forms: yes, like jazz. So he and [*Newport Jazz Festival organizer*] George Wein set up an acclaimed series of Sunday Jazz Nights at the Fillmore East. Fine, so far. As I write this, there have been four of these Jazz Nights and the series is now dead.

Any number of reasons have been put forth to explain it all: among them being the fact that the bills were "too varied" (???). Meaning presumably that the expected audience didn't materialize because no one audience would pay (or stay) to see a (hypothetical) show that included *par exemple* Pharaoh [*we spelled it thusly, according to the "correct" spelling; we had asked Mr. Sanders how he spelled it, just to be sure, and he said good-naturedly that he spelled it "Pharoah" himself, but if that was wrong then by all means spell it right. So we did. Which, I guess, was pretty damn arrogant of us. – PKM*] Sanders, an old-line jazz vocalist and an old trad jazz band, the jump being too much for people to handle all in one evening and so everybody just stayed home.

Bullshit. Have we not had at the Fillmores such diversified (pop) acts on the same bill as the Pentangle and Canned Heat, or Jefferson Airplane and Andrei Voznesensky? No, I think the problem with the jazz series was a little more far-reaching than that, and I think that perhaps it might have worked better than it did had Ornette Coleman been booked with the Grateful Dead, or some similar arrangement: in other words, not keep so tight a fence between "rock" and "jazz." Witness George Wein himself, co-sponsor with Graham: after a soul-searching that included walking out on the Mothers of Invention, George has come to believe that yes, well, rock is indeed worthwhile [*meaning filthy lucrative – PKM*], and this summer's Newport Jazz Fester will boast Jeff Beck, Jethro Tull, Ten Years After, Johnny Winter, Led Zeppelin and Sly and the Family Stone. Reeeally heavy, man.

Well. what now? I don't know. But things like the Fillmore jazz shouldn't fail; if they do, then we must just look around for the cause of the trouble and try again. It's simply a matter of knowing your moment and knowing what to do with it when you see it; there really aren't any contradictions in anything. Me, I'm just hopeful. I expect to see Jeff Beck knock out Newport and Janis and her band finally click and the Doors do something new and just as good as what they've been doing. Ob-la-di, ob-la-da, life goes on...

I HEARD THE NEWS TODAY OH BOY: Those of you who have been wondering much at the apparent time-lag in between issues of Jazz & Pop will, hopefully, have to wonder no more. We have been spinning through changes here: Pauline Ravioli was out of action for six weeks or so with a particularly malevolent bug [*actually, it was peritonitis from a burst appendix, and at one point she was even given the last rites – PKM*], but is just fine now, thank you, and added to that were a few personnel changes that you might have noticed and the usual production hassles. You have all been marvelous patient, and from here on in, issues should be on schedule. End of Statement ... Jack and Jorma Airplane, fulfilling the dear wishes of a good many admirers, have signed with RCA to do two albums on their own. It is not known as yet if the album will include any sitters-in from other groups or if any other members of the Airplane will make a guest appearance ... Jeff Beck cancelled out of the balance of his ill-starred U.S. tour, owing to his collapse in Minneapolis and subsequent return to London under doctor's supervision. Gate loss from the scratched concerts was approximately $250,000 ... Two of the last of the great "underground" groups (whatever that may mean), The Band from Woodstock, New York and Cat Mother and the All-Night Newsboys from East 10th Street and First Avenue, are set for Fillmore East on the same night in May ... It had to happen. Michael Butler, he who is responsible for the growth of *Hair*, will present next season a rock musical version of

Mary Shelley's *Frankenstein*. Rumors that Ginger Baker will play the starring role are both untrue and uncharitable … Mary Hopkin is set to make her U.S. television bow in late April during a 12-day stay, after which she returns in June for a two-week engagement at the Royal Box of the Americana Hotel … Bob Hite, Canned Heat's ursine vocalist, named to *Who's Who in America*, joining the likes of Jefferson Airplane, the Monkees and Janis Joplin, to name but a few … Jim Morrison turned himself in to The Law just before press-time to bear the consequences, whatever they may be, for The Great Miami Exposure of early March. The move was advised by his legal counsel and sounds like something out of a grade B Western … EYE has shut. Pennies on its lids. The announcement was made in late March that the forthcoming issue would be the magazine's last, surprising practically nobody … Metromedia Producers Corporation will do an hour-long special which will be focused on Aretha Franklin, the Lady of Soul and the top female pop recording artist in the country. The special, to be telecast next fall, will be based on soul music and will include other performers, as yet unsigned. Part of the show will be filmed at the Detroit church where Aretha's father is the Reverend and where she received her first musical training … The St. Louis Symphony Society has announced plans for the Mississippi River Festival, to be held June 20 through July 27 at the Edwardsville, Illinois campus of Southern Illinois University. Symphony concerts will take place on Friday, Saturday and Sunday evening throughout the duration of the festival, and top folk and pop artists will be appearing on the weekdays. Scheduled to perform are Buffy Sainte-Marie (June 23), Paul Butterfield Blues Band (26) Janis Joplin (July 1), Joni Mitchell and Arlo Guthrie (7), Iron Butterfly (10, the band (14), Richie Havens (22) and Joan Baez (23). For further information contact Mississippi River Festival,

Edwardsville, Ill., 62025 … Ringo Starr says the Beatles will never again perform in public. (Ringo, by the way, will be doing a Western as his next film, most likely to be shot in California, in the autumn.) John Lennon, speaking ex cathedra from his pillow in Amsterdam during his and Yoko Lennon's seven-day lie-in, declared that the Beatles would indeed make several appearances and this very year, too, for that matter. An Apple spokesman sidestepped: "It would be indelicate for us to comment whilst John and Ringo are so obviously in disagreement." Yes indeed.

June 1969

COVER STORY:
AN INTERVIEW WITH JEFF BECK

My first cover story, though my Doors feature that appeared in the March ish really should have been one, and only wasn't because jazz vibraphonist Gary Burton had already been promised the spot. Pauline's idea. No offense to Gary, but SERIOUSLY?? Gary BURTON? Instead of THE DOORS??? Oh please.

Anyway, the interview with Jeff was conducted with David Walley, by this point in time long since the ex, but he continued to write for the magazine and he wanted to meet Jeff, and we often did interviews as a team (though not the interview with Jim). Quite honestly, I didn't have all that much to ask on this occasion, and had only gone for it in the first place because it was (a) at the request of Jazz & Pop's good friend publicist Pat Costello, and (b) it was JEFF BECK!, one of the three British blues guitarists I liked and who didn't put me to sleep (the others being Eric Clapton and Alvin Lee).

Good thing Jeff was such a pleasant and personable bloke, and so happy to talk, that it came off pretty well…and Pat was hardly an intrusion, the way most publicists back then so often were who insisted on overseeing interviews.

This interview took place during Jeff Beck's second American tour in late 1968. Since then, the group has had a number of personnel changes and at present consists of Beck, lead guitar; Rod Stewart, vocals; Ron Wood, bass; Nicky Hopkins, piano; and Tony Newman, drums. Present at the interview were Patricia Kennely and David Walley for J&P, Jeff Beck, and publicity contact for the group Pat Costello. — *Ed.*

David: What do you really call what you're doing? A lot of people have described it as blues, but do you consider it particularly blues or particularly rock or one thing definitely or another"

Jeff: The blues that we do play is authentic. As near as we can get, you know. But the stuff that we do other than that, is what I'd call progressive blues — blues-rock.

David: Well, what do you mean by authentic blues?

Jeff: The Chicago thing. We've got it polished in the last six months, but before that, it was very haphazard. It's taken at least a year to get the authentic sounds.

David: This is a very unusual thing, you know, Chicago blues from a British group. That's a great thing. How did it get started and when?

Jeff: It started when the Chicago albums started reaching England. And I grabbed them.

David: Which albums in particular?

Jeff: Well, the Folk Festival for one, the blues albums '65. Or '64. With Buddy Guy and Muddy Waters; I think they're just great, you know. There's a special way the guitars sound... the Chicago sound, sort of tinny and rough. It's like nothing else.

Patricia: Well, that's another thing. *Your* kind of guitar playing sounds like nothing else I've ever heard. What are your particular influences?

Jeff: Well, the Chicago thing is the main one. I think a lot of guitar players...well, if they're copying Eric than they probably don't realize they're indirectly copying the Chicago sound. Because that's where Eric got it himself.

David: Yeah, I noticed that... well, your guitar style is kind of unusual, because instead of playing it as an acoustic guitar just electrified, you use it as another type of instrument, 'cause I've noticed you do a lot of messing around with elongating notes and ....

Jeff: Oh, yeah, well, they didn't do that in Chicago...that's the material which is progressive, what we'd like to call progressive music.

Patricia: You do this pretty much on your own. I've never seen anybody else doing it quite that way.

Jeff: Right, right. It takes a bit of nerve to do it, if I may say, because it can end in disaster. In fact, it has ended in *lots* of disasters, because sometimes when you elongate the notes you're playing they go out of tune, go off at a tangent.

David: Are you into jazz at all?

Jeff: Oh, yeah.

David: What kind, particularly?

Jeff: I like the jazz drummers more than anything. I'm not really hip on streams, you know that classification.

David: Third Stream?

Jeff: Yeah, you know. I like Buddy Rich's stuff.

Patricia: Or the avant-garde stuff. Do you dig Coltrane at all?

Jeff: Coltrane, yeah. Some of it. I'm not ready...I couldn't, you know, sit and listen to lots of albums. But I try especially just to take what I can take and use it, rather than force myself to try and like all of it. I like Charles Lloyd, I just saw him in concert; way out, you know, and you've *got* to see him. I would never have appreciated that on records. You have to see him live.

Patricia: Which is a problem, I think, with a lot of the major groups, not to mention yours...like, I heard the record after I saw you in your first concert, the first time you were over here, and then I was very disappointed in the way the record came out. What happened between the studio and the way it came out on the disc was very strange to me.

Jeff: No, well, I was responsible for the recording. I produced it. I know it was my first production. I *am* sorry. [*Laughter*] No, but the next album is going to be produced by a producer who knows what bag I'm in and therefore gets a more true-to-life sound.

Patricia: It has that much effect on the recording?

Jeff: Oh yeah. The producer and the engineer are the making or the breaking of the record, really. You can just lie there and play a lot of rubbish and they can make it sound very good.

David: Good. Will you be doing mostly original stuff on the new one?

Jeff: Oh yes.

David: It was mostly older things, like "Morning Dew" and standard things on the first.

Jeff: Yeah, yeah. Well, that was because we had to rush the album out. I mean, we should not have had to rush it out, because we had a year to make it in, but...we didn't... you're either in the studio or you're not. We just think it's good fun. We just try and extract as much fun out of this as we can. Not batting people with a lot of technical stuff, although there are, really...

Pat Costello: Well, you can tell it's technically difficult stuff you're doing...

Jeff: Where it's at, as far as I'm concerned, is putting the technical stuff over. You know, anybody can go Ooo, you know, but it's putting the technical stuff over that counts. Like when I do a fiddly sort of run on the guitar, for them to listen to the drummer doing it after catches their ear and they think, oh, what's he going to do next time? You know, the more involved my guitar gets, the more involved the drums get.

David: Is that pretty standardized? Do you have that sort of thing down, or do you just come out and do whatever you can think of?

Jeff: No, we just jam it. One basic thing, yeah. One riff and then we're off.

David: It was very… I saw Ravi Shankar a couple of weeks ago, and he was doing that same type of thing, they were just…

Jeff: Yeah, that's really it. This is more simplified, of course, and it's a different instrument, and we have a little trouble with musicality here and there. Well, who doesn't?

Pat Costello: Or a bad night.

Jeff: Yeah, right. I mean, it depends on the audience, If they're absolutely wholly and solely with you, then they're going to extract more out of you than if you're playing to a brick-wall audience, with no one with you.

Patricia: What's the difference between a British audience and an American audience?

Jeff: The English audiences are very blasé, because they've heard so many groups their minds are confused. It's not their fault, but I think that, you know, having music drummed into them, they've been made to believe that THIS is the group and then, a week later….

Pat Costello: Another group comes along.

Jeff: Another group comes along. So, you know, I can't blame them for sitting there dumb, because they really don't know what's going on. But American audiences are closely, more tightly knitted with really good soul and blues music, which is, for me, the greatest thing.

David: Well, the audience last night was…*they* really were into it.

Jeff: Yeah, I like them to be quiet, really. I don't like this ridiculous cat-calling and "yeah, baby" and all that. It's all right, but you know, I'd rather have a hearty appreciation at the end, to know they've liked what you've done. I always feel that atmospheres have a lot to do with it, and sometimes the time is right, the atmosphere is right, and the whole thing just clicks…and another night, even though the stuff maybe is technically right, the group's *there* and like there's a full house and all, it just doesn't happen. You know, it's just one of those nights—any artist will tell you.

Patricia: Is blues, then, the only thing that's pretty much going on in England, because I hear most of the groups coming over now, you and Ten Years After and Led Zeppelin…?

Jeff: Yeah, it reflects it back, you know, but I couldn't really… it's such a state, it's such a state over there, the conditions of everybody's minds. It's mixed up. They're wandering around and don't know what to do.

David: Where do you think it's going to go?

Jeff: In England, I'm sure that it's finished. You know, this is the dominating country. Music-wise.

Patricia: Why do you say that?

Jeff: Well, because two years ago they were all saying, "Yeah, we know where it's at." You know, and like they weren't going to America, none of them, 'cause they were playing in England. If they were going anywhere, they were going to France and Germany and all that, but they were only going for a little while and they were coming back to England again, 'cause that's where it was happening. And then the news got spreading across to New York and California, and it was all Yeah, we must get these English groups over. I mean, you can only go so far. There's a thousand and one groups in one town in England, but they're not good.

Patricia: I think the same thing is happening to a certain extent in San Francisco…

Jeff: Right.

Patricia: ...there are about four layers in San Francisco music, and I think somebody made a count once of at least three thousand groups in the San Francisco area. It's more than that now.

Jeff: Right, there are. There are. It's very difficult to say where it's going because of all these groups. If the whole business relied totally upon, let's say, twenty bands, you could say, "All right, now, that is my bag. I want to follow this group. And that's *my* bag, I want to follow *that* group," and so on.

Pat Costello: Well, what kind of effect would that have on the bands? I mean, say if they *did* just have twenty bands...

Jeff: They would have to work harder to keep their reputations going against each other. It would be a fantastic fight!

David: Battle of the Bands.

Jeff: Yeah, like the old greats. Sinatra's still going, and Sammy Davis, and all those people.

David: Yeah, but it's on a different level. Like, you know, there's different layers of music. There are people that dig Sinatra and Sammy Davis and then there's a whole other group.

Jeff: Yeah, this is the music of the young generation, isn't it?

David: I hate to use those labels, because then people will say "You're making war on us with your music."

Jeff: Right.

David: Or something like that.

Jeff: Pardon?

David: Nothing like that? You don't feel revolution through music, that kind of thing? How about stuff like the Stones' "Street Fighting Man"? It seems to be that it's a very quiet unquiet manifestation of everybody everywhere, forgetting about national lines or the Queen or the President or whoever the hell, De Gaulle, let's say. The hell with them, let's all get together.

Jeff: Right. But let's go back to what you were saying first. The Stones were the first group to start off all this anti-stuff, and that was such a big step. It was a real slice of the market, somebody saw something coming, right? And this is the market. It's going to really be happening, because the kids are going to want to get away from their parents and dissociate with all conformity. No one's done anything like that. They're all done little scenes on their own, like acid and all, you know, the rebelling and all that, but really, they're still just coming back to the same old thing again, and they're beginning to appreciate the basis of the music. In fact, they're conforming.

David: There's a lot of musicians, at least rock musicians, are going into classical music and pulling out riffs…

Patricia: …this group called the Nice..

Jeff: Right, right.

David: …in which the organist [*Keith Emerson*] does a lot of jazz Bach.

Jeff: He does. Bach would probably turn in his grave if he heard it.

Pat Costello: Oh, no, he might like it.

David: But in a way, it seems ironic…you know, rock music has finally brought kids to the awareness of all other types of music as well. All of a sudden, they aren't just listening to r&b, they're listening to the whole continuum.

Jeff: Well, that's good, 'cause it's never been like that, has it?

David: It's…it's an educating function. It's not a cultural thing anymore; in other words, it's not a middle- or upper-class thing anymore, classical music.

Jeff: I think the music scene's never been better. I mean, you can honestly say that it is, you can walk down the street and go see a great act any night of the week, can't you? Kids are so stuffed with this. It's so good. It's the way it should be, in my opinion. Even if there's a terrible group, it still is something to watch, and they're constructing something on stage. It's better than going out and beating up old ladies and kicking in glass windows and all that.

Patricia: We were talking to a classical composer a couple nights ago and we had quite the argument with him. It almost ended with us beating him up and throwing him out the window. He was very dogmatic about it. He said, "Rock is not *possibly* music. It can't possibly be considered music because the people involved in it can't read, they haven't been properly trained, and they don't know anything about the forms and the structure. It *can't* be an art form."

David: This guy was in the conservatory for six years. He's studying to be a composer. He said, "Oh it's all improvisation. It's not laid down, it's not written down. Nobody will be performing this except the group who does it." You know, there are lots of people like that around. It's a question of…I don't know whether ramming it down their throats or just having their kids murder them in their sleep… [*Laughter*]

Pat Costello: Well, it sounds like music no matter what, whether you can read it on a printed page or whether you just hear it inside your head. So they train them to know sonata form and fugues and all of it…

Jeff: …and then where does your originality go?

David: Right. That's what we asked him.

Pat Costello: You know, musicians listen to music and they hear it, and if they can play it, they play it. They might not know the name of the guy that did it or what the form is, but they dig the structure, and they can hear the structure, and they can play the structure.

David: The sound is really all that's important. And the feeling behind it.

Jeff: There's a word for me somewhere, for my kind of

music. but I don't know what it is, because I'm not really a great musician. You can put me up against people like Charlie Byrd and Segovia and those guys, but it's a different scene. I am putting over *some*thing which is obviously of some value. Otherwise, people wouldn't clap, would they?

Patricia: No, right. Because it touches something inside them. I mean, isn't that what art is? This is maybe over-simplification, but it's basically communication.

Jeff: Yeah. So what am I doing to them? What am I doing to them?

David: Reaching them.

Jeff: Am I educating them? Is that it? Am I educating them?

Patricia: Educating their ear.

Jeff: Their ear. For what?

Pat Costello: For all other types of music

David: For everything. If they dig you, they'll go on to dig Charlie Byrd or Segovia or other people.

Jeff: That's good. That's good. I'm quite happy.

David: I mean, you educate the audience, and the audience in turn stimulates the performer to do better and better. It's a natural thing.

Jeff: Right. I thought that perhaps white groups doing blues would lose out to the originals, you know, the spades who started it all. The white groups' blues would be way out, completely finished. But it's not like that. They still want to see white groups play Negro music.

Patricia: It's looking at a picture from two different sides, you know. Different viewpoints, really, is all. You can appreciate it probably the same way, and the value is certainly the same no matter what way you're looking at it. It's just two different things. I can appreciate, say, Big Mama Thornton doing a song and Janis Joplin doing the same song.

Jeff: Music is music, and I think every one should be free to play exactly what they want and where they want it and how and when. If you have restrictions, it's like not being able to swear in your own house, isn't it? You've got to be free to express.

Patricia: Do you think your group now is free to express the kind of music you want or not?

Jeff: Oh yes, we're free in that sense of the word, but musically, you know, we're *not* free, because it's very hard. We have the education of the blues, because I've sort of…I mean, I don't want to give you all that, but I've studied it and I love it. You know what I mean? I love that kind of music. And therefore, anything you love, it impresses you more, doesn't it? And I feel that I've got a right to play it, because I enjoy it and I love it.

David: Well, what other reason do you need?

Jeff: Right. Only I'm not going to stand up there breaking my neck playing a silly song about hate, with insincerity, on hate. Now I've got to look for a basis which is also suitable to get material from which I'm going.

David: You do most of your band's stuff, then?

Jeff: Well, up until now the group has been so hectic; it's the early stages, you know, and it's like 'Break away from the office and get it together'. It just doesn't happen in a year. I'm sorry, I just can't bring out ten years' music, you know. Nor do I want to be two years ahead because I'll miss out on another moment, the start, which is, business-wise, a stupid thing to do. So I've got to plan a kind of music which is just that much ahead, just that far out of reach.

Patricia: You make the people work for it.

Jeff: Right, right. It's like dangling a carrot in front of a horse.

David: What musicians do you admire?

Jeff: I admire any musician, really. I'll tell you who I like. Jacqueline du Pré.

Patricia: Are you much into classical music?

Jeff: When I have *her* turned on, yeah. She's straight down the wall. My parents have had a very good education, which has been an influence, but of course, when you're at school, when you're rebelling and all that, you get out of it; and then, when you leave home, you get to realize there are other things to life. Oh yes, Kathleen Harri…Kathleen Farrier [*actually Ferrier — PKM*]. You don't like Kathleen Farrier? Oh, you must have heard her now. I saw her life story in the television. She was a gas. She's dead now. Really quite something. She was opera…kind of satirical opera, I think. But the only one I can take in that bracket. Now, if that had been forced at me, pushed down my throat, I probably would have hated it. It's always better when you do something on your own hook. It takes someone to die before they come to life. That's what I can't understand. Instantly that she died, right, it was on the television. So when I die, I'll probably get like a one-inch column in the Daily Worker, you know. "Pop Guitar Player Dies. Age 24. Foul playing was not suspected." [*Laughter*]

David: I don't know, I think it might be different, because since we — saying "we" in the collective sense — we're getting more of us than there are them, and possibly the whole idea of appreciation for artists will change, so instead of an artist struggling for forty years, he's going to be recognized, partially because of, well, just what's going on in the media. There'll be a lot more freedom; the artist will be able to create and I think we'll be able to hear them all in a reasonable time.

Pat Costello: So I think, Jeff, you'll probably get a big write-up in the London Times when you die, front page.

Jeff: Oh, thank you, Pat! [*Laughter*]

David: How are the European audiences, on the Continent?

Jeff: They vary. They vary. In Stockholm, in Sweden, they're just awful, just awful, because they get a group like, let me see, the Moody Blues, which is an old group, but they have that kind of scene — the 1965 groups about three years after we've had them. Now they're starting a Mothers of Invention concert tour. You know what I mean? They haven't come up to it in stages, they get who they can get.

Patricia: Then after the Mothers they get the Fugs.

Jeff: Yeah. No, I can't stand going away. It's either stay in London or be in the States. I've been about eight times to the States.

David: With the Yardbirds.

Jeff: Yeah. When? Two years ago. I'll get the date for you, because everyone's asking this, and every time I give a different answer. It's about two years.

Patricia: Are they still around? It seems like they've lost…

Jeff: No, they're not.

Patricia: …just about every lead guitarist in England.

Jeff: Well, you know, they lost this one. [*Laughter*]

David: Can the rock musicians in England…is there sort of a very nice community, like out in San Francisco, where everybody knows everybody else and they've got a real scene?

Jeff: No. England's all a big strange trip. Jimi instigates a lot of jams, Jimi Hendrix, when he's there. But the times that are suitable for jams are so far between. We never seem to have them. 'Cause it's a totally different existence in London. People haven't got any money, you know, and the sort of people that would frequent clubs are all wide-eyed innocent people, They go to a night out, and, you know, they're not used to it. And there is a clique of about twenty that go to the same bloody clubs every night, but for the most part they're all unhip people and they're sitting there. There's a 50-year-old geezer there in a mandarin suit, and next day he's off in his pinstriped suit to work. So therefore, you obviously don't get any atmosphere in these clubs. Once in a while, but not like it is here. I mean, you can cause a right scare at times here, can't you? Hendrix and Winwood…they just get right out there and have a go.

David: I didn't see you the first time you were in town. Then Patricia kept on so about how good the group was and that I should come.

Patricia: You were bottom of the bill to the Grateful Dead, and you cut them cold that night. That is quite something.

Jeff: Well, it was sort of an unexpected thing, which will always remain a great joy to the group but…thank you. Maybe it was a badly planned concert, maybe they should have had somebody like a West Coast group, you know.

Patricia: Oh no. And you've only gotten better since then, even.

Jeff: Oh, do you think so?

Patricia: Yes, and especially now with Nicky…the piano makes all the difference.

Jeff: Well, Nicky's first time on was last night, you know.

David: That's amazing. Piano is just the right touch extra… good and greasy, like Fats Waller.

Jeff: But you did enjoy this.

David: Extremely. Right on top. Like it was real whorehouse piano, really fine.

Jeff: That's all right then. But he's such a sweet guy…I'm so lucky, really, to have him with us.

Pat Costello: He looks so quiet, just sitting there behind the piano, and all these incredible sounds start pouring out of the piano.

Jeff: I've known him for a long time, you know, like two or three years. And like he says to me, you know, we're all going to tea, and he says, "Oh can I come too?" He's so nice it's rude. [*Laughter*]

Patricia: What did you do with the piano? It sounded like… when he got up on the high end, it sounded like he had some sort of amplifier, which…

Jeff: Yes, he's got this piano pickup inside on the very high register.

Pat Costello: It sounds tinny and then it sounds like it's some sort of a sound oscillator.

Jeff: Yeah, that's the amplification. He's got the pickup on the very top strings, you know, touching the strings, so when he hits them, you get this vibration. And in the middle register, it's just a regular sort of microphone….but you can hear it all right? That's good, 'cause onstage it's very different, it's very difficult for me to judge this. I'm playing very loud, and my sound is coming out across this air, and it's like a shield between my amplifier and his amplifier. But when you walk out in the front, you get the two together, you see.

Patricia: How do you keep together with the rest of the group, like the bass player's over in the other corner and Rod [Stewart] is hiding behind the amplifiers singing…

Jeff: Obviously. Don't worry. I'm listening, watching it. The only thing which helps pave the way, with regard to keeping time, is the bass drum, 'cause that's the onbeat. You know you can't go wrong with the onbeat. But when you fool around with two bass drums, you have a lot of work going.

David: What do you see as you're playing? Do you see the audience at all or do you just forget about them, or, you know, like every so often do you look up and see the people in the balcony throwing people down?

Jeff: That is one of the experiences which you can't put in less than about ten chapters, because I want to disassociate myself with where I am. I want to just…you know, it's there, there, there, there, and the sound coming out, and the group. But you realize that you are entertaining, and therefore you have to split your mind up. You have to sort of get the coordination between that, your fingers, your amplifier, the band and the whole auditorium, make sure that it's all together.

David: I read in one of the English music newspapers that you're a vegetarian. Is this true?

Jeff: Yes, it is. I've only been one for six months, though.

David: You're looking pretty good.

Jeff: Well, my girlfriend in England has been one for seven years, and *she* looks pretty good.

David: Health reasons?

Jeff: No, not health reasons so much as the thought of the animal suffering. I just love animals, that's all. And when you're with somebody that loves animals and has like fifteen cats and three dogs, you just begin to adopt their way. And the thought of meat nauseates me now. No, I like the taste of it, I'm not afraid to admit that. I like meat, steaks and all that, but I just couldn't make it.

David: But still, it's like an animal's purpose in nature, isn't it?

Pat Costello: It's a cycle. It's an ecological cycle.

David: Right. You know, everything is all one thing anyway, because we fertilize the ground which grows the vegetables which the animals eat, and we eat the vegetables and the animals and...

Jeff: Quite so, but you can't tell me the animal doesn't suffer, when he gets like a 22-gauge shotgun through his head. He suffers. And also you can live without it. I mean, I'm not suffering. If I was starving myself, I would say I can forget all that.

Patricia: Well, what about the plants? Don't carrots scream when they get pulled out of the ground? I mean, just because you can't hear it...

Jeff: Well, we don't think so. Not so much as an animal, anyway.

Pat Costello: There's a great science fiction story I read where a guy had a machine which could pick up sounds of everything. He'd walk on the grass and he'd hear the grass, he'd hear flowers scream. Well, the guy finally freaked out.

Jeff: Well, who was that artist was walking down the street and he saw these guys pruning a tree? They're chopping off big branches and the guy hears a shriek. I forget who he was. I doubt I would carry it that far, but I can survive without having meat or fish and also I feel a lot better. And it's delicious. Everyone's got this wrong idea about vegetarian food. They think it's boring and bland, but it isn't, and it's so easy to cook. You just get a lot of vegetables and throw them in a pot. And if you really want to go to town, you can make an elaborate vegetarian dish. Tastes great.

Patricia: Sounds ghastly.

Jeff: No, you have fake gravies and stuff like that. Though I did have this incredible hunger last night and went out and had a huge plate of…veal parmesan. [*Laughter*] It's funny, but once in a while I guess…the habits of a lifetime.

David: The habits of what? It's 50,000 years of civilization coming through. What else do you expect?

Patricia: I haven't…Do you have any general pronouncements about anything in particular?

Jeff: Anything at all?

David: Anything. Anything you want. Here's your chance to really lay it on somebody.

Pat Costello: That's usually how the kids start out. [*Laughter*]

Jeff: I could go on for hours. You know, I'd just like to add that I really truly must be one of the luckiest guys, I mean, to have Nicky in the group. He's going to help write songs and put them down in a true musical way, which I can't put over to the others. It's going to be an entirely different group, I think.

Patricia: 'Cause what? You hear things in your head and

you can't put them across?

Jeff: Yeah, I just can't get them out. The music in your head is always better anyway than what you end up doing.

It's not a journalistically dazzling or culturally significant interview, just a rather enjoyable afternoon that four people shared in the Sixties, which I thought you might like to read about. I could have written it up as a feature just as easily, but the conversation flowed so well that I decided to leave it in interview format.

    Even though the interview was done in late 1968, we decided to hold it for release. It took a while to transcribe and edit, for one thing, and the earliest date we could provide to ensure that Jeff got the cover, which he deserved, was June '69, as we usually booked our cover stories three or four months in advance.

Jeff and the band were staying at the Gorham, at that time a rather funky hotel on West 55th Street, considerably upscaled since, which I recently co-opted into fiction for one of my Rennie Stride mysteries; the suite came equipped with a ramshackle kitchen, which as an Englishman Jeff was glad of, as it allowed him to make us tea...

July 1969

POP TALK:
The Doors, "Critique" and Me

Yet another of the pieces I stripped for parts, to use in Strange Days...

Critique *was an arts program of the fledgling PBS network, filmed here in New York at the West Side studios of WNDT, as the local station then was. In the spring and summer of 1969, in the aftermath of the infamous March 1 Miami concert where Jim was alleged to have exposed himself onstage (he didn't) and was busted for it retroactively, Doors concerts had been cancelled right, left and center, and pretty much nobody would give them a gig for fear of what might happen.*

But Critique *took a chance on them. They wanted me on the program because I was a known Doors enthusiast and a magazine editor; also because, unlike the other three participants, I was a long-haired chick in her early 20's who might wear a really short skirt and possibly go braless. I was not in the least bit enthusiastic about the whole idea, since for the most part, under pressure, I do not think cleverly and memorably fast on my feet (hey, I'm a writer, I, you know, WRITE THINGS DOWN), and don't do well in debate situations; as it turned out, this fear was justified...*

Recently I had the opportunity to appear on a National Educational Television program devoted to a study of the Doors and their music. I got on the show, which was an installment of the weekly series *Critique*, on the strength of my piece on the Doors in the March issue of J&P, and was to engage in a panel discussion of the group with Richard Goldstein [*Village Voice rock critic*], FM rock disc jockey Rosko [*Bill Mercer*] and writer [*New York Post*] Al Aronowitz. With the nervous naïveté of a media virgin, I planned a couple of possible discussion approaches, allowed for unforeseen circumstances, and even had a number of points writ large in my mind that I thought worthy of bringing out; and I figured pretty good odds on being able to do so.

Older and wiser now, thank you, and the next time I accept an invitation to a panel discussion I am going to set my spear early on—like about two and half seconds after the moderator finishes the introductions—and just dig in. The rule seems to be "He who gets (verbal) foot in door first does not wind up with foot in mouth", and next time I shall remember that and not bother very much about off-camera politenesses like not talking if someone else is already talking; when your three fellow panelists are all articulating simultaneously and/or contrapuntally, one more mouth isn't gonna make any difference. (After a while it all got to resemble nothing so much as a ping-pong game, doubles, with a paddle in each hand and eight ping-pong balls...) But about the program.]

The Doors opened it up with some film footage that had been shot at the Miami concert of last March: typical entrance, crowd making animal noises, ring of rent-a-cops around Morrison; then they performed twenty minutes of back-to-back songs: "Tell All the People", "Alabama Song", "Back Door Man", "Wishful Sinful" and a marvelously scabrous, unnamed blues number. Goldstein then did a ten-minute interview with the band, Jim in Che Guevara drag, shades cigar and beard; the panel discussion followed, and the Doors closed with a twelve-minute piece called "The

Soft Parade", the title track of the fourth album.

I have not got any superlatives strong enough or happy enough to tell you just how good the Doors were on that show. If you didn't get to see it, you won't believe me anyway, but the Doors have made it back from wherever they've been for the past, and man, that makes me glad. There seems to have been a sea change all the way round into something richer and stranger from beyond the borders of the possible, Jim Morrison's beard being the most immediately obvious f'rinstance.

Not to go into any sort of fan–mag psychologico-spiritual connotations (because it doesn't have any, apparently: "Well, uh, it just kind of happened. You'll get used to it." Which strikes me as a pretty feeble reason, but who cares?), but because as Richie Goldstein pointed out on the show, it seems as good a place to start as any other.

So here is Jim Morrison, then, Door, Lizard King and alleged felon, looking like John the Baptist after a rough forty days in the desert and singing like Jim Morrison on the first Doors album. Perhaps significantly, perhaps not, the beard, the bust and the new music all commenced roughly around the same time.

Historically, then, to put things into perspective, the Doors had been treading water for nearly a year; the undeniable mad magic generated by "Light My Fire" and "The End" was rather grimly holding on only through such things as "The Celebration of the Lizard" and the film for "The Unknown Soldier". Live performances, at their best absolutely indescribable (their last set at the Fillmore East last year rendered me catatonic for three days afterwards), were turning into set pieces, a standardized bag of predictable tricks that they would zip through like a well-rehearsed troupe of trained seals. However, there is no getting around the fact that when the group was up for it, and the audience was up for it, and that great rule of Coleridge's about a willing suspension of disbelief was in general effect, the Doors could produce a sheer force of power and psychic violence that would freeze you in your seat.

Now the trouble with this kind of thing is that you can't keep it up over a prolonged period of time: not if you're giving of yourself honestly. After a while you just naturally have to do less and less, or die; and after a while longer the semblance of the power comes to replace the substance and people can tell the difference immediately. If you yourself do not believe in what you are doing , how can you reasonably expect others to believe it? So the word was out, and the word was "shuck". One album under three separate titles, they said, and Haven't progressed one inch since "Light My Fire", and Theatre-of-ROCK??? (This last accompanied by hysterical laughter.)

(Let me digress for a bit. Now Theatre-of-Rock is a very strange thing, but I am a whole-hearted believer in it and multimedia and all the other tenets of the McLuhan handbook. I have seen *theatre* that wasn't theatre, so don't talk to me about theatre and rock being mutually exclusive, because rock and roll is by its very nature physical, presentational, HERE, and yes, theatrical. Falling off the stage or being mock-electrocuted by the microphone are not what I consider essentials of either good theatre *or* good rock, and if I may be so bold as to make a statement on the basis of one performance, I am glad that that phase is finished. There were no instances of either on the telecast, just vibrant, in-response movement that was so much a part of the song being performed as to be virtually unnoticeable. And it was ten times more effective than all the acrobatics of the past; if the Doors keep at it as they did on the tape, a lot of people are going to have to eat a lot of words. End of digression.)

The Doors' *music* is something else again. I seem to be the only person I have run across who thinks that the Doors' third album is superior to their first (the fourth is going to be the best, I think, judging by what I have heard from it. If T. S. Eliot had been a rock group he would have been the Doors and done "The Soft Parade", but more of that in a future issue.) I hear the shrieks beginning just about now. Good. Dig this. First albums are always special albums simply because they *are* first albums, and the Doors' first put us all away because we none of us had ever heard anything like it before. Sure, it's a great record, but it's three albums later now and all of us are older. Underneath the excitement and the new, it was more than a little repetitive and a bit philosophically simple-minded, and a good deal of the music was incestuously close-related. I think *Waiting for the Sun* is a better album, for a number of reasons: it has got musical and psychological layer-cake levels that really appeal to me, the evidenced emotion is in sharper focus over a wider spectrum, motives are specific and not merely general rants, and Jim *sings* instead of the half–mad chanting that characterized his work on the two preceding LPs. I am aware that all this is a definite minority opinion; but I play *Waiting for the Sun* two or three times a week, which is a lot of times to play a ten–month-old record, considering all the other albums I find it essential to hear, and I invariably play it twice through each time.

Still, that first record communicates a vibrancy and an excitement in Morrison's singing that I haven't heard since, until I sat in the control booth of the Channel 13 studio the other week and watched the color tapes of the Doors' performance.

The producers of *Critique* wisely kept everything as simple as possible; the group had plenty of open space, a platform for John Densmore and his drums, a remarkable (for TV) sound system, intelligent lighting, a plain cyc for a backdrop. Everything focused on the music. And the music knew it. The Doors knew it. *I* knew it. The magic was back.

Speculating idly, I think the change was primarily a function of coming out, of realizing that there was still a world out there that needed to related to; heads (collective as well as individual) seemed to have been turned around. The Doors manifested there in that studio a positive creative belief in what they were doing and the intrinsic worth of it. The music is recognizably Doors music, which sounds like nothing else, and it is neither repetitious nor a frantic effort to find a new and workable formula. It just moves along, nicely balanced; the blues thing was believable, blues-from-where-the–Doors-are-at, with no attempt to come on black; and it worked, everybody was bouncing up and down in their seats, studio technicians were dancing around the cameras. "Alabama Song" and "Back Door Man" (which generally bore the hell out of me) seemed totally new, and I have never heard the Doors do the latter song so well. "Tell All the People" was probably the weakest of the numbers, and "Wishful Sinful", which died the death on top-40, sounded surprisingly lovely. But "The Soft Parade" was the one: graceful, musical and full of Euclidean simplicity. Along with everything else, the Doors have learned to be subtle. And relaxed: there was no strain apparent in their performance, no posturing; everything was free, unpressured, and very good entertainment.

That may be the key concept: entertainment instead of ritual. Rock can be either, or neither, but if you are very clever you can manage to do both at once. (The Who is a good example.) Watching the group, Morrison in particular, I was struck by the fact that for once the band had subordinated itself to the music; they were letting the material carry itself instead of relying on the Doors mythos that has gotten them through in the past. I do not think Jim Morrison will ever fade into *any* background, but somehow he managed, on the program, to become just another instrument in the band, neither more nor less important than the other three. Oh, the old charisma is there, all right, alive and well, but my mind kept flashing on Frank Sinatra, for some reason, and the comparison isn't as far out as it sounds. After all, Morrison did tell a New York Times reporter that Sinatra was his favorite singer…

Anyway, the Doors are back, and, to paraphrase Mark Twain, reports of their demise have been greatly exaggerated. I think the NET program proved it, and I heard :"Touch Me" on Muzak today; tell me what *that's* all about…

I got a very nice thank-you note from the president of the Doors' label for this, and Jim sent me copies of his just-published private-edition books, which I treasure to this day. But it was no more than the band deserved, and I certainly didn't write it for the thanks. Or the books.

Many years later, after the execrable Oliver Stone movie blotched the face of the earth, a magazine whose name I do not recall did a rather nebbishy piece on rock poetry, Jim and his poetry in specific, which, to its credit, included a reference to this very column: "…while critic Patricia Kennealy wrote, 'If T. S. Eliot had been a rock group, he would have been the Doors and done The Soft Parade', *prompting Morrison to haul off and marry her." I was so proud. And it was even true.*

August 1969

"Criticism...talks a good deal of nonsense, but even its nonsense is a useful force. It keeps the question of art before the world, insists upon its importance, and makes it always in order."

—Henry James

"A critic...rock and roll critic...that seems like a pretty nutso thing for anybody to be doing."

—Rob Tyner

There are times (more and more frequent of late) when I find myself inclined to agree with Robin Tyner in his pronouncements on the critical trade in general and rock critics in particular. But mostly not.

The Problem of Criticism has always been around. When the cave paintings were going up at Lascaux, there was undoubtedly some Cro-Magnon equivalent of John Canaday [*then the New York Times art critic — PKM*] standing off to one side and commenting on the proceedings. Like the shark and the cockroach, the critic has come unchanged through the evolutionary mill; like the shaman, the critic (performing in his proper role) serves a necessary function in the societal structure.

The art of criticizing, as the above-mentioned Mr. James once noted, has nothing in common with the practice of reviewing; the latter being chiefly a convenience of roughly the same importance quotient as a vacuum cleaner or an automatic dishwasher. Criticism, on the other hand is concerned with—ultimately—much more than yes-it's-good or no-it's-not-good.

Real criticism is a process of selection, a functional energy: it pulls in all the goods, considers all variants, and then goes on to pronounce conclusions. The best criticism concerns itself with direction and flow, general trends, and it logically follows that the best critics are the ones who can double as visionaries, who can see simultaneously where it's been and where it's going and how it is right now. I consider myself an observer, not a critic; critics are people like Walter Kerr and H. L. Mencken and probably even Jimmy Breslin: people who perceive and then apply their own selves to the perception. Criticism is a reflection of both the artistic creation upon which it is based and of the society that fostered the creation; criticism provides insight, not doctrinaire pronouncements. No critic is infallible, and any who speak ex cathedra without having first considered all possibilities are only fooling themselves.

On to rock criticism, then. Richard Goldstein undeniably launched the whole trip back in 1966; before that, there was very little in the field of rock and roll worth talking about Writing in The Village Voice, Goldstein allowed as to how rock now needed a critic, and for the next three years (despite his wondrous sins of error—i.e., panning *Sgt. Pepper* and *After Bathing at Baxter's*) probably did more than anybody else to further the cause of rock as a to-be-taken-seriously art form. Oh, what a falling-off was there; early this year Richard rethought his position and noted that now, instead of a critic, rock is in need of a shit-detector, and apparently unwilling or unqualified to volunteer, retired from the lists.

Now, shit-detectors are a necessary adjunct to any area of achievement, and certainly rock and roll needs all the help it can get in that department (being noticeably more overstocked with shit than most others). But somehow I get the feeling that a Real Critic is more than ever essential to the music; I do not think that as yet rock has had one (the Goldstein Era notwithstanding, Paul Williams [*founder of Crawdaddy! magazine*] is probably the closest anyone has gotten so far).

Rock is a field which is admirably suited for (and in definite need of) the function of criticism. Its very temporariness is its greatest asset: rock moves the way no other art form can, and therefor it can reflect conditions and shifts in a way no other art form can begin to approach. If criticism, then, is the process of progressive selection, and the critic's proper function is that of liaison between artist and audience, rock would seem the ideal critical proving ground, as its motions are progressive (cyclical as well) and its potential for audience (and artists) is limitless.

Moreover, rock is bound up inextricably with other of the potent shaping forces of the time: politics, race, sociology, sex, all of which are part of the critic's range. With all this going for them, then what have rock writers been doing diddling around on the way to legitimate criticism? I think perhaps what has happened is that people writing about the music have gotten hung up on individual trips within the form and not bothered/not been able to treat with the subject as a cohesive social whole. Thus, we have politically-oriented rock writers, racially-oriented ("Can the white man *really*...", etc.) rock writers, revolutionarily-oriented ("Kick out the jams, motherfuckers!") rock writers and any number of other-directed people putting words on the music, but no one yet who has really succeeded in tying it all together: no *critic*, not yet.

I haven't any concrete suggestions to advance concerning development of the craft of rock writing into the art of rock criticism. (And that's really where I think it's at, right now: "craft" as opposed to "art".) I do think, however, that the compleat rock CRITIC, whoever it turns out to be, will have certain definite characteristics, chief of which will be a love for the field he is involved with (an area in which I suspect a goodly number of rock industry people fall down hard). A built-in immunity to superhype would help, too, and more than anything else he should keep it in his mind and not forget that responsibilities are a three-way interaction between himself and the artists and the audience (prospective as well as actual). Rock will have a critic yet: just give us time.

I'd like to be able to say that eventually rock got one. But I don't think that's true. We got several people who came quite close, but we have had no one, except possibly Greil Marcus, who brought rock sensibilities together with a tonnage of cultural clout the way the big guns of literature, music and drama did. We did get a lot of cultural commentators—reviewers—some clever, some not; and perhaps that is as good as we were ever going to get...

September 1969

> Peace, peace, he is not dead, he doth not sleep;
> He hath awakened from the dream of Life.
> 'Tis we who, lost in stormy visions, keep
> With phantoms an unprofitable strife...

Mick Jagger read Shelley's words to a crowd of 250,000 on a sunny after noon in London's Hyde Park, two days after Brian Jones died, drowned in his swimming pool with drugs and alcohol in his bloodstream

Brian Jones was 27 and had been with the Rolling Stones since 1962, when the group was formed. Mick Jagger sang it, Keith Richards played it, but Brian Jones lived it; he was one of those people who jump into things with both feet and never care whether what they jump into is a mud puddle or the Abyss. Time got tight for Brian Jones, and maybe it was never on his side at all.

> He is a portion of the Loveliness
> Which once he made more lovely...

When Brian Jones left the Rolling Stones, all he would say was, "I want to be able to play my own music." Nobody could have guessed that it would sound like this. But after six years Brian Jones was two thousand light-years from home already and getting farther and farther away all the time.

The Rolling Stones said goodbye to Brian with three thousand butterflies loosed into the air at Hyde Park and thirteen songs to follow: a rock and roll Irish wake. Nobody painted it black.

> **He lives, he wakes, 'tis Death is dead, not he!**
> **Mourn not for Adonais: thou young Dawn,**
> **Turn all thy dew to splendor, for from thee**
> **The spirit thou lamentest is not gone.**

I'm only glad I never had to write J&P's eulogy for my Jim— writing Strange Days *was hard enough—but if I did, it might have sounded not unlike this...*

October 1969

FEATURE:
FLYING HIGH – JEFFERSON AIRPLANE

Another piece I strip-mined for use in Strange Days. *Not much of a story and no real reason for it, except that I just liked writing about the Airplane and it was fun to hang out with them: hence this little scribblet. The fuller version in* Days *is the more accurate one; persons present for the hotel part of the interview were Grace Slick, Paul Kantner (for the past few months Grace's new consort), Airplane press agent Diane Gardiner and me.*

An acetate, for the younger generations who grew up digitally, was a special kind of record: a lacquer-coated, metal-cored disc, hence also known as a "lacquer". They typically degraded after only a few playings, not being made for longevity, and were primarily used as demo discs or test pressings so that artists could hear and approve what a record sounded like before mass vinyl pressings were undertaken. Because of their fragile nature, despite their surprising heaviness, they have always been collectors' items, and once past their original purpose seldom if ever played.

Down at the Fillmore East to watch Jefferson Airplane rehearse, two nights before their first performance at said Rock Palace since last Thanksgiving. The Airplane doesn't like New York very much: this time in, they refuse to leave their hotel rooms during the daylight hours, coming out around eight every night like some bizarre sort of collective nocturnal psychedelic snail.

The Fillmore looks like a construction site: huge wooden planks stretch across the seats, fat ropes are swinging from the ceiling. I sit in the front row with Spencer Dryden and quote him: "Our band doesn't look good onstage at all."

"Did I say that? Well, it's true; we look like living shit. Right. No stage presence whatsoever: just six people standing there giggling, not together and can't even count to one…"

I am thinking nothing coherent except that they all look healthier than I've ever seen them, like they've been eating once in a while, and Jorma Kaukonen even has a tan. Jack Casady drops down from the stage behind like Cyrano from the balcony, tells Spencer they're going to start.

The formless jam that the Airplane calls a rehearsal begins; Grace leaves a cluster of people and heads for the stage. Everybody comes up front to sit; we get wine from one direction and a pipe from the other…

The jam, with Jack, Jorma, Spencer and Paul participating, is a punctuated soundtrack to the quippies and Fillmore stage crew moving around behind them; Jorma's guitar takes off like a runaway horse and the jam disintegrates into a pigpile of miscellaneous notes. The group huddles, briefly, then begins work in melodic earnest.

An Airplane rehearsal, when they've doing it seriously, is probably better than the regular performances of ninety out of a hundred other groups. This one gets serious with "Eskimo Blue Day", a new song written by Grace that raised static over at RCA Victor because of its inclusion of the word "shit". They do it three or four times; at the moment they can't move on to anything else because Marty Balin is missing and they are waiting for him. Jack steps to one of the vocal mikes, grins and asks, "Was that inhumanly loud?", clearly delighted that it was. Some hassle begins between Jorma and Jack; it resembles internecine warfare, but among the Plane it passes for merely mild dissension.

Some time later, Marty Balin slouches down the aisle with more wine and hair that is now nearly as long as Jack's; good, *now* they can work, and for the next hour it is nonstop hard playing and singing.

Jefferson Airplane is one of the original San Francisco bands, and probably the only American band who has managed to make it in more varied milieus than any other: the Bell Telephone Hour, gigging with the San Francisco Symphony, an August appearance at the venerable Tanglewood (Mass.) music shed, heading a bill of the Who and B. B. King.

This diversity is due chiefly to the diversity of the Airplane itself. Founded in 1964-65 by Marty Balin, the group at first played in a Byrds–Spoonful bag of very melodic folk-rock sounds; with the addition of Grace Slick and Spencer Dryden, the sound changed into a more complex blend of rock, raga and jazz. Commercial success struck hard with the release of *Surrealistic Pillow*, the group's second LP, in early 1967, and the two singles taken from that album, "Somebody to Love" and "White Rabbit". In subsequent releases, the directions the group has taken have become increasingly sophisticated yet never once losing sight of their past.

The result is a nice synthesis; and a totally original sound. No matter what the Airplane does, they never sound like anything but the Airplane. And that's just fine.

"Come on up, we're having an acetate party!" says Diane, Jefferson Airplane's press lady. Me, I'm up for anything that sounds reasonable, so I go over to the Holiday Inn, of all places, where Grace Slick and Paul Kantner have been working all afternoon and are now free to entertain.

I have been told Room 200; accordingly, I get off the elevator at the second floor. No Room 200. It's one of those Twilight Zones scenes, I think, having just talked to Diane in Room 200 not three minutes before. I call again. Diane says she'll meet me at the elevator, and this time I hit the right one; nothing so exotic as a time warp, only the wrong wing of the hotel.

Grace is sitting on an unmade bed, playing an acoustic guitar. Paul, who is much better–looking than his pictures, greets me affably and everybody settles into conversation. The acetate?

"It's been and gone," Paul admits. "The record player they sent us was a piece of crap, so we didn't play it. I have a cassette, want to hear that? You could do a review right now from it…"

He pulls a cassette from a stack on the night table and wrestles it into the tape player. It doesn't go in. "Spencer's goddamn machine…" He succeeds in getting the cassette into position; it stays there exactly four seconds and then pops out, flying through the air and under the bed.

"Wasn't that the best record you ever heard?" Grace asks earnestly. She is dressed in pale-purple velvet pants and tunic, and wears no makeup; she looks about nineteen years old. Paul whips out his little blue and white tin box.

"There's this thing [Edward] Kienholz did," he says. " 'Confessional'. You walk in off the street, go into it and do whatever you feel like, be father–confessor or penitent. And this other one—he had a vacant lot, and he filled it up with trash, you know, papers, old tires, and he fenced it off, and that was the work of art. Then one afternoon, some old wino wandered in and fell asleep, and he was part of it too! That's a nice approach to things: to our music, if you like."

Paul leaves to go down to RCA so he can hear the

acetate, which will be their sixth album for the label [*Volunteers*]. Grace settles back and asks wouldn't we like something to drink….

We are now exploring the Airplane's more bizarre intra-personal relationships ("Paul, yeah, he's the Nazi of the group. Very logical. Shit, you *know* you've had it with Paul when he gets this little smile on his face, and then he stands up and puts his hands in his pockets and starts talking through his teeth. Sitting down, he can still be talked to. Once he stands up, you haven't got a prayer.") when the phone rings. Diane grabs it.

"Hello — no, she isn't — no, I'm not her sister — no, I really don't sound like her at all. [Grace: "Say I'm dead!"] No, she really isn't here — "

Diane breaks off, stunned, and hands the phone to Grace, who listens with an expression of entirely suspended judgment. Diane turns to me. "He just said, 'I sing, too', and then he started to sing 'White Rabbit'."

Grace gestures to the effect that apparently he is still singing it, and when she finally hangs up, she adds, "Yeah, *all* of it, and 32 bars of 'Somebody to Love'."

The conversation shifts to media and journalism, and I lament the fact that nobody seems to read much anymore.

Grace sits up. "Yeah, *right*. Remember when you used to read? I mean, sit by yourself and turn the pages of a book and read the words and maybe take a week to think about it all. That was nice; I liked it. Now everything is mainlined. Books, TV, knowledge. Mainlined life. Just shoot all up."

Phone rings again. Grace picks it up. "No, there iss no one here, no one atall…Yess, I vill leaf a message. Thank you."

Diane giggles. "That was Margareta, if I ever heard her."

"Yeah, Margareta, Jorma's wife." Grace says, grinning.

"Margareta was into this really bizarre thing one night; everything Jorma said she would say to him, 'Jorma, a voman vould not say that'. 'Jorma, a voman vould not haf a cat like that.' He was flipping out after about fifteen minutes."

The whole thing is rapidly degenerating into three chicks sitting around being wiped out and gossipy; it would be nice, but it's time for me to head back to the office.

"Are you coming to the rehearsal?" Grace asks . "We're only just learning the songs, you know."

"But you've recorded them already?"

"Yeah, sure, but we're still learning how to play them. We'll probably never learn to do then really right."

It was always fun talking to the Airplane. We never became friends—my job was to write about musicians, not be friends with them—but we were on friendly terms, and I generally spent time with them whenever they came to New York. It was invariably enjoyable: they were all smart and funny and well-read, and of course I loved the music…and they were probably the single most important reason that I got into rock in the first place. Thanks, JA!

POP TALK :
SAY THE WORD AND YOU'LL BE FREE

The bookend to the previous piece. Ultimately, RCA and the Airplane reached a compromise on Volunteers: *the group could sing the offending words ("shit" in "Eskimo Blue Day" and "motherfucker" in "We Can Be Together") as much and as unmixed-down as they liked, but the liner notes would have to carry the words written out as "fred." Yeah. "Fred." As in "Up against the wall, fred!" Quite the radical little slogan, that.*

Oh, and there was a further controversy over the album title: the band had originally wanted to call it Volunteers of America, *but the conservative organization the real* Volunteers of America *had a fit and made them snip it to just plain* Volunteers, *though JA did manage to sneak the full name into the hook.*

RCA Victor, that father–figure record company monolith with the receding hairline, has just finished up the latest in a long-standing series of best-fall-out-of-three tussles with, who else, Jefferson Airplane. Seems that the Plane had these dirty words on two songs ("Eskimo Blue Day" and "We Can Be Together") for their sixth album that were giving the RCA execs heart failure every time they thought about it.

The group, approached by the company, refused to change a syllable. RCA pleaded that certain record-store chains would refuse to carry the album in stock. Jefferson Airplane said fuck the record-store chains, the words were going to stay. ("It's very strange," Grace Slick mused. "I mean, everybody talks like that all the time, and it's natural to use those words in songs because they're so familiar. But then along comes somebody and says, Look! What's *that*?, and then you start to wonder, Yeah, what *is* that? What's it doing there? Who put it there, what does it mean? The emphasis becomes fixed on the wrong thing.")

And the words *did* stay, and RCA ran a full-page inside cover ad in the Fillmore program that announced with somewhat pitiful bravado, "If you think Jefferson Airplane has problems with each other, you should see the problems they have with us." Funny, no?

No.

People have been getting it for years on the question of artistic freedom (and by implication, of course, the other end of the stick: artistic controls): Michelangelo, James Joyce. It is only very recently that the problem came up in relation to rock.

The majority of rock and roll performers never make a real confrontation with the censorship forces; they turn out their songs, cut their albums and don't make any waves. I mean, really, no disrespect intended, but how controversial is Cher? A small but definite minority group, on the other hand, seems to put their liberated foot into it every time they tune up, and it is this particular segment of the rock and roll that I am concerned with here.

Being sat on by your record company because your lyrics are, according to said record company, too inflammatory, too dirty, too weird or too otherwise unacceptable can be a disillusioning experience. What it eventually comes down to is a question of priorities: record companies — of necessity — lay a whole extraneous business trip on the "product", as they dub it. And there's nothing basically wrong with that: as long as the company stays on the business side of the fence and concerns itself with such matters as proper promotion and effective distribution and quality sound reproduction; in short, doing everything possible to insure that the record makes it on technical and business grounds.

That's it. No meddling with the artistic end of things: that is a matter strictly between artists, producer, and public. Rock is a business, sure; so're the 57th Street art galleries and the New York Philharmonic. The record company's sole function is to merchandise: to be a clearing house for the group's efforts. Ideally, the only contract a rock band should ever have to sign would be a distribution and promotion contract; all recording, artwork and final putting-together of the album in progress should be controlled solely by the people responsible.

Who but the artist, ultimately, should have the unqualified say-so over what will eventually appear before the public under his name? I find it almost incredible that artists such as the Airplane and the Rolling Stones and the Mothers should have to go through seven different sorts of shit with their respective labels over such inane details as jacket artwork (the Stones and their graffiti bathroom wall) or Anglo-Saxon nouns and Oedipal expletives (Airplane). Along with the other lords of the media, record company powers (with a very few immediate and well-known exceptions) tend to grossly underestimate the general sophistication or shock level of their potential audience. People are in general a lot less flappable than they used to be, most especially the kind of people who *buy* those records by the Stones and the Airplane and the Mothers, and nobody is going to be turned into stone by a perfectly normal little unremarkable four-letter noun that is used (somebody figured it out) on an average of once every twenty words. And maybe that wouldn't be such a bad idea after all.

I HEARD THE NEWS TODAY OH BOY: MC5's first Atlantic album probably out by the time this appears, titled *Back In the U.S.A.* ... Arthur Lee and Love's current Elektra

LP will be their last for that label .The group goes with Blue Thumb after that, first album to be called *Out Hear* ... Ex-Cream producer Felix Pappalardi has got himself a brand-new bag: bass in former Vagrant Leslie West's new group, Mountain ... Chambers Brothers set for return tour of Europe in early fall ... Jefferson Airplane and Santana did a free concert in Central Park's Sheep Meadow August 10 ... Jimi Hendrix, the ubiquitous Airplane and the Who got it together on the Dick Cavett Show, ABC-TV, August 19. The Doors are also reportedly considering a Cavett appearance or a gig on David Frost's show ... Elmer Johnson put in an appearance recently at the Mississippi River Festival in Edwardsville, Ill., sitting in with the band from Big Pink. Or at least that's how he was introduced — it didn't take long for people to recognize him as Bob Dylan ... Speaking of the Doors, the word from L.A. is that Jim Morrison has shaved off the beard and wants to record "Heartbreak Hotel". I guess that's the way God planned it...

REVIEW:
THE SOFT PARADE, The Doors

My first Doors review. Perhaps a bit more, um, bipolar than it might otherwise have been. But I really did think, and still do, that it was an extraordinary album and the title track is still my favorite long-form Doors song...

DOORS ♦ *The Soft Parade* **(Elektra EKS-75005). Jim Morrison (vo); Ray Manzarek (keyboards); Robbie** [*as he was spelling it then*] **Krieger (g, chorus vo on "Runnin' Blue"); John Densmore (d); Harvey Brooks or Doug Lubahn (b); Curtis Amy (tenor sax); George Bohanon (trombone); Champ Webb (English horn); Jesse McReynolds (mandolin); Jimmy Buchanan (fiddle); Reinal Andino (congas); orchestral arrangements, Paul Harris.** *Tell All the People; Touch Me; Shaman's Blues; Do It; Easy Ride; Wild Child; Runnin' Blue; Wishful Sinful; The Soft Parade.*

Run, do not walk—nay, *teleport* yourself—to the nearest record store and take this record home with you, 'cause the Doors can still do it and we all ought to be glad and I hope it shuts up the bad-rappers for good and all.

The Soft Parade: none of it is bad; most of it is very superior music, and some of it is absolutely glorious. The first major bitch—of two—that I have against the album is that of the nine songs presented, five were released in single versions over the past eight months. Now this does nothing to take away from the intrinsic value of the songs, it just serves to make more than half the record instantly familiar, and I don't think that is a particularly good idea.

On the other hand, though, this type of programming gives new importance to such a knockout song as "Wild Child", which in its previous avatar was the B side of "Touch Me" and didn't have much chance to do anything. You figure it out.

The other complaint is the orchestration. I was forewarned about this back in January, and so had ample time to develop immunity. Happily, most of my steeling myself in advance was unnecessary. Paul Harris's arrangements are for the most part tasteful and effective, and the Doors are smart enough to *use* the backing, not just let it happen, or, worse, use *them*. The big loser on the orchestration trip, though, is Ray Manzarek. Ray, who plays an ascetic, thoughtful, professorial and appealing organ, is very often snowed under by the brass Harris has added, and most of the time he is dastardly under-recorded. He gets it on, as they say, whenever he can, however.

The chief thing the orchestra does do, when it happens, is expand upon the Doors sound until it all becomes both ends of one supremely smooth musical continuum, and the one thing it does more than anything is set off some of the best vocal work Jim Morrison has done to date. Morrison demonstrates that indeed he can sing in other keys besides D modal drone, or whatever it was that most of the Doors' songs have been written in up to now, and his voice has never seemed in better shape: he shrieks without cracking, and he can hit semi-spoken low notes without driving his chin into his chest.

All *right*! The record opens up with "Tell All the People"; not very auspiciously, I might add. Robbie's guitar stutters around underneath the Easter Parade horn voicings, and Ray does some cocktail-party jazz piano. Of the heavily orchestrated, numbers. "Touch Me" fares the best, but "Wishful Sinful", a really pretty song written by Krieger, is done in by the instrumentation: much better just the group should play it.

"Do It" is prefaced by some bizarre cutting-up by what sounds like Jim and Robbie (only audible through 'phones, boys and girls), followed by Morrison's wickedly gleeful chortles over the lead-in. I suspect that "Do It" is a studio concoction, a Doors rave-up in the non–tradition of "A Small Package of Value Will Come to You Shortly"; it's got two lines, several variations, and some powerful pounding music (particularly from Krieger) that could have been put to excellent and far more suitable use on something a bit more serious. "Easy Ride", which closes out Side One, sounds approximately like Don Rondo and his old outfit trying to make a rock and roll comeback having been heavily influenced by Jim Morrison and the Doors in the interim. Goddamn.

The aforementioned "Wild Child" is a real Doors song: hypnotic, dark, surreal, evil. Check out the bass and guitar figures. And oh yeah, "Runnin' Blue"; wow, Robbie Krieger on chorus vocal! It's things like this that make you properly appreciate Jim Morrison... Jim and Robbie's duet on the closing chorus verse is, ah, historic. "Runnin' Blue" is a good rock and roll song, though: a double-time tambourine would have been nice, but there's a really funky Bulgarian folk-dance fiddle and some classical (even) contrapuntal action, and the horn reinforcement on Jim's vocals is superlative. A tight, bright song that could make it big as a single. (No! Please! Not another!)

But the real beauty of *The Soft Parade* (album) lies in "Shaman's Blues" and "The Soft Parade" (song); and, to a lesser extent, "Runnin' Blue". None of these songs sounds like anything the Doors have done before: they are all technically sophisticated, well-balanced and definitely positive in statement, and I hope like hell that they are indicative of the new direction the Doors appear to be taking: because if that is the case, gonna be a lot of doomsayers standin' around with their faces hanging out, and that would please me mightily.

"Shaman's Blues", then, is a Morrison-composed, scatty-sounding amalgam of jazz and blues that its author sings most convincingly. This song involves a totally new rhythmic approach for the Doors: free, choppy, much stretching and bending of measures and a lot of jazzy licks, vocal as well as instrumental (especially in the backup sax runs). John Densmore's background as a jazz drummer shows up full inventive strength here and in "The Soft Parade" (in contrast to his work on, say, "Wild Child", where he sounds like a troglodyte with one (1) new Christmas drum. there's some obscure *recitative* at the end: all in all, a surprisingly beautiful song and to my mind one of the Doors' very best.

And "The Soft Parade." Dazzling as this piece is, it becomes more so when considered in the light of a beginning: using "The Soft Parade" as a point of departure, the Doors are in a position to move into previously untapped regions of musical exploration, AND IT DOESN'T SOUND ANYTHING LIKE THEIR FIRST ALBUM.

The song is built on tidal shifts of music and kinetics, declamatory poem trips: sections strung together like contrasting beads of melody and surreality. The Doors play some very original studio games with "The Soft Parade": Ray triple-tracked on piano, organ and harpsichord or marimba or possibly both—the Manzarek way with keyboards is so beautifully involuted it's hard to tell just what is happening. Morrison comes in for some unison and harmonic doubletracking later in the piece: the effect is startling, it sounds as though he's ten feet tall, and later still it gets into a pattern of four-track vocal, tape delays of half a beat, all staggered, separated, stereo whiplashed and reverb'd into a God-of–Doom finish.

Technical effects, however described, can give by themselves no real idea of "The Soft Parade", and I don't want to lay an exegesis trip on anybody, with this song particularly or with the album as a whole. Lyrically, the record is an even split between Morrison and Krieger, with one collaboration between the two ("Do It"); Morrison has let it be known that individual writer credits are now being stated because the unity of the group is no longer so much in danger and "I thought it was time people knew who was saying what." Well, now we know: I am not going to be so ill-advised as to attempt to draw any parallels, analogies or other comparisons between Jim's and Robbie's respective songwriting heads. All I will say is that I am glad to know Robbie wrote "Touch Me", and Jim "Shaman's Blues."

The Soft Parade is all the better for the knowledge that it is only a start. "The Soft Parade has now begun…"; come on.

Written before we got together, though after our friendship had begun…

November 1969

I ripped off this story for not only Strange Days *but for my Rennie Stride rock murder mystery series.* Go Ask Malice: Murder at Woodstock, *the fifth book in the series, has a different and totally fictional take on the festival—two murders and a poisoning, which to the best of my knowledge nothing remotely like that ever happened there—but I took a lot of the backstage background for it from my experiences and the account I wrote of it here. The versions in* Days *and* Malice *are greatly expanded, from my notes, diaries and outtakes, as I didn't have that much space in the magazine (as you will see) and couldn't do the festival full justice.*

I was there with aforementioned former roommate and sorority sister Susan P. Donoghue, who also wrote for J&P and who later became the managing editor of Rock magazine and a publicist for Warner Brothers Records; she had a dark-green Mustang that we drove up in, and we thought we were just too cool for school. Thankfully, we didn't have to sleep either in the field or at the crammed motels: we were staying with our college friends Ron and Mary Janoff, who lived near a little town called Long Eddy, about fifteen miles away on the far side of the festival, along the banks of the Delaware, and we had every luxury—food, beds, a nice warm house, not being rained on. As it turned out, it was very good that we had a bit of distance and remove...

"That festival was probably the strangest thing that's ever

happened on this earth," David Crosby commented on the day after. Imagine, if you can, a city of 500,000, most of whom were well under the age of 30, a city with no buildings and no conveniences to speak of, a city that lived on an upstate New York hillside for three days with no violence whatsoever. (500,000 people is about half as many as live on Manhattan Island; there has yet to be a three-day period in which half of Manhattan Island is totally non-violent. Think about it.)

The city started happening on Wednesday, August 13, two days before the start of the festival, officially known as The Woodstock Music and Art Fair at Bethel, N.Y.: An Aquarian Exposition. Bethel (the name means "house of God" in Hebrew) is a village and township in the southwestern Catskills, with a permanent population of around 3,000 and the usual influx of summer visitors to the resorts that are all over the area.

An unlikely place for a rock festival, perhaps. But Max Yasgur had said they could use his dairy farm's 600-acre back pasturage, and that was when the city began. By Friday morning the campgrounds were full, the huge natural amphitheater that was to be the site of the festival was full, the roads leading to Bethel were impassable, and as many as a million and a half were still on the way.

We run into the traffic backup at the first Monticello exit on Route 17, going west; radio reports say forget it, so we cut to Liberty via Routes 55 and 97. The country house where we were to stay was about 20 minutes' driving time northwest from Bethel, and we are congratulating ourselves on our cleverness in avoiding the crush, heading to the festival later that afternoon. We have a press sticker on the car, so we are allowed to drive into the grounds along Hurd Road, a rather twisty one and half lane road now nearly solid people. We inch forward and they shuffle out of the way. I am flashing on oil-rich Bedouin sheiks in a black Cadillac plowing through crowds of dusty, barefoot peasants on pilgrimage to Mecca. It is not an association I particularly like.

We reach the press parking mudhole and get out to join the multitude. Coming over the crest of the hill I see it for the first time: the city is there .It looks like the biggest gypsy camp in the world, the bazaar at Samarkand, both Fillmores, the new Jerusalem, and London during the blitz, all in one. It is absolutely staggering. Richie Havens is on, and he sounds just fine as we walk along just behind the last of the people, on the hill sloping down to the stage a quarter of a mile away.

Press passes, as we quickly find out, pull weight only to get you a telephone to call your paper in New York or wherever; the press section was overrun the first day by the kids who arrived early, and no one with a mere press pass is allowed onstage, backstage or in the performers' pavilion: in short, nowhere near the action. Friday evening, therefore, is spent trying to obtain what someone sardonically refers to as "upward pass mobility", and by the time I have gone through my routine for at least six people [*making sure they see the package I'm carrying bearing the Doors office address, "Oh, this little thing? Only my copies of Jim's private-edition books that he sent me just yesterday, of which I am burstingly proud in the possession of and could not bear to be parted from even for the weekend…" – PKM*] and managed to get performers' passes, I feel that I have earned them.

By this time the crowds outside are of truly biblical proportions and evangelical fervor. The performers' pavilion, in the midst of all this, is an oasis of relative serenity; once you are there, you do not want to move again, ever, just sit facing the stage and write your piece from there. But we get up to move around, flinching at the helicopters that are taking off from a few hundred yards up the hill, airlifting the musicians and the emergency cases in and out. There is a bridge constructed from the pavilion over the cyclone fence surrounding the field, over the road, over another fenced work area, right into the stage. It looks like a down-at-heel Bridge of Sighs and is outlined in red Christmas lights. We gingerly cross over and come onto the vast wooden stage, where Tim Hardin is just going on. The m.c. asks the audience to light matches, to "see how bright we can make this place." This is a familiar riff to anyone who attends Doors concerts, but the fire that is almost instantly on the hillside puts Madison Square Garden to shame; it really is almost bright enough to read by. Hardin begins to sing; I overhear a stage guard, seriously concerned, mutter something about not letting anybody else onstage, because it can't support the weight. Not wishing to be a party to the Bethel Mining Disaster of 1969, we leave the grounds for the evening.

Saturday begins with pours of rain, thunder, lightning and bigger than ever crowds. The people who have slept out are sodden and tending toward pneumonia, but everybody is smiling as they slog through the ankle-deep red mud. We have found where Hurd Road comes out on the other end from the festival field, so most of the early afternoon is spent trying to get through from that side. Unfortunately, about five hundred other people have had the same idea before we had it, and it takes us two hours to go a distance of six miles or less. The rain has stopped and the sun is out; there are people skinnydipping in Max Yasgur's pond, much to the dismay of his neighbors. I have been hearing incredible stories of twelve-hour waits to get from Monticello to Bethel, ten-mile hikes to parked cars, brigades of little old ladies from nearby towns distributing free water and sandwiches to the hungry masses in the cars lining Route 18B; it's too weird, it must *all* be true.

God always rewards the patient, though, and He does so this time with a parking space right in the middle of the festival, at the crossroads facing out. I am feeling like a rather uncomfortable elitist, so instead of making a beeline for the pavilion, we set out to explore. Half an hour later we are back in the pavilion. I am not usually put off by crowd situations, but this is something entirely different. The onslaught of varied vibes is psychically deafening, and the physical fact of 500,000 wiped-out people sitting perched on a hill like an acid avalanche is just too much. I am at the point where if one more person says to me "Good vibes, huh?" I am going to punch him in the mouth.

So we're back in Valhalla, the performers' pavilion, an open-sided psychedelic mead hall, surrealistic pillars roofed with canvas and floored with redwood chips. I am sitting there like Phoebe Zeitgeist [*a contemporary underground-newspaper cartoon character, rather sexistly renowned for haplessness and bosomage, in a strip written by Michael O'Donoghue and drawn by Frank Springer – PKM*] asking myself, "What does it all *mean*?" when Ellen Sander breezes in. In the course of an idle rap I allow as to how the scene is splitting my head.

"Have you been Out There?" she asks earnestly. "GET Out There, then! Those kids are beautiful! They're beautiful and together and you'll see it. It just amazes me how magnificently people can behave in a crisis situation. You'll see it, too."

I look at her. CRISIS? This is supposed to be three days of Peace, Love and Music, what happened to *that*? Yes, the kids are beautiful; yes, I was Out There with them, and I did see a great deal of beauty. But also I saw thousands upon thousands of the walking wounded of this Revolution we all talk so much about: kids who haven't got faces yet, filled up with drugs they don't know how to make proper use of and only take because the Scene makes it easy. Kids like that hurt me: I feel media guilt, that maybe we who are older and supposed to know better did this to them (they're turning on in the elementary schools now....) before they were ready for it: the kids that try to hitch a ride in your car with a V-sign, then snarl viciousness at you when you tiredly explain you have a full car and can't take any more passengers, the kids who have all the right hip clothes and know all the right words and drop all the right stuff but whose heads haven't been affected in the slightest; the kids who have come to this festival and are going to consume vibes and dope and music, but what are they going to take home with them? Just as importantly, what have they brought?

So I sit there looking at Ellen Sander as she tells me about the beauty of the children, and part of me is yelling "Right on, sister!" but most of me is feeling like Scrooge at the Christmas party. Unregenerate to the end, I check out the rest of the pavilion. A majority of those present are probably of Ellen's persuasion, but I don't notice too many of them flinging their guest passes to the ground and rushing out to *join* these beautiful children....no, they are sitting in here, French aristocrats huddled together while the citizenry press outside the cyclone fence.

There has been music going on all day and all evening, somehow it is of only peripheral importance. Even the Grateful Dead, who finally make it onstage around ten Saturday night, can't turn it on, and leave the stage looking disgruntled. There has been a rather ugly incident, to my way of thinking, earlier this afternoon, which occurred when somebody's equipment man tossed acid in the fruit punch cooler; an unsuspecting chick drank some of the now-electric punch and freaked. Really, acid in the punch? I ask, thanking God I stuck to champagne. Yeah, some blond cowboy giggles, isn't that wild? I fail to see the humor in the situation, though, and the memory of that girl, who probably wasn't more than eighteen, was with me all night. Just one more thing to wonder about.

Buy now I am running on survival vibes; the pavilion is rapidly taking on the aura of being the rock world's Ultimate Press Party, the groups are taking longer and longer to get onstage, and there is a cat sitting next to Albert Grossman in a black porkpie hat, yellow shades and a trenchcoat, with *short* hair, who I am *convinced* is an FBI agent. When I realize it's Johnny Winter, incognito, with his hair stuffed up under the hat, I know it's time to go home. Even with a performer's pass, I was not permitted onstage that night ("You a performer?" Noncommittal "mmm..." "You on tonight?" "No..." "Sorry, only people who are on tonight can go on the stage."), nor was I allowed in the pit, despite my press pass ,because you had to have a press pass, a camera, *and* be doing some kind of number on the group you were photographing before you were let into the pit. And even then they cleared the pit completely in between groups. My total musical experience, therefore, consisted of four minutes of "On The Road Again" from the repackaged Canned Heat, and a briefly ecstatic epiphany from the Grateful Dead before they started to sulk.

[*Pauline cut and edited this sequence drastically, basically amputating the entire Saturday/Sunday section from the Dead on, for reasons of space, which annoyed me considerably when I saw the issue blueprints, especially since she didn't ask me and I thought I could have stitched it together way more sensitively. But, apart from a few hours on Sunday morning, to go back to the Janoffs' and eat and crash, Susie and I were at the festival right through till Crosby Stills Nash & Young played, though by Monday morning, at the moment Jimi was onstage making rock history in front of a mere 50,000 diehards, we were wending our weary way back to New York. So I did indeed hear considerably more music than Pauline's hack job would indicate. In* **Strange Days** *and* **Go Ask Malice** *I added back what I could from my journals and my memory, to give a more complete picture. — PKM]*

It didn't matter, though. There were people I spoke to who never got closer to the music than two miles away, and they were just as happy as those who camped out in front of the stage. The real show at Bethel was simply being there, and the real worth of the festival lay not in the music, but in the incomparable community closeness that sprang up, for whatever reason. There was no rioting at Bethel because everybody was, to one degree or another, *there* for everybody else; there was no gesticulating George Wein uptight onstage, there *were* people who warned the crowd public-spiritedly about bad acid going around. The lack of violence was so natural that I and others had to remind ourselves that it was not the norm outside this valley, that for this one weekend real life had expanded to include us but it wasn't going to be like this once we all left Max's farm. That didn't matter either. The important thing was that it happened, and we will be talking about it for a long time; more to the point, THEY will be talking about it for a long time too, that half a million of their children, muddy, tired, hungry, thirsty, without sufficient sleep or shelter, did what they did.

On the way out of the festival, we were held up in traffic for the longest wait we'd had so far. On the trunk of the car in front of us, a little girl was sitting in between two men. She had long blonde braids and was wearing a fringed buckskin jacket, and was about six or seven years old. After exchanging smiles and peace signs, she spoke to one of the men, obviously her father, and then hopped off the trunk and came round to my window and proceeded to discuss with incomparable aplomb the faults of the festival's programming, sound system and facilities, how much she had wanted to hear Ravi Shankar but he was on too late and they had to get back to their motel. Seven-year-old kid. Then all of a sudden she *was* a seven-year-old again as she caught sight of my sleepy kitten and demanded to be allowed to hold her. Traffic started up far ahead, the girl's father called her and she handed back the kitten, smiled at us and said, "It's a nice festival but not for music. I feel safe here."

Out of the mouths of babes...but I don't suppose anybody who was at Bethel for those three incredible days felt otherwise. Rock and roll fit the battle of Jericho on Max Yasgur's back pasture on an August weekend, and nobody who was there will ever feel alone again. In spite of everything, I'm glad I went.

And I still feel that way. Basically, I went to Woodstock with a VIP pass and a clubhouse ticket, but Woodstock doesn't get a pass from me. It was overhyped, autohyped, retroactively embellished with glittery sparkles, and pretty much a preeningly self-satisfied heap of hokum. I'm glad I was there for it as a first-hand witness to a sociological phenomenon and piece of history, absolutely; but more as devil's advocate than anything else. Still, I was young and as subject to the self-persuasion of the time as anyone. Pete Townshend, among other musicians, says he can always tell who was really at Woodstock and who's lying about it, by the fact that people who were there say the music was horrible and those who weren't rhapsodize about it. True, that.

But Woodstock stood alone and oddly out of its era; Altamont was only four months in the future, so the Woodstock Nation was particularly short-lived even in its own moment. It was never meant to endure, hadn't been built to last; it was as evanescent as a butterfly's wing and as temporary as one of the showers that soaked it.

And yet, from another viewpoint, Woodstock Nation never stopped *enduring, and even prevailing. Its ideas and ideals, many of them, became, almost unthinkingly, by default even, the law of the land and a fait accompli in people's minds and hearts: equality of race and gender, care for the Earth and its creatures, healthy food and clean air and unpolluted water, effective political activism, compassion and concern for the less fortunate.*

All these policies, startling and radical in their time, are now standard issue for just about every right-minded individual— you will notice how with great care I say "every RIGHT-minded individual", as there are some beings around these days who are minded far more harshly and more cruelly and more viciously than any of the enemies we had to contend with back then—and it was at Woodstock where those policies became codified.

And it was also at Woodstock, of course, where the music became classic...

EDITORIAL:
AQUARIAN AFTERMATH

The events in Bethel, N.Y. over the weekend of August 15-18 have caused wildly disparate reactions from every imaginable quarter. Most of the backwash of opinion was predictable: i.e., those who were there themselves, or who understood what was happening, were full of praiseful words; those who are opposed to what Bethel represented took the opportunity to vent their frustrations with impotent invective. What is far more significant, however, is the *un*predicted reaction.

The Short Line Bus Company, for example, took a half-page ad in the New York Times, using glowing quotes from its own drivers who conveyed the multitudes to Bethel, asserting that "We learned a lot about the young people around us. We love what we learned." Mrs. Max Yasgur, whose husband's pasture was the scene of the Scene, had nothing but praise for the comportment of the festival-goers, as did the vast majority of residents of the Bethel area who came into direct contact with them.

The New York Times, on the other hand, blew whatever cool it may have had by an outrageously jaundiced editorial appearing on August 18 entitled "Nightmare in the Catskills", comparing the sanity of the festival crowd to that of lemmings precipitating themselves into the sea. (The Times was remarkably schizoid on Bethel: its editorials said one thing, but stories from the reporters who were actually there said quite another, and in subsequent editions the editorial was changed, withdrawn, and, the next day, contradicted by a favorable one.) So much for the journalistic perceptiveness of the Establishment press.

If the Short Line bus drivers and Mrs. Yasgur had their heads turned around and their opinions reversed, so did those who went to the festival full of preconceptions regarding the straight people whose homeland they were visiting. It was a cultural interchange on the highest level, and the knowledge each participant gained of the other will not be lost.

This, perhaps, is the real meaning of Bethel.

January 1970

REVIEW:
ABBEY ROAD, The Beatles

BEATLES ◆ *Abbey Road* (Apple SO-383). John Lennon, Paul McCartney, George Harrison, Ringo Starr. No instrumentation specified. *Come Together*; *Something*; *Maxwell's Silver Hammer*; *Oh! Darling*; *Octopus's Garden*; *I Want You* (*She's So Heavy*); *Here Comes the Sun*; *Because*; *You Never Give Me Your Money*; *Sun King*; *Mean Mr. Mustard*; *Polythene Pam*; *She Came In Through the Bathroom Window*; *Golden Slumbers*; *Carry That Weight*; *The End*.

The new Beatles album.

Elaboration would seem to be unnecessary, beyond that simple statement, but then things are seldom what they seem.

Abbey Road is a schizoid record, but lovably so, and that makes all the difference. Stylistically, it comes across as a hybrid, a reloaded (and reconstituted) *Revolver*, by *Rubber Soul* out of the Rock and Roll Revival. Owing relatively little to the fancy-flash of the White Album, *Abbey Road* nevertheless seems more to be marking time than to be stepping ahead.

Which is not necessarily bad by any means. "Something" is perhaps George Harrison's most beautiful song to date, a lovely, graceful lyric. "Maxwell's Silver Hammer", out of the same insanity mulch as "Honey Pie" and even "Country

Pie", is gloriously perverse, and Ringo's "Octopus's Garden" is a crashing bore. "Come Together" and "I Want You (She's So Heavy)" are the two successes (out of three attempts — the third party being "Oh! Darling ") at playing good ol' rock and roll; the lyrics are on the one hand bizarre and on the other simplistic, but the overall effect is fairly vital.

Not so the second side. It opens promisingly enough with another Harrison charmer, "Here Comes The Sun" — just thinking about it is enough to warm your shivery bones in the chill of a Manhattan autumn. But the medley that ensues, and continues to the end of the side, is shaky in structure and lackluster in tone; there is the distinct impression that the songs are huddled up against each other for warmth and security-in-numbers reassurance. "Carry That Weight", though, and "The End" are fairly responsible, and, in context, quite beautiful ("And in the end/The love you take/Is equal to the love you make" is an unimpeachable and righteous sentiment), while the little ditty about Her Majesty being a pretty nice girl though she doesn't have a lot to say comes as a totally unexpected and very funny surprise: betcha Her Majesty even liked it herself.

Abbey Road is supremely accessible, it's there for you any old time, and though sometimes it may not be as there as at other times, that's all right too, because nobody else is either.

MOVIE REVIEW:
ALFRED THE GREAT

Alfred the Great ◆ starring David Hemmings (Alfred), Michael York (Guthrum), Prunella Ransome (Aelhswith), Colin Blakely (Asher), Ian McKellen (Roger), Vivien Merchant (Freda). Directed by Clive Donner.

On the Medieval Flick Index, which ranges from Excellent to Painful, *Alfred the Great,* sad to tell, tips the scales at Medium Dreadful. Just whose fault it is cannot be precisely ascertained, as all those involved ought to know better: director Clive Donner, stars David Hemmings, Michael York and Prunella Ransome; but it really doesn't matter in the long run.

Alfred the Great purports to be about the exploits of the ninth-century Saxon war leader Alfred, styled King of Wessex (southwestern England), in a time when Britain was divided up into petty kingdoms and the invading Danish Vikings were picking them off one by one like winkles from a rock.

In a subsequent series of plot thickenings, Alfred is (a) coerced into marshaling the fight against the Danes, (b) forced into giving up the priesthood by his love for Aelhswith, princess of a neighboring kingdom, whom he marries, (c) trapped into assuming the kingship on the death of his brother Ethelred, (d) defeated by Guthrum, the Danish leader, who tricks him into giving Aelhswith to the Danes as a hostage against treaty–breaking and then takes Aelhswith as his not-unwilling mistress, (e) deserted by his lords, vassals and armies, and driven to take refuge with a band of outlaws in the marshes, where he learns humility, and (f) is ultimately victorious. The lords, vassals, armies and Aelhswith all come back to him, Guthrum is defeated in battle, and all ends happily.

Well, not exactly. (The really best thing about this film is the authenticity of the settings: therefore, we get the mud-and-wattle-daubed Great Hall of Wessex's kings and not your WPA-rococo medieval Loew's Palace.) Ultimately, of course, what matters in a film is not how cleverly they've tricked up the back lot or how many groovy locations were used for the shooting, but rather the interaction between the various components of the cinematic process. and *Alfred the Great* just doesn't make it: the players are stiff with each other (exceptions: Ransome in her scenes with York; Colin Blakely as the Welsh priest Asher), the camera is cheesecloth'd à la *Elvira Madigan* far too often, and worst of all, the lines, oh, the lines (Alfred: "What? King? ME? Oh no. Athelstan, you'd do it better, YOU be king!"). Good medieval dialogue is probably the hardest to write of all period-piece scripts: the temptation is equal to be fulsomely archaic or else contemporary cute. Either way, the anachronisms are staggering. In any case, it hardly matters. *Alfred the Great* may not be great cinema art, but it's a damned good popcorn movie.

— Shamrock O'Toole

My first encounter with Guthrum the Dane (protagonist of my historical novel Son of the Northern Star), *in the ever so photogenic person of actor Michael York. I doubt the real-life version was half so cute—York played him as a kind of charismatic blond Viking Beatle.*

The historical inaccuracies were legion, the most egregious being that hostage-romance between the dishy Viking king and

Alfred's bolter queen—which never happened. The script really was appalling: York, in his memoir, is quite funny about it. In fact, it was so bad, he writes, that actress Vivien Merchant, Harold Pinter's wife and as such accustomed to far better fare, insisted on playing her entire part—a kind of Saxon Maid Marian, wife to Ian McKellen's guerrilla leader—as a mute, in a form of protest when the promised rewrites failed to happen!

Also this was McKellen's first big movie role (well, biggish, anyway), and you can see Gandalf the Grey already twinkling in his intelligent eyes.

But looking back, and having seen it a couple of times since on DVD, the movie wasn't quite as dreadful as I made it out to be. Jim and I saw it together, in fact...

This was "Shamrock O'Toole"'s first appearance in J&P; her bio will come up later, and also some of her other reviews. As I mentioned earlier, we all used aliases from time to time; it made it seem as if there were more folks reviewing than there actually were...and spared our blushes.

February 1970

One of the many great things that Bill Graham did during his Fillmore East tenure in New York was the institution of various "nights", often free or at least very cheaply priced (hard to achieve when the regular prices ran from $5.50 top to $3.50). These nights, held at the venue during the week when the theater was otherwise dark, were a kind of give-back to the scene and the music. Jazz night, community night, poetry night...and audition night, when unknown, untried bands actually had a chance to get up on the same famous stage trod on weekends by rock gods, and present their own music to an audience of their peers.

It must have been incredibly exciting for the groups selected for the honor—I was on the stage a few times myself on various occasions, and it was amazing to stand there and look out at the house and think of the legends who'd stood in that very same place. On the other hand, audition night was pretty much a crapshoot for the audience, though it was fun to try to predict if any of the acts might go on to catch the ear of some a&r guy and get signed to a deal. As far as I knew, that never happened. But it was still a good idea...except when it wasn't.

POP TALK:
WOMEN IS BLUESERS

At the first of the Fillmore East Tuesday audition nights a while back, second act on the bill was Ariel, a group from Vermont, a five-member band who with the exception of the drummer and one song were uniformly dreadful and who received a dismal reception from the audience. Why then spend good column inches on them? You may well ask. Because Ariel was a group of chicks.

Now there is nothing new about all-girl bands (Ace of Cups, Freudian Slips, et al.), but what particularly interested (and incensed) me about the evening in question was the audience reaction.

Ariel was a nice, well-scrubbed, collegiately hip group of girls in their late teens, early twenties: the sort of band (and girls) that you could see playing for (attending) a Sunday afternoon sorority tea-dance, Glamour Magazine College Girl-pretty, long straight hair and rich-hippie (but clean) outfits. Their music, though godawful, was not totally unredeemable: mostly icky-poo medleys from *Hair* and ball-less treatments of soul standards (spare me the obvious remark: as far as I'm concerned, Tina Turner has "balls" — and a sexier lady I haven't met. You know what I mean), but with a lot of work and more substantial material they could be quite a respectable little band.

At any rate, nobody is harder on women than other women, and so I was sitting there anticipating probable disaster, though full willing to be impressed if they proved good. It started when the girls came out to tune up; naturally, they had trouble. Kip Cohen, the Fillmore's intrepid house manager, and the stage crew behaved like gentlemen and professionals. Ariel behaved like ladies and professionals. The audience behaved like professional pigs. There were cretins who applauded each note as the girls tuned up, shouts of "Get them off the stage and ball them!" from daring males who probably couldn't get it up with a splint, and sundry other manifestations of the most staggering display of rudeness and the double standard that I have ever seen.

And all this before Ariel had even begun to play. So,

they were not a good band: at least they deserved a hearing. You would grant that much to an all-male band, would you not, Fillmore audience? Yes, and you did, because I saw you that same night with the other two acts on the bill, one of which was fair, one of which was excellent, both of which were composed entirely of men. And both of which were treated with enthusiasm and respect.

Women in rock are something of an iffy subject anyway. In contrast to other music-performance areas, with their legions of Julie Andrewses and Petula Clarks, rock boasts a scant handful of participant ladies. When compared to the number of men actively and artistically involved in the field, female rock-and-rollers dwindle almost to the point of vanishment.

Almost, but not quite. A woman's *chances* at superstardom are probably enhanced in inverse proportion to the scarcity of women in the rock business. Whether she makes it is something else. Grace Slick on the subject: "If you had a group of five cows and a pig you'd look at the pig because it was different"; and a woman singing in an otherwise male band is almost traditional practice.

An all-female band, though, apparently poses too much of a threat: or at least the *idea* it represents to all those music-lovers out there with uncontrollable castration complexes. Though I have yet to see a chick group really get it on, in the parlance of the trade, I feel that this is due to overt and/or covert discrimination, rather than to any innate lack of musicality among females of the species.

Reaction: "Not that many chicks interested in musical careers." Perhaps, but I find it difficult to believe that all those millions of girls are interested unto retirement age in being secretaries. It seems to me that if it were easier for a girl to get into professional music, a lot more would jump at the chance and not just take some bullshit job because they weren't able to do what they wanted.

No, that's a cop-out, and I've heard it from people who ought to know better; it's a rationalization of the same stripe as "There are very few black lawyers (or doctors or politicians) because none of them are interested."

Substitute "chicks" for blacks", change the context to a musical one, and there you have it: Ariel at the Fillmore. I hope we don't have any more of it.

I HEARD THE NEWS TODAY OH BOY: In a noble attempt to fill the gap left by the closing of Steve Paul's Scene, New York clubs are working double-time and more. Ungano's is probably the most immediately successful, and rightly so: less claustrophobic than most, though drier than just about everybody (the strongest concoction Ungano's offers is an excellent cherry fizz), Ungano's has been the locus of late for the kind of jamming that used to be a treasured part of after-concert hours at Steve Paul's establishment. On the downtown front, Tarot on Union Square West has also moved into the breach, billing itself as a "discoraunt", with recorded music alternating with live bands. A little more of this and New York's rock club scene will be on the road to recovery after all ... Poppy Records celebrated Thanksgiving with an all-label show at Carnegie Hall on T-eve. Dick Gregory headlined, giving his first New York appearance in almost a year, and accompanying him on the bill were folksinger Townes Van Zandt and group Mandrake Memorial. Poppy set a uniform reserved–seat price of $2.50 for the event; oh, that other record companies would only follow suit. It's one of the best ways there is to get a label's acts before a good audience ... Diana Ross and the Supremes are once again just plain the Supremes, as Diana departed for a solo career which will include musical and dramatic appearances in films, Broadway productions and television. The break was completely amicable on all sides: both Diana and the "new" Supes have renewed their contracts with Motown, and the group now consists of Mary Wilson, Cindy Birdsong and new member Jean Terrell, sister of former heavyweight boxer Ernie Terrell ... Lou Rawls performed in a rather unusual setting recently: the controversial New York City school, I.S. 201 in Harlem. Lou was there on behalf of the "Stay In School " campaign, and was presented with a special citation form the City of New York for his continuing efforts in that regard (he has even formed his own Dead End Productions, a program which allows students to become involved in show business while completing their educations ... Jefferson Airplane, like rock-age Pilgrims, came to New York for their annual Thanksgiving concerts (and attendance at Bill Graham's Fillmore East turkey banquet, held in the Fillmore itself and participated in by hordes of hungry freaks from the Fillmore staff, press and music strata ... Area Code 615, Nashville supergroup, have been planning a tour which may have become fact by the time this is out. Dates have been tentatively scheduled in New York, Los Angeles, San Francisco, Boston, Philadelphia, Denver, Chicago and Seattle ... What I would like to do, if demand and response warrant it, is list here from time to time places in and around New York that out-of-town musicians and like-minded individuals would find interesting, convenient, cheap and something to do in between interviews and rehearsals, apart from just hanging out. It is my private contention that much of the bad rep New York has among out-of-town bands is due to the fact that they are not here long enough or often enough to really find their way around outside of the Max's-Fillmore-Ungano's-hotel room circuit. It's an old game for New Yorkers, and crucially connected to our problems of day-to-day living, but everybody can play, even if you're only in town for two nights at some club. Any suggestions, reactions or comments from anybody are of course welcome.

March 1970

My take on the Rolling Stones' American tour of 1969: the one that climaxed with Altamont...the anti-Woodstock.

POP TALK:
AFTERMATH: THE ROLLING STONES

The Rolling Stones have been and gone, no moss on their tails but astronomical grosses in their pockets, leaving a wake of gladiator concerts, a stunned populace, ecstatic writers, four people dead and some pretty roiled rock and roll waters. Altamont was only the logical outcome of it all.

It all began for me at a press audience granted by the Stones the day before Thanksgiving (I realize how after-the-fact this is in reaching you, but bear in mind that it is but three days after Altamont as I write). The conference was to be held in the Rainbow Grill on the 65th floor of the RCA building, and featured an open bar and a string quartet hired from Juilliard to entertain the press with Haydn and Mozart while we waited like courtiers for the Stones.

Long before the group even appeared, the conference had turned into a pitched battle between straight press and underground/hip press: "Move OVER, hippie, *I'm* here to get a story!" "Well, so am I." "Oh yeah? Then why aren't ya taking any notes?" Interspersed with periodic omnidirectional shouts of "COMMUNIST!" from one particularly puzzling TV gentleman.

When the Stones finally arrived, they were greeted with a ripple of applause, which seemed to sum up the whole thing. Past the first three rows, visibility was nil due to TV camera tripods and bodies standing on chairs, so I spent most of the next twenty minutes at the windows watching a truly spectacular sunset and listening to Mick Jagger skewer his interrogators.

The conference was remarkable in that not once did anybody from the hip press get to ask a question and also not once did *any*body ask the Stones *any*thing having to do with their music. (Samples, yes, honest to God they asked him: "Mr. Jagger, you once wrote a tune called 'Satisfaction.' Are you really satisfied?" "How do you like America?" "Mr. Taylor, how do you feel taking a dead man's place?" to which Mick Taylor properly refused a reply). Finally Jagger rose, stretched, and they marched out, again to applause and a few scattered clenched fists.

Going down in the elevator, it was agreed that any five of us could have played the roles of the Stones and the press conference would have been no different. Which says less for the straight press than it does for the Stones.

The concert at Madison Square Garden was something entirely different. I had never seen the Rolling Stones live before: now I can only say that I wonder what I missed that I should *still* feel I have never seen the Stones live. Annie Fisher wrote a piece in The Village Voice that sums up my general feelings; not so coincidentally, she was sitting directly behind me at the Garden Thanksgiving night, and that probably has a lot to do with it. At any rate, as Annie observed, critics are usually given what amounts to the best seats in the house; for this occasion, we were seated, a lot of the press, in one of the rear side sections of the Garden floor, still top-priced seats and there were thousands of worse places to be sitting. No complaints, God knows it was hard enough even to get *those* seats: but, continuing Annie's point, it was interesting to observe a concert from a civilian viewpoint for a change, and I, like everybody else in the trade, have never been willing to sit through a show as paying customers do up in the $3.50 attic.

From where we were, Jagger was a stoned marionette, his face a blur over his new Superman suit of black with a gold omega on his chest, studded black leather belt and long red scarf that he fancy-twirled like a honky-tonk lady. Everybody was up on their seats, instanter, at his entrance, swaying back and forth like Christmas ferns, for "Jumpin' Jack Flash"; down properly attentive for the quieter blues stuff (with Keith Richards on acoustic); back up wild for "Satisfaction" and stayed up until the end. The dynamics of the occasion were strange: about halfway through, Jagger called for the house lights to be turned on, "Let's see what you look like," everyone blinking like owls in the glare. It was the Woodstock Nation, all right.

But there was something missing. Maybe because the Stones had performed their concerts as set pieces: I had been hearing about "Jumpin' Jack Flash" and the black outfit and the riff with the house lights since the group played the West Coast. There was, for once, no quarrel with the Garden itself: the proscenium stage arrangement and the sound system worked just fine. The Stones played well enough, certainly. but nowhere throughout the entire evening was there anything that would seem to justify the reaction the Stones were getting, other than the obvious fact that these were the STONES, man!!!, the assumption clearly being that that was the only justification necessary. To be honest, I was turned off. YES! Turned OFF! By the ROLLING STONES!!

Maybe I'm just getting old — pushing 24, man — -at least that was what I thought until I heard about what happened at Altamont. Briefly, the Stones had agreed to play a free concert in Golden Gate Park, got hassled out of that, and accepted the gratis offer of Altamont Speedway. Jagger, Stones manager Sam Cutler, Rock Scully of the Grateful Dead and others concerned with setting up the program had asked the Hells Angels to serve as the "security force" for the occasion, which the Angels agreed to do for $500 worth of beer.

Three hundred thousand people or more turned out for the concert, and the Hells Angels enforced the security of the Rolling Stones by beating people away from the stage with wooden sticks, pool cues, belts and bare fists. Marty Balin, during the Airplane's set, leaped off the stage to the aid of a black guy the Angels were working over and was punched unconscious for his trouble; the black 18-year-old, Meredith Hunter, was later stabbed to death by assailants unknown.

It is all too easy to lay the blame on the Angels or the Stones or Scully or all of them together; but hair-shirting it at this late date isn't going to do anybody any good. Following Hyde Park and Woodstock and the Isle of Wight, the joylessness that prevailed at Altamont came as a rude awakening to heads conditioned by the give-and-take of the other atmospheres. The realization that, indeed, we are capable of being (and, at Altamont, were) just like Them is a jolting one. It was a down way to end a decade, and I hope it does not portend so for the future. Ralph J. Gleason, in a superb column for the San Francisco Chronicle, pointed out that although the concert was ostensibly a free one, "there *was* a tab, in money and ego. The Stones did it for money... the name of the game is money, power and ego, and money comes first and means power. Whoever goes to see that movie [*the Maysles brothers'* Gimme Shelter, *the excellent and disturbing film that was made of the Stones at Altamont*] paid for the Altamont religious assembly."

The point of all this is that it didn't happen at Hyde Park or Woodstock or the Isle of Wight, it happened at Altamont, after a cross-country tour during which the Stones behaved indeed and truly like people who were only in it for the money. Maybe it was divine retribution, God punishing the Rolling Stones for being more concerned with their ego trips than with their audiences and their art. Who knows? But when the Stones got back to England, word has it that they immediately gave a series of interviews to the British press in which they said that Altamont and their tour were the greatest things that ever had happened to the United States.

Love their records, though…

The Stones, though the headliners, weren't the only band at Altamont. A number of Bay Area big names, from Jefferson Airplane to the Grateful Dead, Santana and Crosby Stills Nash & Young, had also been conscripted to play. They had wanted to show the Stones how American bands did free concerts, how it had been at Woodstock, and they were expecting to put on the kind of concert they were used to putting on in San Francisco: laid-back, mellow, dreamy, dancing. But nobody paid any attention to what they had to say, and signals got crossed from the first. At the very least, San Francisco bands were thoroughly experienced in staging outdoor concerts in their hometown, and the Stones should have listened to them.

But egos prevailed, and mellow, dreamy and laid-back was not what anyone got. So malevolent were the vibes and so sour the atmosphere that after hearing about Marty Balin being attacked, the Dead just turned around and choppered right back to the city without so much as setting foot onstage.

Some attributed the debacle of Altamont to the baleful influence of retrograde planets, or the weather, or negative ions: only two days later, down in Los Angeles, Charles Manson and his ghastly groupies were indicted by a grand jury and charged with murder, so perhaps a dark star was indeed shining down on the rock world. The fact remains that Altamont was in the end a Stones production, and murder was on the bill.

As the Dark Side Woodstock, Altamont has been endlessly deconstructed, and I'm not going to get into it here more than I already have—if you're interested, you can't do better than to watch the Maysles' movie. But I think it's fair to say that whatever dolt thought it was a clever idea to give armed motorcycle thugs five hundred bucks' worth of beer and free license to pummel all comers ought to be smacked upside the head.

REVIEW:
VOLUNTEERS, Jefferson Airplane

JEFFERSON AIRPLANE ◆ *Volunteers* (RCA Victor LSP 4238).
Marty Balin (vo); Grace Slick (vo, or); Paul Kantner (vo, g); Jorma
Kaukonen (lead g, vo); Jack Casady (b); Spencer Dryden (d, vo);
Nicky Hopkins (p); Jerry Garcia (pedal steel); David Crosby (g);
Stephen Stills (or); Ace of Cups (vo); Joey Covington (chair). *We
Can Be Together*; *Good Shepherd*; *The Farm*; *Hey Frederick*; *Turn
My Life Down*; *Wooden Ships*; *Eskimo Blue Day*; *A Song for All
Seasons*; *Meadowlands*; *Volunteers.*

The word is generally never Volunteer for anything; in
Jefferson Airplane's case, almost, but not quite.

The Airplane, after six albums and five years, is
developed to the point where they don't really get "better"
or "worse", whatever those terms may mean, from record
to record; just different, wandering round from place
to place, taking each other's place in line and cleverer at
some things than at others. Though *Volunteers* has not the
sophistication of *Crown of Creation*, nor the celebratory joy
of *After Bathing At Baxter's*, it manages to dance for the most
part sure-footed and spontaneously jiggy.

"We Can Be Together" and "Volunteers" bracket the
record with similar sounds and similar sentiments: they are
the Airplane's first overtly political songs, and I find them
rather tiresome. No, folks, the Rev ain't gonna happen this
way, and as a writer friend of mine put it, one always finds
it amusing to hear people who pull in upwards of twenty or
thirty thousand dollars a weekend sing about tearing down
walls and wires.

But there are other things: "Good Shepherd", for instance, a lovely traditional churchy song arranged and sung by Jorma and one of the two best things on the album. Jorma dazzles so as a guitarist that one rarely thinks of him vocalizing to any degree (except on the dismal and abysmal "Rock Me Baby"; his voice, though not so conventionally melodic as those of Grace and Marty, is to my mind tremendously appealing, and he does a superb job on "Good Shepherd". When Jorma is doing vocals (as he is now, more and more, in live gigs, and in the new Airplane spinoff group, Hot Tuna), his lead guitar work tends to take on the tonal color of his voice, and his timing balance between guitar phrasing and vocal phrasing becomes razor-sharp; his originals ("Last Wall of the Castle", "Star Track"), though recognizably Plane, have a totally different flavor than a Balin-Kantner, and this has not been sufficiently noted in the past. Hopefully, with "Good Shepherd", this will change. (I'm still waiting for a Jack Casady original...)

"The Farm" is a stompy romp with Jerry Garcia doin' that rag on pedal steel; "Hey Frederick", "Turn My Life Down" and "A Song for All Seasons", though pleasant, are substandard.

Which brings it to "Wooden Ships", of Crosby-Stills-Kantner authorship. "Wooden Ships" is another in the grand old apocalyptic tradition of "House At Pooneil Corners", sci-fi rock, but this time from the other side round, gentler, and more positive in ultimate outlook.

Finishing out the album are "Meadowlands", a brief and lovely folk hymn played by Grace on the organ, and also her "Eskimo Blue Day", the second of the previously mentioned two best things on *Volunteers*. "Eskimo" has a strong melody, nicely obscure lyrics and one of the two dirty words that RCA objected to so strongly.

And that's it: strangely spotty for an Airplane album,

but all together well above a uniform standard. Packaging is stunningly eccentric, mixing is acceptable, but volume level, for some reason, is unusually low. Tear down the walls, fred.

April 1970

Just a little snippet...again, pillaged for use in Strange Days, *and again, Shamrock was called in as designated hitter, or really as a beard, as by this time Jim and I were deeply involved....*

IN CONCERT:
THE DOORS IN NY

"YEAHHH, we're really gonna git it on t'night," Jim Morrison leered encouragingly from the stage of the Felt Forum. The audience, apparently not too willing to suspend disbelief, merely giggled and emitted a few polite catcalls, but by the time the evening was over, they were thronging the stage area, arms upstretched, Touch Me, Touch Me, as though the white-shirted Morrison were a piece of the True Cross.

Not that it mattered. The Doors were in town again, for The Second Annual January New York Doors Concert, though this time, wisely, they had chosen not to perform in Madison Square Garden's vasty main arena, but in the 4,000-seat downstairs Felt Forum, a crescent-shaped, acoustically cheerful auditorium; and they were recording the entire proceedings.

Anyone who thinks the Doors are dead should have been tied to the orchestra railing and made to listen to all four shows that the group did. The Doors are rusty, they may even be jaded, but they are not dead. They are just someplace different. Though Morrison received approximately the same reaction he has been receiving for the past few years (i.e., vocal adoration/vituperation, flung tokens of affection such as bras, panties, notes, rings and lighted cigarettes), one had the impression he would have been equally happy, nay, happier still, had the audience sat quiet and listened to what the Doors were doing.

And perhaps the audience would have been happier too, because the music that was going on was the sort of Doors music the East Coast never gets to hear: unrecorded raunch like "Sunday Trucker" (or "Ten-Foot Woman", depending on whom you talk to), or "Money" or "Who Do You Love", unrecorded ritual like "The Celebration of the Lizard", last heard in these parts a full twenty-two months ago.

Eventually the sustainment factor broke down, of course, as it was bound to, and Morrison announced with amiable truculence, "Now we're gonna give you a famous radio song," and Robby Krieger smirked into "Light My Fire." Predictably, the oldest songs were the best-received; newer things like "Roadhouse Blues" or "Land Ho!" went right on by. But Morrison can't control his crowd the way he used to: there was very little of the mystical momentum that used to nail the audience to the chairs, and a number of times he was outshouted — now you KNOW that never used to happen.

The evening after the concert, the Doors hosted a party in the penthouse suite of the New York Hilton; falling somewhere between a Hieronymus Bosch engraving, the party from *Blow-up* and a college homecoming mixer, it was suitably decadent, a thumping success and everybody from New York had a lot of fun. Ah, but if the party had been the concerts, though...

—Shamrock O'Toole

The Doors did four shows at the Felt Forum, eschewing the main Garden area and providing a surprisingly intimate environment for the fans, though I would have thought four shows at the Fillmore East, which they never played after the March 1968 second weekend of its existence, would have served the purpose just as well. But the Forum was low-ceilinged and the stage was low and right out there, a terrific funnel for both energy and sound, so on balance it was a really good choice.

I had been given a pass for the sound check before the first show, and actually got to stand on the stage with Jim, who grabbed my hand and pulled me up there beside him as the band was blasting behind us. It was an amazing experience, which I borrowed shamelessly for my Rennie Stride book Scareway to Heaven: Murder at the Fillmore East, *and which totally confirmed me in the correctness of my decision never to be a rock star.*

I was at all four shows, and my outfits for both nights were carefully planned, thinking especially of my backstage moments. My more notable ensemble was thigh-high black leather boots topped by a black jersey microskirted dress with a laceup bare back about a foot across, and I wore it back-to-front, no bra. A genuine bodice-ripper: Jim had a hard time keeping his eyes above my collarbone, and after a while he didn't even bother to pretend.

The party was pretty good, too: lots of New York society and media Beautiful People, plus shoals of us mangy undergrounders. I wore a lovely cream leather tunic and pants outfit I had made, sleeveless, navel-revealing, open-fronted and scoopnecked down to there, with a coiled snake arm ring. Jim said I looked like Genghis Khan's favorite wife. By this time, of course, we were heavily and secretly involved, and after the concerts and party were over, he stayed on in New York and we spent almost two weeks together, mostly in my apartment. We did an interview and public lunch, chaperoned by his publicist, hoping to throw people off the track, as well as a private dinner at his label president's Greenwich Village apartment...with mixed success all around. You can read about the entire interlude in Strange Days, *if you're interested.*

May 1970

I didn't write a Pop Talk column for this issue, because we ran the results of our Readers' Poll and it took up too many pages. So I contented myself with a one-two Jim punch (or kiss) instead...

REVIEW:
***MORRISON HOTEL*, The Doors**

DOORS ✦ *Morrison Hotel* (Elektra EKS 75007). Jim Morrison (vo); Ray Manzarek (p, or); Robby Krieger (g); John Densmore (d); Ray Neapolitan or Lonnie Mack (b); G. Puglese [John Sebastian] (hca). **SIDE ONE: Hard Rock Café:** *Roadhouse Blues*; *Waiting for the Sun*; *You Make Me Real*; *Peace Frog*; *Blue Sunday*; *Ship of Fools*. **SIDE TWO: Morrison Hotel:** *Land Ho!*; *The Spy*; *Queen of the Highway*; *Indian Summer*; *Maggie M'Gill*.

I confess, for starters, to extreme and lasting critical ambivalence concerning *Morrison Hotel*: on one level, it is pre-eminently satisfactory, on another (save for a handful of songs), it is nothing of the sort.

For all you first-Doors-album freaks out there, *Morrison Hotel* (an actual L.A. hostelry; the album is so titled because it is in contents about 87% J. Morrison) [*To quote him on it, when I asked: "It's called that because I wrote all the words and most of the music." — PKM*], could have made a great second album. Musically, it is no great shakes: nothing inspired, nothing dazzling, but competent, very workmanlike rock—when it IS rock. There are good polyfuckrhythms, Densmore's great clumping mastodon beats, resonant vocals, always Robby Krieger's underrated, charming, smug and snaky guitar (Aiyeee! Will we NEVER get a Krieger solo?), John Sebastian's tie-dyed harmonica and the first new Manzarek organ riffs in three years (and guess what, they're jazz). But sad to say, some pret-ty faggy-sounding piano work, and all too often the album takes on a Fanny Farmer Valentine quality that is not only lacy but craven.

The songs are oddly sporadic: they come from all levels of straight-line time in the Doors history—early, middle, late, present, future—and they seem to reflect the increasing tug-of-war now going on between the opposing camps within the group. This conflict of musical interest makes for an album stunningly devoid of temporal identity (except for the fact that it *is* devoid of temporal identity). The Doors are a severely patterned band: some would say repetitious, I would too but I like the pattern. Before you even take a new Doors LP off the shelf, you *know* there will be an up-tempo number for openers, you *know* there will be two or even three songs segue'd together by nature and by the grooves, you *know* there will be a long, somehow ominous and significant final track. *Morrison Hotel* is no exception.

Good songs first. They are: "Roadhouse Blues", "Waiting for the Sun" (left off the album of the same name), "Peace Frog" (protest-political), "The Spy" and "Maggie M'Gill". To a lesser degree, "Ship of Fools" (ecology-rock) and "Land Ho!" (Morrison's formative years as a Navy brat coming to the fore). All of these are clearly Doors, sinewy, interesting and well-constructed, with "The Spy" and Maggie M'Gill" by far the best.

But. There are no Great songs on this LP (with the marginal exception of "Maggie M'Gill"), nothing to stand with "The End" or "Shaman's Blues" or "Crystal Ship" or "Five to One" or "People Are Strange" or "The Soft Parade". Ordinarily this would not be so grave a sin of commission, indeed the good songs could have carried *Morrison Hotel*, were it not that the rest of the album is so plain tacky.'

The true disasters are "You Make Me Real" (a cop from Steppenwolf's "Everybody's Next One" mixed with a little "Easy Ride" from the *Soft Parade* LP), "Indian Summer", "Blue Sunday", and most particularly "Queen of the Highway"; the last three are actually embarrassing. C'mon, Jim, you're not Perry Como *yet*...your following doesn't deserve such Hallmark greeting-card sentimentalities as "I love you the best/Better than all the rest" or "My girl is mine/She is the world/Now I have found my girl."

Oh fie. Where are the DOORS, those musical brats? (Certainly not on the jacket, which art is nothing worse than sick-making: inside foldout photo, scummy bar, Doors trying their best to look equally scummy and not making it by a country mile, Morrison looks as though he just missed the urinal).

All this sounds down on *Morrison Hotel*; not true, I like it very much for what it does. It's just that on *Morrison Hotel*, the Doors' reach seems to have exceeded their grasp; having heard he was getting back, I expected more from Dionysus.

Well, I guess we had progressed by now to the hair-pulling, pigtails in the inkwell stage of the relationship...only Jim was the object. Actually, he responded rather good-naturedly to the semi-bashing, even going so far as to autograph the review for me, so apparently I was forgiven.

It's funny how my opinions of this album changed: I still think the sucky songs sucked bigtime, but I now consider "Roadhouse

Blues" to be one of the best Doors songs ever, though it didn't impress me to that extent at the time, and I now think "The Spy" and "Land Ho!" are pretty lightweight.

It was suggested by author Chuck Crisafulli, in Moonlight Drive: The Lyrics of the Doors, that "You Make Me Real" could well be Jim writing about me and our relationship ("You make me feel like lovers feel", which I always heard as "You make me feel like a lump of steel"—not quite the same thing), but I never got that out of it. Jim did tell me that "Love Hides", which appears on the Absolutely Live LP as part of the great, great medley on Side One, is indeed about me ("Love hides in the strangest places/Love hides in familiar faces/Love comes when you least expect it"). It would be nice to think he was telling me the truth...

BOOK REVIEW:
THE LORDS & THE NEW CREATURES, James Douglas Morrison

Although we had a regular book review page in the magazine, I didn't review for it all that often, as you may have noticed by the sparseness of book reviews here. No special reason for avoidance, it's just that back then there weren't all that many rock books around that needed reviewing, or indeed merited it: it was all either compendiums of lyrics or gushing fanboy books. But I made an exception for this one...Jim certainly got it with both barrels in this issue, I have to say. Still, he came back for more...

The Lords & The New Creatures, Jim Morrison. Simon & Schuster, 1970. Privately printed, 1969, in editions of 100 copies.

It would be one thing if this were a collection of notes (_The Lords: Notes on Vision_) and poems (_The New Creatures_) published by your typical struggling, insightful, young and hungry poet. But this is a collection of notes and poems published by a culture hero of the first water, a rock superstar who at the apex of his popularity deserved every bit of it, chief minstrel of the Doors, celebrated for, among other things, incisive lyrics and poetic rock dramas, and as such, of course, it is quite another thing.

Therein, fellow Lit. majors, lies the rub.

The Lords, then, is a somewhat glib compendium of notes from Morrison's UCLA career as a film school problem child, and unfortunately does not amount to much more than a collation of determinedly minor observations that were apparently scribbled down in the margins of his notebooks during particularly dull lectures. *The Lords* abounds in neoprofundity and stream-of-consciousness overkill; some few of the would-be aphorisms might make first-rate essays, for, say, *Cahiers du cinéma*, had they been developed, but as small, hard, resolved, gemlike comments (which, judging by the presentation, is what I am assuming Morrison was trying for), they simply and sadly do mot make it.

The New Creatures is another problem entirely, and its deficiencies are ultimately much sadder than those of *The Lords* because its scope, its potentiality and the poetic success that does break through are all so much larger than those of the other work.

Morrison is so economical, so splendidly spare and disciplined in his choice of words and structures when lyric-smithing for the Doors that the poems come as a vast disappointment for one who expected more of the same, only better (because Morrison was not here tied to the requirements of a melody line). A re-rereading at the earliest opportunity of Aristotle's *Poetics*, or better, the Preface to the *Lyrical Ballads*, might assist to a re-establishment of poetic priorities sorely needed. Morrison is by no means a peon of the creative imagination, having the makings of a fine Irish poet of the old school—once he learns the rules.

His poetic style (undeniably poetic, even at his worst) demonstrates a buttery satisfaction; it is self-indulgent in the worst degree, because almost nowhere in all the poems does he attempt to bridge in any way the gap between his own experience and the reader's experiencing of that experience. The poems, especially the shorter ones, are stuffed with highly personal allusion, images and events that only Morrison himself, his wife and his press agent could possibly claim to understand: I am sure that a goodly percentage of even those poems could perhaps have meaning to others—if only we could grasp the hidden codebreaker. Morrison, however, whether through intent or carelessness, has failed to supply any poetic Rosetta Stone, and much of *The New Creatures* remains studiedly inaccessible, and tiring to try.

More's the pity, for Morrison does exhibit in his better moments the same evocative and expansive command of word tension and plasticity that makes his lyrics so superb. [...] The bulk of the poems, though, offer no such felicity of wedded word and mood. Morrison himself describes *The New Creatures* as having been patched together over a period of several years, and it is much to the volume's disadvantage that there was apparently no unifying factor but whim to tie the poems together.

If there are strange truths here, they are well concealed.

Ouch. Much to his credit, Jim took this in the constructive spirit in which it was intended. Well, mostly; that "wife" thing, for one—a not so subtle dig meaning myself, of course, and no other person who might have been going around calling herself that. In fact, it was probably the first time that a slap-on-the-wrist review occasioned a formal proposal of marriage from subject to reviewer, a few days after said subject read said review. Proving beyond all doubt that Jim Morrison was not only a man in love but a very brave man indeed.

And an intelligent one: he totally got what I'd intended him to get out of it—after reading the review, he sent me a telegram in the middle of the night, consisting in its entirety of "Thanks for the pat on the back." At least he considered it a pat and not a stab... And he was right—it was indeed meant as constructive criticism. Elektra executive Bruce Harris, encountering me backstage after the Doors' Spectrum concert in Philadelphia, which I'd been invited down to, marveled that Jim couldn't get over the review, and was telling anyone who would listen that it was the first time someone had actually reviewed his work and not him. Well...yeah. Maybe I was the first girl who'd ever come along who actually could.

He'd given me private-edition copies of both books the summer before, and I of course was over the moon about it. But I withheld reviewing them until their official publication; he didn't ask or require it, I just felt that that was the correct procedure.

He did tell me he was quite cross with Simon & Schuster for not using "James Douglas Morrison" as his author name, the way he'd asked them to and the way it was on the private editions; even just "James Morrison" would have been fine by him. The publishers' reasoning being that "Jim Morrison" was more recognizable and familiar to his fans. But he didn't care about that; he just wanted to establish and preserve what he considered a proper distance between his songs and his poetry, and he and I both thought that it was a more than reasonable request.

The publishers hadn't used the photo he'd wanted either, choosing to go with the all-too-familiar bare-chested, Alexander the Great-coiffed, prettyboy publicity shot from 1967 that everybody knew, rather than the bearded, brooding 1969 photograph he vastly preferred (well, of course he would—boy vs. man, no contest). Though, he wearily remarked to me, resigned, at least he had succeeded in getting the shot he wanted as his author photo on the flap, and it had been a battle to get even that much, so he was grateful for small favors.

But he should never have had to fight like that to have his work presented as he himself chose.

June 1970

The first thing that came to mind when I heard that Bill Graham, Parks Commissioner August Heckscher and the City of New York had something to announce was "I bet Bill's taking over the city."

Wishful thinking, as it turned out, though I remain convinced that he would do it (a) more efficiently, and (b) more imaginatively, than the present city archons. What they actually had to say was that Graham will be producing his regular Fillmore East programs for the summer in the Pavilion, once the New York State Pavilion out at the Flushing World's Fair grounds and city property, beginning June 19 and running through until Labor Day, when the Fillmore East will reopen for music.

Putting aside for the moment the aesthetic considerations, and they are many, what looms largest in the decision for the Pavilion is a not-so-simple matter of rock economics, and by no means is it limited to Bill Graham.

It is a blatantly well-known fact that rock and roll is a big-money, fast-money operation: huge advances, substantial guarantees, monster percentages, astronomical ticket and album prices. Since, of course, we all like to believe that the artists are Our Own, fighting the good fight on our side and not out to *get* us the way some other people are, who but the concert promoter is left to take the pipe of blame.

Well, liking to believe is not the same as knowing. It

may have become quite fashionable in certain circles to damn Bill Graham as a capitalist (a truly deadly epithet, I guess), but the fact fairly shrieks that Bill Graham has probably done more to get more music before more people, and more money for more rock artists, than anybody else around. (I choose Graham as chief example because he is so visible, so successful at what he is doing, so competent and so professional in his work. "Professional" means adult, responsible and self-disciplined. I like that. No, I do not know Bill Graham personally.) [*Well, I met him on numerous occasions, of course, and he knew me by name, but we did not hang out. – PKM*]

I have no intention of taking up the cudgels for the rippers-off, but it is my personal observation that promoters as a group have been pretty badly mauled by people who ought to know better. Granted most freely, a large percentage *are* in it for the money; but what is basically wrong with that? Most rock and roll performers are in it for the money too, though you will not hear them say so for publication. But the actual numbers of promoters who are into Medici-style power plays, who are out for themselves no matter how much to the detriment of others, are not so great, and comparable numbers can be found in most any field of work.

No, the reason for open season on concert promoters seems to stem from the fact that, of necessity, the promoter is the one most vulnerable to charges of price-gouging, rip-off, fixing, cheating, etc., simply because he is the one responsible for setting things up. It is all too easy to take a gratuitous swipe at Graham or Howard Stein or Sid Bernstein, much easier than taking the time and the mental energy to figure out where the "blame" – if we're really going to get into it properly – actually resides.

And that is (a) with the artists, and (b) with our fat

little selves.

If artists want to maintain in any degree their ostensible position of community sensibility, they will have to do something both concrete and relevant. Fast. When a festival or concert is being promoted by a thoroughgoing Rasputin, and everybody knows it, and evil things are going to go down, and everybody knows that too, ideal behavior would be a general boycott of that particular festival or concert, artists and audiences both. After all, if you play with pigs in the pigsty, it stands to reason that you will get muddy. But of course you have never seen anything remotely resembling such a boycott, nor will you, because the artists have to meet the payments on those Aston-Martins and the audiences have always to be reassured still further how grooooovy it all is (The Festival Mentality, and more of that next month).

Not, heaven knows, that I begrudge anybody astounding material success: when I see groups that used to play artistically and at length for hamburgers and beer money go to ten or twelve thousand dollars a night, that's one thing, and good for them, but when suddenly they find they just can't see their way clear to play for ten or twelve thousand any longer but it must be fifty thousand and a percentage of the gross for a forty-five-minute set, and the ticket price must then go up to seven-fifty or ten dollars top because of the group's demands, and when the promoter, who has to pay the band and cover overhead costs and staff salaries and often as not post a guarantee to the corporate owners of the hall or festival site and still hope to make a few bills for himself out of it all, gets *blamed* for all this, then I think change is due, and past due.

And this is where we come in. How long, think you, could a band make such demands last, if we as consumers (and make no mistake about it, that's exactly what we are) refused to support them? Or how many productions could a rip-off promoter mount, if we as consumers refused to buy the tickets? Ultimately, it all comes down to us, and how much we are willing to countenance.

Who is to say that rock and roll performers should *not* make a great deal of money? Not I, certainly; there is nothing whatever to be said against voluntarily paying for the pleasure music can give, provided we receive in return goods and services equal to the money we invest. What I *do* object to is being implicitly exploited by rock: by artists singing about The Revolution and hiring bodyguards to protect themselves from any distasteful contact with their revolutionary minions, by loud claims that "WE'RE not in it for the bread, that's the other band" and then pulling out for home with backbreaking bankbooks, by "Oh hey, man, it's not *us*, we're your *friends*. It's those fuckin' promoters (or record labels, depending on the rap) ripping' us all off."

And they get away with it. They get away with it BECAUSE WE BELIEVE THEM. We believe them because they have long hair and weird clothes and smoke lots of dope; we believe them because we all know how much they love us; we believe them because everybody knows that only straight businessmen in suits and ties and short hair are out to burn us; we believe them because they chant Revolution and the rock and roll Byzantium and that's what we want to hear more than anything else and we'll pay anything to hear it.

As long as we appear to have decided that this is what we want, and we don't mind, we would do well to assign the effects more accurately to their causes, for the first documented case of Art exploiting Life. The middleman promoter, who is after all only taking care of business and trying not to be thought of as too much the Philistine, is involved only to the extent that he allows himself to be involved. There can be such a thing as "creative promotion", after all, imaginative bookings and interesting programming and efficient set-ups and lighting, and all of this, though certainly an effort, is by no means out of the reach of all save a Bill Graham.

You get what you pay for, ultimately, and we are certainly getting that, but purchasing a Revolution doesn't cut it. One way or another, we are all being burned.

Amusing, really, to think that we were complaining about ticket prices going up to ten dollars, considering that today we're happy to pay four figures for a front-row Garden seat for some of the same acts we paid a few bucks, or no bucks at all, to see back then. But when such acts played for a ticket spread of $3.50–5.50 at the Fillmore East, where even for the biggest bands the prices stayed the same, a price rise to $10.00 was a huge increase, and music fans by definition didn't have a whole lot of bread to begin with.

Nobody was saying that the artists shouldn't get paid, of course, and better paid than, say, label execs; except some artists, like Janis, were even at this late date still advocating the hippie-dippie Haight philosophy of free music to go along with the free love, minds, bodies and dope, which was admirable but just ridiculous. It had never really *been free, of course, any of it; there had always been a price tag attached, and sometimes it was the artists paying it and sometimes it was the audience. But when Jefferson Airplane's publicist released a story about Grace going to buy herself an Aston Martin with her handbag stuffed with the full $17,000 purchase price in cash, after she'd been insulted at the dealership by a salesman who apparently thought this bejeaned hippie trollop was wasting his time (kind of a pre-*Pretty Woman *moment there), things started to feel all mean and narrow-eyed.*

Even Bill Siddons, Doors manager, thanked me in person for this particular rant, backstage at the Philadelphia concert, and so did Bill Graham, later at the Fillmore East—which made me feel... uneasy.

July 1970

It took almost a whole year to really codify how I really felt about Woodstock; and still it's a bit schizoid. Two heads, indeed...

POP TALK:
THE FESTIVAL MENTALITY

Ohwowfarouthiptripdopefreakmusicgroovypeacelovegoodvibes BULLSHIT.

The above string of free associations is what results when someone, anyone, mentions in my hearing, in any context at all, the words "rock festival", and I think I have been to enough of them, in both civilian and professional capacities, to know.

Like locusts, rock festivals burgeon best in summer, and this summer there will be a veritable plague of them, in locations that range from England to upper New York State to the West Coast to Virginia to the Midwest and various places in between. Though I wonder how long the big-business entrepreneurs will continue in the field without the law of diminishing returns coming into effect, the general, ground-level reasons for being that attach to rock festivals are far more significant, and provide a rather interesting study along the lines of Sociological Phenomena Among Our Peer Group.

Unlike most, if not all, other festivals that concern themselves with the bringing of music to its audience on a mass, outdoor, more or less informal level, rock music festivals are by and large operating not for the music, nor for those solely interested in hearing and/or performing that music. First off, generally the audiences are so huge (Woodstock, 500,000; Altamont, 400,000; last year's Newport Jazz with rock added, upwards of 20,000 in a milieu geared for half that; giant crowds at Tanglewood to see Jefferson Airplane and the Who in that old bastion of classical music; at Atlantic City; at Miami) that optimum or even halfway decent viewing and listening conditions are virtually nil for large portions of the attending audience.

So. If people don't go to see and hear the performers, then what? We go to be reassured. We go to be informed by the very spectacle of so many others like us that we're all special, all young and beautiful and nonviolent. Groooovy.

God. How fucking self-righteous we have all become. When will we learn that there is no such thing as good karma by association? That we have to do it alone? That tie-dyed pants from The Different Drummer or that little boutique in L.A., some two-toke grass, the latest esoteric paperback in our pocket, and a ticket (or better, NO ticket) to the festival of the week do not a beautiful person (as opposed to Beautiful Person) make?

We are, I hope, sophisticated enough by now not to wonder that all the people at Woodstock and the other shrines of the litany (with the notable exception of Altamont) were so wonderfully nonviolent. Not to spoil the beauty of it, because that part of it truly was, but outside of the fact that everyone there was too stoned to *move*, let alone fight, if you think about it for a minute, the peaceableness should come as no shock whatsoever—after all, why not? Real importance would then have been those 500,000 people going home and working consciously to translate that peace into reality. But there is the rub: the vast gulf between whatever numbers of people were there to do just that, and those other numbers who were there merely to cop the vibes, enjoy irresponsibly, take and take and leave, to fall into a lovely, natural, comfortable pattern for four days not because it was their belief or their style but merely because it was the thing to do and fun to do for four days but longer would be an effort, longer would be WORK.

The true insidiousness of the Festival Mentality lies in itself. Robert Christgau once termed a similar concept "autohype", and the Woodstock Syndrome is no less dangerous. It sets up standards of expectation yet encourages no participation, only a form of environmental (psychological, not physical) consumerism that takes but does not make. The Festival Mentality is the worst of the world's ready-mades, a set of fashionable attitudes one can slip into or out of with ease and minimum guilt, at the expense of those who also hold the same attitudes but hold them with comprehension and responsibility and the certainty of active choice. The Festival Mentality makes no demands on its believers, and because it makes no demands, it becomes a haven for the undemanding and the undiscriminating, a rock and roll soma holiday, sanctified by those who have proven themselves unable to distinguish between semblance and substance, by those who take trappings for reality and cannot be troubled to look beneath the surface to find real roots and reasons.

I have not been to see the Woodstock film yet; I attended the original and am one of the few individuals who were there and are not ashamed to say that they hated it. Not because I dislike being cold, wet, muddy, hungry or otherwise inconvenienced (I've done it before), but because the attitudes evinced by that groooovy mob literally made me fear for the future of the Movement. It was peer-reliance, and let no one tell you otherwise. Peer-reliance rather than self-reliance: a psychically crippling leaning together in symbiotic (and what I have no doubt will prove ultimately destructive) relationship on others of the breed rather than utilizing the individual self-strengths that are most abundantly there, using the ambient togetherness of the moment and the too-readily available drugs to reinforce this sort of self-estrangement and build up a warm, secure, reassuring and utterly false eidolon of things as they are, all at the expense of things as they could so easily be.

Now there is nothing wrong with huge mass gatherings, to hear music or for any other reason, though if one is seriously interested in music, the shotgun approach of rock festivals is probably the worst way imaginable to indulge one's interest. What incenses me so about Woodstock is the fact of half a million people doing the right thing for the wrong reasons, and believing as only the fanatic can that their reasons are not only right but above reproach, and that anybody who should be so misguided as to doubt this truth is, well, just not groooovy.

Believe it, the real beauty of Woodstock happened in spite of all those groovers, not because of them; and it will continue to happen in spite of all the festivals that are proliferating in the wake of Woodstock like earthworms after a rain. Woodstock Nation has nothing to do with last August in Max Yasgur's cow pastures; that only brought it into the open. Woodstock Nation is real, and it's there for us any old time once we learn the proper way to come into it. For everybody's sake, I hope we learn quickly.

And yet we never did...

August 1970

Another in a string of Pop Talk rants. Being publicly (by now) in love with Jim and dealing with the strange days of our private lives seemed to be conducive to such intensity. This one was set off by the milquetoast musical offerings and tendencies, as I perceived them, of assorted big names, which names I had no difficulty naming in my text...

POP TALK:
THE THEORY OF SELECTIVITY

I saw the blue bus on Second Avenue the other day, and it wasn't the first time either. The blue bus has been coming around a lot lately; sometimes it's full, sometimes there's nobody in it. I never notice any license plates. One of these days it will pull up in front of me and there will be somebody at the windows waving me on, and then we'll see some proper action.

Maybe. The bus, of course, is only symptomatic, not causal, and everyone who hasn't been lobotomized recently knows that. Kent State, Cambodia, Jackson: anywhere at all. But what about the expected reflection of all this? Art, said to be any deliberate attempt to represent the human condition, does not seem to be doing much actual representation of late (though perhaps that *is* the real representation—but I doubt it), and *our* art, which should by theory and practice be doing the most accurate representation of all, has fallen into some sort of sluggish self-indulgence the look of which I do not like one bit.

Here we have the opportunity and the necessary tools for a rare piece of consciousness-raising, and what do we get instead (and accept) but McCartney, Starr, Crosby, Stills, *et* all the *al.*, like a co-equal row of thick and thoroughly fatuous Christmas puddings. Not a spark of honest reaction in the lot, unless you want to count David Crosby writing a song about how he *al*-most cut his hair.

Well, "almost" doesn't count, not these days, and perhaps rock *isn't* art anymore, but the problem is even less complicated than that, and no one is going to tell me that Paul, Linda and the carefully nontesticular CSN&Y reflect the temper of the times. What they do reflect is a rather — to my mind — ostrich attitude: if we don't sing about it, it isn't there, and if you just listen to our pretty songs it won't be there for you either.

At any rate, what I think it can all be reduced to is wholesale lack of discrimination, on the part of just about all of us. Now, discrimination (or selectivity, if the racial overtones commonly associated with the former word upset you) has always been one of my favorite things, one of the qualities I look for first in people and in situations and in works of art, and it means in this context nothing more nor less than an active, intelligent exercise in good critical judgment, on the basis of individual or artistic merit. All the words in that very personal definition are equally operative; and, defined as such, selectivity somehow does not seem to be overly difficult of achievement for anyone with more than the intelligence God gave a goat.

Not if you are open to it. And there, I think, is where the trouble lies. There appears to be, in Woodstock Nation, a widespread tendency to avoid just this sort of exercise, and embrace instead intellectual prepackaging in all its new, Now, extended forms. You can see it everywhere you go: for each of the half-million mental somnambulists at Bethel, there were who can say how many more at home eating their hearts out with wanting to be there. Truck yourself over to the Fillmore on one of its big-league nights and dig the Pavlovian nightmare: all those bodies and so few minds, practically nobody working out in any way whatsoever any discriminatory capabilities whatsoever, and practically nobody caring. Any attempt by a band to try and raise the level of general audience consciousness has been a sorry failure; every time an artist tries to drag people kicking and screaming a bit farther down clarity road, they just dig in a little harder and refuse to come along.

The reason no one cares to discriminate, of course, is because no one cares to think. "Think" on these levels means "work", and it is undeniably hugely easier to have your thinking and your opinions done for you, and at the same time to have your social acceptability assured, all without a stroke of effort on your part except that required in standing up on a chair in Madison Square Garden or the L.A. Forum and raising your fist over your head.

Certainly conscious selective reasoning is work, and, like all forms of productive work (and we should be concerning ourselves with no other sort), the resultant benefits are not generally immediately apparent but most definitely worth waiting—and working —for. You derive from something only as much as you put into it, and if, as is now happening, you present to the artists of your society nothing more than a passive, unthought-out *Lumpen*-appreciation, it is only logical that very soon you will begin to get back exactly the same, in spades. Nobody operates in a vacuum, and we are serving no one by furthering in any way this sort of non-selective attitude.

Indeed, we end up cheating ourselves most of all: first, we deprive ourselves of the pleasure to be obtained by real appreciation, on all levels—the mind is not more valid, certainly, than the emotions, just different; essential to any claim of either true appreciation or true understanding, and we would do well not to slight either approach. Second, the more non-selectivity we practice, the more non-selective material comes back to us in response, and the more such fatheadedness as that of McCartney and confrères is allowed to perpetuate itself.

This all becomes obvious in live performances: the automaton response of an uncritical audience transmutes itself between seats and stage into what can be—and on occasion have been—the most colossal displays of self-indulgence ever seen in public: drum solos are what comes to my mind as the most immediate example, the fifteen-minute variety inflicted upon us by—invariably—the, uh, less gifted members of the drumming profession (you will find, with only a few exceptions, and they've got problems anyway, that the really top-flight musicians don't go in for this sort of extended public self-reassurance. They don't have to). But it is by no means limited to drummers: how many excruciating guitar solos, now many organ solos that were so boring your legs started to hurt, how many meaningless vocal improvisations, have we all sat through? And at the conclusions of all of these various monuments to rock ego, how many standing ovations have we bestowed? Exactly.

And there it is: non-selectivity on the part of the audience equals non-selectivity on the part of the performers. A non-critical, all-approving attitude elicits a non-artistic, all–ego response. And what are we going to do about it?

There are no glib solutions to offer: what would you suggest, telling the entire Woodstock Nation to go out and take a course in critical thinking? If they did, would it do any good? I don't know, and would rather not guess. But until something radical happens with regard to the demands we make and the response we offer in return, the non–selective slush is going to continue to permeate rock music and pervert its adherents and its practitioners alike.

Looking back now, I see that the climate in which that rant was ranted seems to be an Augustan golden age by comparison to the mental and spiritual bog that exists for young people today. Oh, well; at least I recently wrote a song along this theme for my guitar-stud protagonist in the Rennie Stride books, and called it "Clarity Road"...a little bit of meta self-consolation.

September 1970

This is the only piece in here that I did not write myself. Edited, cleverly and creatively, yes; but didn't write. The writer was Bruce Harris, then a publicist for Elektra and friend of both Jim and me, hence the anagram de plume to avoid accusations of favoritism or conflict of interest.

But Jim knew exactly who had written it, because I'd told him, and the piece pleased him very much. Many years later, I was told that he had been carrying the story around with him right up to mere days before his death in Paris, in July 1971...nice to think that at least my magazine was there with him, as I couldn't be there myself...

When I was with him in Miami for his trial in August of 1970, I brought down with me forty copies of this issue to give him to distribute, with the intent (thwarted, as it turned out) of getting it entered into evidence to attest to his cultural validity and seriousness as a person and an artist—which, we both hoped, Bruce's article would demonstrate.

This issue also had as its cover story the first publication of his poem "Anatomy of Rock", which he'd rather diffidently asked me back in May would I care to do ('Oh yes PLEASE!' being the only possible sane response to that request, needless to say). I still have a handwritten manuscript of the poem, and a typescript he sent as well. The poem had originally had as its subtitle "(The Whole

Thing Started With Rock & Roll, Now It's Out of Control)"; but in a subsequent phone call he asked me to remove it, no reason given, and I did so at once. And I truly, really, majorly liked the poem; to the point of sending him a sort of critical annotation of it, which he professed was the best thing ever, particularly appreciating my Othello-reference comparison to a line or two.

He also told me he loved what I had done with the cover (a spectacularly beautiful photo of him at Maximilian's Palace in Mexico City, in front of a rather weird and creepily apocalyptic mural by the wonderfully named Juan O'Gorman (check it out on my Facebook page—and dig the dog in the gas mask!. So beautifully composed is the photograph that Jim, gorgeous and incredibly studly in a dark burgundy shirt I knew well and hair to his shoulders, actually looks as if he's painted into the mural— my favorite picture of him, and for twenty years after his death the only one I had on display in my apartment and office). He was pleased too with the inside layout for his poem, and he read this piece eagerly and immediately. His first comment was, "I see you've been talking to Bruce..." Which, of course, I had.

Anyway, I thought "Morrison Hotel Revisited" should be rescued for new generations of Doors fans who have never seen it before; it deserves it, as do they—and Jim. It is reprinted here by kind permission of my old friend and former colleague at RCA and CBS, Marion Harris, Bruce's widow. Thanks, my dear!

Bracketed ellipses in the text [...] denote places where Bruce used Doors lyrics to bolster his critical points. I was required to redact them, as I lack permission to quote them (though for publication in the magazine, of course, it was just fine) and certainly wasn't about to ask. If you don't already know them, you can always look them up online if you're interested. Any remaining lyrics quoted are according to fair use.

Morrison Hotel, the Doors' fifth album, is not what it seems. And anyone who tells you it's the Doors' return to that "good old rock and roll" has either confused Fabian with Walt Whitman or has just been listening to the Moody Blues for too long. (After the Moody Blues, even Mantovani starts to sound like the Great Rock And Roll Revival.)

No, the Doors have revived, even resurrected, a lot of lost arts in *Morrison Hotel*, which lyrically encompasses everything from poetry to parable, but in their hands rock and roll and all its magic have always been full of life and have never needed any special care. More accurately, Jim Morrison and the Doors have finally found a way to create the long-overdue, much-needed "Great Revival Revival." The elements of Theatre, so essential to the group's central musical ethic, have not been forsaken, but have rather been condensed and compressed so that while they are now less glaring and obvious, they are all the more overwhelming simply because of their subtlety. *Morrison Hotel* is then an involving album on several levels, so you shouldn't be surprised to find yourself pounding your fists or tearing your hair out in addition to tapping your foot.

The Great Revival Revival. That's it. Fever and fervor. Screams of religious ecstasy. Shouts of "Glory Hallelujah", "I gotta get to God", and "Love the Lord", and "Save us, Jesus" and "Sing, you Sinners!" and "A hearty Hosanna to you all!!!!"

Poet, singer, shaman, high priest, prophet, poet, politician, Messiah, Father, Son and Holy Ghost.

Jim Morrison.

Film-maker, actor, writer, director, composer, and all-around, kiss-'em-on-the-lips rockandrollstar.

Teenage Idol

Sex symbol.

Superstud.

Superstar.

Jesus Christ.

What all this muck really demonstrates is that Morrison's effect on his audience, great as it is, cannot *begin* to compare with his massive effect on critics. Morrison and the Doors make writers fairly foam at the mouth with verbiage. He arouses us to such fits of intellectual masturbation that we all begin to spend our days sitting around racking our brains trying to find more awesome roles for the singer to perform in the social milieu: "And now, for the first time in any overblown windbag rock column, see the young artist, in the very act of painting his own portrait, attempt the death-defying stunt of being Elvis Presley, Mao Tse Tung, Lord Byron and Noel Coward all at the same time, while balancing himself precariously over the audience on an empty can of film and a full can of beer."

Oh, well.

Jim Morrison is a masterful songwriter, a provocative and inventive lyricist, a worthy composer and a motherfucker of a singer. His full-length feature motion picture, *Hiway* [sic; *actually HWY*], soon to be made available for exhibition by the national underground cinema, is a filmed poem overflowing with beautiful, evocative images, sensitively depicting man in relation to Nature and in relation to himself. [*Of course, Bruce hadn't actually* seen *HWY yet...* – PKM]

Morrison's poetry, released in book form as *The Lords and The New Creatures* by Simon and Schuster, is sometimes a bit obscure, even murky, but somehow through the power of its language and the depth of its thought, is always stirring.

But never mind all this. The best way to discover the Doors is to investigate the critical reaction against them. The people who dislike the Doors the most, in their attempts to demonstrate what's wrong with the Doors, never fail to point out just what it is that makes the Doors so great. Critics raving about the Doors often get so carried away that they have to be, well, carried away. The best picture of the Doors' brand of insanity is best drawn by the sane man who hates them. Only he can truly do justice to the group.

Critics who react harshly against the idea of Morrison as Messiah tend to question Morrison's qualifications to be leader of *anything*, including a band. What such a critic is really objecting to is the entire concept of leaders, and is spouting a kind of anarchistic let-it-be-we-were-all-a-bunch-of-asparagus-at-Woodstock-anyway type philosophy. But in a time when leaders are scarce, we need leaders the most. Well, we ain't gonna look to our mommies and our daddies and we ain't gonna look to our teachers, and we ain't gonna look to the Pope and we ain't gonna look to the Vice President, so all we got left is ol' Jim. (Actually, it is one of the great saving graces of this generation that its most significant leaders have been artists rather than politicians. You might follow [*Senator Eugene*] McCarthy all the way to New Hampshire, but you know damned well you'd follow Morrison or Lennon or Dylan to the ends of the earth, or at least as far as L.A....whichever comes first.)

The critic arguing with the concept of Morrison as leader has to tried to restrict Morrison to only one of his many social functions. Morrison's performance, for instance, tends to be far more religious than it is political: Morrison has always been more a prophet than a pied piper, and if he cannot teach us how to live, he can at least teach us how *not* to live: "*Cancel* my subscription to the Resurrection: and "You *cannot* petition the Lord with prayer." (Italics added.) After you've cancelled your subscription to the Resurrection, it's entirely up to you whether you will find "sanctuary" and "soft asylum" or will remain "lost in a prison of your own devise." Morrison has not so much attempted to destroy religion as he has attempted to replace it.

Which takes us right back to *Morrison Hotel*.

Autobiography has always been a central focus of Morrison's wr4itings. Even though his work often masquerades as the history of a generation, it is more often the history of a man. We forgot too easily that all those times that Morrison was speaking for us (in "Five to One" and "When The Music's Over", for instance), he was also speaking for himself. The justifiable fear of linking too closely an artist's personality with his work kept us from realizing that Jim Morrison's songs were as personal as they were universal, as much about Jim Morrison himself as they were about anything or anybody. This does not mean to imply that Morrison simply wrote down whatever he felt and that it just happened to coincide with what a lot of other people were feeling. On the contrary: Morrison is sensitive enough to what is going on around him to know which aspects of his own personality will most accurately reflect the personalities of his audience. Thus, "The End" is about all of us simply because it is also about Jim Morrison.

All Doors albums have been deeply autobiographical, especially the unjustly criticized *Soft Parade* LP, which was really on the whole an awful lot better than an awful lot of awful people wanted to have to admit. More than any other of the group's albums, *The Soft Parade* is most specifically an album about the Doors and their meanings in our society. Its unfortunate and unfitting appendages, "Wishful Sinful" and "Touch Me", have a way of just being there, and even being in the way. But the rest of the album, for better or for worse, tells us a great deal about how Jim Morrison sees himself (or at least saw himself at that time). "Shaman's Blues" is obviously a self-referring statement, as is the more precious and schmaltzy "Tell All The People". "Tell All The

People", written by Robby Krieger, is obviously Krieger's view of Morrison and clearly tells us far more about Krieger than it does about Morrison. We see Krieger from the inside out: in describing Morrison, he succeeds primarily in describing himself.

Morrison's self-description in "Shaman's Blues" is decidedly more revealing. [...] And there is really no end to the autobiographical implications in a suggestive verse like: "[...] (You'll be dead and in hell before I'm born) Sure thing/ Bride's maid/The only solution [...]"

Perhaps a lot of people liked *The Soft Parade* LP least because it referred to them least. Like a Beatles album, it was highly internalized, an album about itself. In the *Soft Parade* LP, we are related to Jim Morrison only as "Wild Children" or as "Please-please-listen-to-me Children." Morrison talks *to* us here, but rarely *about* us.

Morison Hotel, on the other hand, for all its flurries of autobiography, is really more directly an album about America. But like *The Soft Parade*, it is about you and me only by inference. Most of what has already been written about the album has been about the music, about how it is a return to the tight fury of early Doors music, of how it abounds with funk and guts and earth energy. All this is true, and there can be little doubt that *Morrison Hotel* is one of the major musical events of Rock '70. But perhaps even more important, and far more overlooked, is the lyrical accomplishment which Morrison, who wrote all the lyrics for the album, has made. A little chronology is in order.

The first album, *The Doors*, was pure experimentation. It is made up of a number of greatly contrasting moments, the successful non-lyric of an anti-song like "End of the Night", which is simultaneously sparse on words and rich in thought, opposing the not-so-successful rock 'em, sock 'em pseudo-something of "Take It As It Comes". After all, the line from that forgettable ditty, "Specialize in having fun!", though it became the creed for legions of would-be greaser-hippies, is neither particularly poetic nor particularly profound, as in an idea Morrison has elsewhere made more subtle and more precise: "Deliver me from reasons why you'd rather cry, I'd rather fly" ("The Crystal Ship").

The *Strange Days* album is earnest and consistently poetic, while the *Waiting for the Sun* album, though more loosely entertaining, is spasmodically brilliant, or maybe just clever, and leaves the listener with the vague impression of a chaos of sounds and ideas.

As suggested earlier, *The Soft Parade* exhibits the schizophrenia of a group struggling to encompass both the amiable nonsense of Robby Krieger's "Runnin' scared, runnin' blue, goin' so fast, what'll I do?" ("Runnin' Blue") and the awesome imagery of Jim Morrison's "Tropic corridor, tropic treasure, what got us this far to this mild equator?" ("The Soft Parade").

Morrison Hotel is all Morrison and thus even at its most charming and most banal ("My girl awaits for me in tender times, my girl is mine, she is the world, she is my girl" —"Blue Sunday"), still a little fearsome. What happens, for instance, when the tender times are over?

The suggestions for interpretation that follow are founded in the belief that there is a basic sense of order at the core of Jim Morrison's songwriting. It is really very doubtful that Morrison settles for blank visions of empty chaos in his lyrics, and we ought to have faith in his integrity as an artist. He does not throw words around in his work but rather tends to be simplistic, direct and painfully concise. Yet it is remarkable how much meaning he can pack into tight little lines like "Remember when we were in Africa?" Unlike his harsh critics and detractors, Morrison does not need to use a million words to state a single idea. Often in a single word, such as "Lord" in "The Soft Parade", he can conjure a million ideas. We should then proceed with the faith that at least a significant portion of what we find in Morrison's work was placed there intentionally.

Each of the songs contained in *Morrison Hotel*, even the innocuous "Blue Sunday" and "Indian Summer", is constructed around one or both of two central image patterns, which in the end combine to form a vision of America in all its savage splendor and awesome beauty. These two central image patterns deal with either roads or houses, the imagery of roads being expanded into the imagery of traveling and journeys (either through space or time). This is what gives the album its unity and therefore its impact. The songs play off each other, comment on each other, complement each other. And not in the unsubtle and obvious (though powerful) way in which "Moonlight Drive" works together with "Horse Latitudes" on the *Strange Days* LP or "I Can't See Your Face in My Mind" contrasts with "My Eyes Have Seen You" on the same album, or "Wintertime Love" contrasts with "Summer's Almost Gone" on the *Waiting for the Sun* album.

In *Morrison Hotel*, all the songs work together very deliberately. They flatter each other, both musically and lyrically, by setting off each other's strong points and intensifying each other's meanings.

Finding these image patterns in *Morrison Hotel* should by no means astound us. Imagery of travelling and making journeys and of endless roads is nothing new to Morrison's work. What with all those "highway[s] to the end of the night" ("End of the Night") and the "blue bus" ("The End") and the Crystal Ship and the Spanish Caravan and the "still sea [conspiring] an armor" ("Horse Latitudes") and the Moonlight Drive and the "alleys on an endless roll" ("My Eyes Have Seen You") and the Love Street and "nothing left to do but run, run, run" ("Not to Touch the Earth") and "My Wild Love" "rode to Japan" and "I gotta go out in this car with these people"("Five to On") and "fleeing down south across the border"("Celebration of the Lizard") and the Easy Ride and the Soft Parade. All about roads and journeys. The journey is a kind of voyage, one way to "break on through to the other side", "one way to get unraveled."

The imagery of houses is equally abundant in Morrison's work. At different times, we are inside the Soul Kitchen, inside the "ancient gallery" ("The End"), inside the "strange rooms" ("Strange Days"), inside the "prison of our own devise" ("Unhappy Girl"), inside the "house of detention" ("When The Music's Over"), inside the "store where the creatures meet" ("Love Street"), inside the "mansion on the top of the hill" ("Not to Touch the Earth") and of course, inside the "seminary school" ("The Soft Parade"). Houses are wombs, tombs, homes and hells. Always it is left for us to "wonder what they do in there", since "we won't know a thing till we get inside."

The title of the album is not without its share of significance. The hotel is a special kind of house, where there are many visitors, many different views and ways of life. *Morrison Hotel* is obviously the hotel of Jim Morrison's mind. The subtitle, *Hard Rock Café*, also clearly denotes a house of some kind. The first song title on the album is "Roadhouse Blues", clearly signifying the two central image patterns, roads and houses. As the album opens, we are told "Keep your eyes on the road, your hands upon the wheel". Obviously we begin our journey in a car, which is a house with wheels, a kind of road house in itself. We are going to the roadhouse, we are optimistic, we are "gonna have a real good time." This is Irish beer-drinking Americana. And what can we expect from an Irish beer drinker like Morrison? [*In fact, Jim was a* Scottish *beer drinker…which doesn't have quite the same ring to it, I suppose – PKM]* The only warning we must keep in the back of our minds is that the journey may be dangerous. If we don't keep our eyes on the road and our hands on the wheel, we may not survive. We know where we are going, but we might well ask what it is we are coming from. Obviously, a place where *no one* has a real good time. Isn't that how America began? All those people fleeing tyranny, searching for a land of freedom. Perhaps we are witnessing the birth of a nation.

Morrison's chorus in "Roadhouse Blues" is the first instance in the album of a phrase which is worked time and again throughout the songs: "Let it roll, baby, roll! [...]" This is an invocation to the audience, that they join Morrison on his journey. He doesn't want to let us be, or even to let us bleed, but wants us literally to let it roll: to act, to become a part in something turning.

In the last verse, we glimpse the broader meanings of the idea. We get up in the morning and have our Irish-American beer. What still hangs over us on our voyage is that "the future's uncertain and the end is always near." This is where we stand now. What we can do is to let it roll.

"Waiting for the Sun" continues the journey. "At first flash of Eden, we raced down to the sea/Standing there on freedom's shore". We are now travelling to the ocean and finally on the ocean. It is the first flash of Paradise, our first vision of freedom. The sun is "scattered" all over the land. We must search for it now. For too long, we have been simply waiting. The time is Now.

"You Make Me Real", though masquerading as another bang-bang rock 'n' roll excursion into Morrison's cock psychology, is in its own moronic way a similar statement. It too tells us "Roll, baby, roll", in a manner that seems to border on obscenity but has much more to do with tying the album together. "You Make Me Real" also ought to get an award for containing the all-time great Morrison slur: "So lemme tie a binder rounder don't you see", which is on the lead sheet written out as "So let me slide into your tender sunken sea."

"Let me slide into your tender sunken sea", eh? Where were we going at that first flash of Eden? Not bad, Jim, not bad.

"Peace Frog" is Jim Morrison's throwaway protest song. If Paul Simon, or any other college sophomore, had given it a title, it might have been called "Hey There, Mr. President, What Are We Gonna Do About the Blood in the Streets?????" Morrison had to wince at all this and couldn't do any better than to leave the song essentially untitled and burden it with a bad joke. Peace frog, indeed!

At any rate, "Peace Frog" is the song that gives us the best picture of the current America. It isn't the good guys vs. the bad guys America we can find in *Easy Rider*, either. It's a much more terrifying America, a land of death and violence and horror. A land in which everything is a giant. The land of dinosaurs. And then too, some of that blood in the streets is caused by traffic accidents made by careless travellers who don't keep their eyes on the road and their hands upon the wheel: "Indians scattered on dawn's highway bleeding/ Ghosts crowd the young child's fragile eggshell mind". America, land of traffic accidents.

But of course, there's much more to it than just that. For one thing, it is an Indian that's been killed. On the highway of dawn, a dead Indian. The dawn of America. As Morrison says in "Peace Frog", "blood will be born in the birth of a nation." And after all, "blood is the rose of mysterious union". America is a very mysterious union, and blood is the rose of her flag which sometimes is striped red, red and red.

But there is something else in "Peace Frog" which

cannot be overlooked. Morrison can only make a joke out of peace, because he looks upon it much the way that "Blood and Guts" Patton looked upon it. Blood in the streets, blood in the streets, blood in the streets. There is blood in the streets in Chicago (remember?), in New Haven (scene not only of the slaughter of a number of innocent black people in a police riot, but of Morrison's first onstage bust, back in 1967), blood in the streets in Venice (Venice, California, remember?) and of course there's the "bloody red sun of fantastic L.A." We were waiting for the sun, but when it came, it filled the sky with blood.

"Blue Sunday" is pretty much what it seems, except that it places the journey in time. The album opens in springtime ("Can't you feel it, now that spring has come?") and moves through the "terrible summer" of "Peace Frog". Now we hang suspended on a "Blue Sunday."

"Ship of Fools" and "Land Ho!" both deal with new voyages. The human race is dying out because we are making journeys to the moon. Smog, caused in part by polluting car engines, is going to get us all, and pollution is the most dangerous traffic accident there is. "Along came Mr. Goodtrips, looking for a new ship [...]". Some trips are false. Maybe "Mr. Goodtrips" is Morrison himself, and we had all better watch out. In any event, we are on a ship of fools, all on a journey toward death.

"Land Ho!" tends to operate as a historical footnote to "Ship of Fools". We begin to see America as America. Somewhere along the line for all of us, "Grandma loved a sailor"; that's what America is. It is a land no one is born in. Everyone is really from somewhere else. And everyone is going somewhere. The great journey westward. Toward the sunset, toward death.

The three ships with the sixty men that Morrison talks about in "Land Ho!" could be any three ships, but they could also be the Niña, the Pinta and the Santa Maria. All of us are "going crazy from living on the land [...]". We've gotta get out of this place. Remember?

"The Spy" is in a house of love. That's where we're going. To the house of love, to the Roadhouse. In our cars (houses on wheels), in our ships (houses on water), in our minds (houses on ideas), we all travel somewhere. What we seek perhaps is to become more than just spies.

"Queen of the Highway" strengthens the imagery of the journey. This is not only an album about America in some abstract form but also about Americans. You, and me, and Maggie M'Gill. Our heroine is the princess, the queen of the highway, the constant traveller, whose realm is anywhere she visits. "Sign by the road said, 'Take us to Madre!'" Where else in a Jim Morrison song but to Madre—Mother? Our hero is a motorcycle "monster". The two marry and they are like two young lovers. [...] How touching. But what is important is that they are going to have offspring, which is what you get if you're not careful while sliding into someone's tender sunken sea, and their offspring, we are told, will start it all over. That's America. Cycle upon cycle. Birth, life and death. And then more birth. They are the "American boy, American girl, most beautiful people in the world". Well, how's *that* for patriotism, Spiro [*Vice President Agnew*]? And like all of us, they are children of the frontier. Children of the wilderness. Americans. They will dance on and on. But again, we hear the threat. "Hope it can continue a little while longer". The human race is dying out.

Winter is almost upon us. Soon it will come with pain and destruction, desolation and emptiness. We are surviving in an Indian summer. The end is always near.

And after all, as the album draws to a close, what have we in Maggie M'Gill but the archetypical American heroine? She is a rural woman in a setting almost frontier-

Western in nature: "[...] So she went down, down to Tangie Town." With no other course left her, Maggie turns to what a frontiersman might have called a life of sin. Tangie Town is a good place to be, because the "people down there really like to get it on." Hang out at any roadhouse in the vicinity of Tangie Town and you can have a real good time. Maggie M'Gill makes the journey. She leaves her life on the hill. She goes to a strange land. Which she finds has its drawbacks. It seems ugly, sordid, tawdry, but it is the end of the road. If you can't get it on in Tangie Town, there ain't nowhere you'll be able to get it on.

"Maggie M'Gill" fades out on what seems to be another of Morrison's parenthetical monologues, but is really a consummation of the thematic development of the album. As a last song, it obviously has much to accomplish. For one thing, it serves as a unifying factor. The album opens with our riding in a car, on our way to the roadhouse, and, in "Maggie M'Gill", ends with a scene of Mom meeting Dad in the back of what Morrison facetiously calls a "rock and roll car." The car is parked now. The journey is at a end, and yet the last voice we hear cries out, "Roll on Maggie, Maggie M'Gill [...]..." Once again, we are told to roll on, to let it roll. The cycle continues endlessly. Life somehow goes on. Morrison says, "I've been singing the blues ever since the world began."

He has indeed. But he hasn't been alone. Maggie M'Gill has been singing the blues ever since the world began as well. And so have you. And so have I. And all of us will be singing them forever. It's what Morrison means about "rolling on." Begin to live the life that's unfolding before you, because if you don't, it will unfold without you. The American quest for the sunset, for the house of love, for the Roadhouse, for the rock and roll car, for Tangie Town, for Morrison Hotel. For Something Somewhere. Morrison tells us that it's everywhere. Life is all around us. It just rolls on and on.

Kind of a long goodbye, isn't it? Especially knowing now that Jim had this with him, and read that last paragraph, in Paris, maybe many times. It breaks my heart and brings me to my knees even to think of it: I can't imagine what he *must have thought or felt, keeping it with him, so close...but perhaps he found some comfort in it. I like to think that he did, that he thought of Bruce, and of me, as he did so, knowing that we, at least, got what he had tried to do...but all I wanted to do was hug him. Even still. Even now.*

Although I discussed this piece with Jim on several occasions, in Miami and L.A. and over the phone in New York, I never asked him the one thing I should have: "How does stuff like this make you feel when you read it?" I mean, if someone had written something like this about me and my work, I'd probably have quit rock and roll on the spot and joined a convent. It would have made me so self-conscious and so hyperaware of everything I did that I would have found myself incapable of doing anything at all.

But Jim had this amazing ability to separate his private, inner self (Jim) from his professional public image (Jim Morrison), which always astounded me. He couldn't do it so well in his personal life, tragically for us all, but that's another story. Or book. See Strange Days. *But although I never asked him straight out about it, he would from time to time drop little hints about how he felt, or confide in me about it frankly and openly from his pain, and those hints and confidences were megaton weight...*

POP TALK:
ALTERNATIVE WHAT?

Up at freaky little rustic little Goddard College in Plainfield, Vt., there was held in mid-June a four-day conference, sponsored by the college itself and a rather amorphous entity calling itself the Alternative Media Project, which was attended by some 1300 or so of the prime movers in progressive radio (AM and FM), underground press, trade and consumer publications, record companies, tape and video and film people, and just plain high-energy unaffiliates.

On the face of it, it all sounded like a fine chance for an informational interchange at really high operative levels (which, I swear to you, is how someone described it to me); what it all came down to was, unfortunately, hype, dope and dogma.

Formally organized (perhaps naïvely, in view of later developments) into a well–programmed series of seminars, workshops, special interest meetings, general meetings, entertainment and discussion, the conference emerged as a sort of mini-Woodstock for the freak elite, a stoned MLA convention, R&R for the battle-fatigued warriors of the rock scene. Though all spoke much of "alternatives", no one seemed to know quite what to do about setting them up — or making them viable.

And it wasn't so much the fault of the manner in which things were arranged: the AMP planners had scheduled such workshops as Record Companies & The Underground, Women & The Media, Rock Criticism: Its Validity and Role, The Third World & Mass Media, Media Ecology, Selling Progressive Radio…well, you get the general idea, and the people chosen to "moderate" the sessions were at least good monitors, if not particularly effective and/or imaginative moderators. No, the whole Alternative Media Express temporarily derailed itself on the thrown switches of the various trips, role conflicts, pocket games, acid affinities and more-revolutionary-than-thou sanctities of certain of the participants; but only, I do reiterate, temporarily, and not because of any basic flaw in theory or implementation.

Because "alternative media" is a good concept, the disgruntled (or ungrammatical) low-grade revolutionary who went around muttering, "Oh fuck it all, media is media" notwithstanding. The core of the problem, I think, is information, and, by logical extension, communication itself, the actual mechanics of conveyance of ideas. The negative side of the conflict would appear to be, then, *mis*information — intentional or otherwise — and voided connections. Now, the average child of nine knows the standard (read, established) media channels have run up for themselves a reputation — deserved in only some cases, I must point out — of credibility failures awesome to behold, and so it would seem to be that the chief priority of any alternative media setup desirous of avoiding the sins of the parent would be to somehow ensure that this sort of loathsome informational short-circuiting does not occur.

Well. When I was back there in journalism school, there was a professor there who put forth, indeed, this identical proposition, instilling into all of us potential James Restons that one does *not* go around petitioning the readership with lies, not if one wants to continue to have a readership. A veritable Hippocratic oath of the working press. (I might add here that sometimes certain readerships do *desire* lies, but that is another story.) Information, then, becomes only as valid as those who impart it want it to be, be they journalists or junior-high teachers or rock and roll singers or politicians, and this is where those thrown switches I spoke of earlier come round again on the typewriter.

When all the cool talk begins to fly about alternative media, we tend to forget, in the passionate conviction of our righteous revolutionary rhetoric, that we are the ones who will be required to operate the mechanisms of these new media, and that if we are ever to coalesce into anything remotely resembling an effective media setup, we will without a doubt have to clear away all those extraneous little bullshit trips, out front; then, and only then, will we have a chance at real meaning, and real power, and real significance. If we are going to have alternative media, let them be *real* alternatives and not merely slightly hipper versions of the existing product. I am not indicating a need for wholesale head tests, or mass analysis, or general application of Robert's Rules of Order, but judging by what I saw at Goddard, it does seem to me that some serious rethinking is needed.

When intelligent, productive, creative people are trying to work something out in verbal style and debate format, it should be allowed to happen with minimum harassment, discourtesy, interruption or interjection of somebody else's doctrinaire ego trip. And that goes as much for the San Francisco *Om*-ers who insisted on resonating their way through every crucial moment as it does for the Jerry Rubin Cretin Brigade who specialized in gratuitous pig-calling.

All of this, of course, resulted in massive energy defeats, unchanneled movement and a whole lot of frustration, all of which could so easily have been avoided, and I tend to see Goddard in this context as the microcosm: if we cannot get it together on this level, we who were at Goddard and who are supposed to be laying it down for everybody else to see, then, folks, I honestly fail to imagine how we can possibly expect those whom we are attempting to reach to do any better .

We recently received here in the office a letter from political prisoner John Sinclair, parts of which missive are quoted in this month's Mailbox, and towards the end of the letter he very graciously commends my July rant in this column on The Festival Mentality, concluding with "Patricia, it isn't ever the *kids'* fault — please remember that. They will support whatever is offered to them if it's offered to them in a way they can relate to, and it's up to us to make the alternative available to them. Dig that. And right on."

Now while I violently do not agree with some facets of John's political-social-economic expository philosophy, I think that this excerpt packs weight in view of the events at Goddard College. For it is most certainly we ourselves who must set out the alternative for the "kids." All the musicians and artists and dj's and writers and record company executives and anyone else whose job, reputation or predilection puts him or her into position to communicate on mass levels (which means with more than one other person).

There is a particularly noxious antidrug commercial spot on one of the big New York FM rock stations which contains as a reason for not fucking around with scag the line: "How can you get your people together when you're a slave who reinforces his own slavery?" Simplistic as that may be, at least it has some paraphrase value to the question under discussion here: how can we, indeed, get our people together when we can't even do it for ourselves yet? A question, I think, well worth the asking; and the answering.

That was pretty much it for the Alternative Media Project; I don't think it lasted much beyond that weekend, if at all. At least it was a nice four days in the leafy, lovely Vermont countryside. But I think the raggedness of the whole thing quite correctly mirrored and metaphored the raggedness we faced every day in our politics and the way we dealt with the world: as a collective entity of hipness, we did not play together particularly well, and I think that that's maybe one of the chief reasons why we, as a culturally influential cohort of our generation, never managed to take power in any real way in the real world. Herding cats. And those of our vintage who did *actually manage to come by some power* were not people like us but either the earnest nebbishes (sorry, Bill and Hillary!) whom we scorned in our schooldays and who didn't inhale, or at least who said they didn't, or else the snobby dumb Ivy legacies like Dubya. Just about none of "us" ever managed to get into positions of control. Makes me sorry Jim never had a chance to run for President, even merely as a pure, or not so pure, symbolic gesture.

Still, it was a most pleasant weekend as long as one kept away from the dogmatists and spent one's time instead running around stoned and naked (not me! I'm only reporting), just enjoying the warm summer rural landscape. I never heard such a loud dawn chorus of birds as I did up there...it sounded like the Garden audience before a big concert. And it was fun telling Jim all about it when he showed up in New York the next week for our wedding...

REVIEW:
LET IT BE, The Beatles

BEATLES ◆ *Let It Be* (Apple AR 34001): John Lennon, Paul McCartney, George Harrison, Ringo Starr; various musicians. No instrumentation listed. *Two of Us*; *I Dig A Pony*; *Across the Universe*; *I Me Mine*; *Let It Be*; *Maggie Mae*; *I've Got A Feeling*; *One After 909*; *The Long and Winding Road*; *For You Blue*; *Get Back.*

Somehow it seems that the fatalism contained in the title of this particular record was premonitory: when the Beatles changed it from *Get Back* to *Let It Be*, we all should have been forewarned, and perhaps some of us were.

Not I, at any rate; the Beatles had long since begun to pall, and after a while I noticed that I just couldn't be bothered ringing all the changes they appeared to be going through. By the time *Let It Be* finally made it out, it didn't matter any more, and the record has been out long enough now that I should feel rather foolish giving specific rundowns on the songs as entities.

Not only that, but I wonder if it would even be worth it. "Two of Us", "The Long and Winding Road" and of course "Get Back" are the only cuts I can bear to listen to; all the rest seem to me filled with strain and difficulty — headache music, if you will. You can hear the group unity groaning everywhere on this record, like wood under stress, like wires in a high wind.

Sad, really, that what will probably be the last collective Beatle record had to turn out like this. Karma, I guess, but it seems to me that *Let It Be* might well be retitled *Rest in Peace*; it wouldn't change a thing.

Which pretty much says it all. I loved early-middle Beatles, things like "Don't Bother Me;", "Thank You Girl", "P.S. I Love You"; even late-middle stuff like "Love You To" and "She Said She Said". But though I fully recognized Sgt. Pepper for what it was—though only on the second listening...the first time around I played it straight through, both sides, then I sat back, took a deep breath, said "Huh" and turned the record over to start straight through all over again—even with all that, I didn't love it. I never LOVED the Beatles the way I LOVED the Airplane and the Doors.

Sgt. Pepper may have been groundbreaking and earthshaking for the musical world, and yes, I could see that it was. But I really couldn't hear why it should be. "A Day in the Life": yes, amazing, but I would never put it on the turntable for pleasure, for casual listening. The other songs seemed commonplace and, frankly, kind of dull. So for the Beatles to gently fade away like this didn't upset me as much as one might have thought. They made me very happy, at least with some of the early stuff. They made me way happier than Hendrix or even the Stones. But they didn't give me real joy.

I guess here is as good a place as any for a confession that may seem heinous and disloyal. Even though I loved the Doors to distraction, I would have to say that what I consider the three best (not the three most popular) Stones songs are better than the three most popular (not the three best) Doors songs. I would have to say that "Gimme Shelter" just about wipes the floor with "Light My Fire"—in fact, with pretty much every other rock song in the world in space in the universe. (In case you're wondering, the others are "Jumpin' Jack Flash" and "Ruby Tuesday"; on the flip side, no Stones song can possibly measure up to "The Crystal

*Ship", "People Are Strange", "The End", "Waiting for the Sun",
"Roadhouse Blues", "The Changeling" and "The Soft Parade".)*

*But I don't love to listen to the Stones, apart from maybe six
songs all told, and I could listen to the Doors for hours on end.
Well, not these days, of course; I can't, it's far too painful, and
has been ever since Jim's death. Which is yet another thing to be
pissed off at him for: taking his music with him when he went.*

October 1970

POP TALK:
ROCK AROUND THE COCK

Until now, this column was the only Pop Talk piece that had ever been reprinted anywhere: in Evelyn McDonnell's and Ann Powers' groundbreaking 1995 compendium Rock She Wrote: Women Write About Rock, Pop and Rap. *I was very proud of having been asked by them to submit a piece for inclusion, since no one else had ever requested to anthologize any of my stuff (except for a couple of Doors reviews in some coffeetable book). Quite honestly, I had been feeling slighted and ignored in the grand scheme of rock-criticism narrative and history, not having my undeniable status as a Founding Mother of the Genre recognized in any real sense. So when Ann and Evelyn asked me to be in their book, I was thrilled, and though my pique did not vanish, I felt better about it.*

I still feel that way—the resentment and pissed-offness. Everybody focuses on the guys who were there at the dawn of it all and not the few chicks who were there every bit as much and who were every bit as erudite and serious and musically opinionated as their male counterparts. It's always been deeply annoying, which is one of the reasons I put this present collection together—to get my work of that day, perhaps not as shatteringly ever-so as Richard Goldstein's or R. Meltzer's or Lester Bangs's, but certainly as valid, out there for people who never saw it, to claim my place and speak up for not only myself but my rock-critic sisters. It's not wrong to want credit for what you achieved, and we achieved a LOT.

❖

Then again, even women rock critics who came along much later were similarly ignored by the boys' club...just like women musicians and women executives, who also complain, and quite rightly, about being slighted. Anyway, I chose this piece to appear in Rock She Wrote because I think that of all the things I wrote for J&P, this was probably the most important.

Plus, in the company of fellow anthologees like Patti Smith and Kim Gordon, I naturally wanted to look my best...

Rock and roll has come a long way, baby, from the strange days when the streets were thick with sobbing chickies come to throng the pavements outside hotels housing the Beatles or the Stones. Times've changed, for sure; now the interested phenomenological observer can go to the Fillmore or similar habitats and behold an audience comprised chiefly of young men, alone or in groups, some of whom may be accompanied by young ladies but very often not, and almost nowhere will there be seen (a) three or more women together and not looking uncomfortable, or most especially (b) a lady by herself.

Odd indeed for a branch of popular art that once was almost exclusively female in its constituents, but by no stretch is it limited to the concert situation: I haven't any figures presently available as to the gender percentages of the record-buying public under 30, but it comes to my mind that I do see mostly men patronizing the record stores in my neighborhood, and it takes only a quick glance at J&P's rate card demographic breakdown to see that for a music magazine *put together entirely by women*, the readership is some 92% male.

Not to mention women in the business end of rock, and women artists, and the LYRICS...but all in turn.

Welcome to the Camp,
I Guess You All Know Why You're Here

Given: rock and roll is a middle-class phenomenon. All the following rant, with the exception of that statement of I think unarguable fact, is purely subjective and based entirely on my own observations in the field, supplemented on occasion by solicited opinions from various sources friendly and not; of course, any further reader observations, experiments and/or hypotheses are more than welcome.

Now. Concerts, contrary to popular opinion, are not devised chiefly for the hearing of the music therein performed, though that music is a major factor in deciding who attends which concert, but rather as a socio-economic ritual, of some solidity, in which all participants know the roles and moves assigned to their specific level of the whole and generally carry them out with a good will, whether it be Jethro Tull at the Whisky or *Cosi fan tutte* at the Metropolitan Opera House.

Rock concerts, up until a few years ago, used to be primarily female occasions, screaming seas of young girls with tear-streaked, ecstatic faces; the whole interchange was largely gonadal in orientation. Along about 1967 the change came: rock and roll became rock. More sophisticated, more self-conscious in lyrics and techniques, more mechanically oriented, the new music lost large numbers of its old fans — and in so doing, picked up even larger numbers of male music-lovers who had previously avoided it. (Not to say that there had been *no* male rock and roll fans all along, but they had definitely been lying low, or listening to folk or jazz or blues, and came to rock in open and significant numbers only when it became — dare I say it? — more intelligent. I have no idea how far it is possible or desirable to go with the proposition that most women do not dig 'progressive' rock, but I think it is pretty clear that lots do not, the reason being that it is, indeed, too much of an effort to make; hastening to add that this is not necessarily due to any cerebral defect on the part of these women but more likely a reflection on their education — the same could be given as a reason why many women do not enjoy jazz.)

So concerts then became largely male occasions, and, outside of the very small number of women who attended because they had done some listening and actively decided that they preferred the music of Group X to others and had real musical reasons for so doing, females at rock concerts tended to be there chiefly in the role of attendant to some man — either in a pre-arranged, "date", situation or as a free-floater, invariably in tandem with another girl, there to check out the action and hopefully score with, depending on tastes and opportunities, either an unattached male fellow audience member or a musician.

I comment once again on the noticeable scarcity of solo women at rock concerts; whether this is due to vestigial social embarrassment at being seen without an escort or understandable fear at being out alone late at night, I do not know, but I tend to think it falls somewhere in between — having made such scenes, for whatever reason, primarily social, it has become incumbent upon women to further elevate them into "occasions", something to look forward to, and not to treat concert scenes as casual entertainment the way most men do, just running out and buying a ticket and going, alone, to hear someone they really appreciate.

All of this, of course, merely serves to illustrate that given proposition: rock is most truly a middle-class phenomenon, and these are all most truly middle-class attitudes; for all the screaming we do about how free the women of this generation are, things show up quite otherwise in practice.

Sexy Sadie

Congruent to the situation of women: rock concerts is the position (no pun intended) of the groupie. Judging by all the criteria available, the role of groupie seems to be the only one that most rock musicians are willing to allow females to fill. Carrying the concept of woman-as-object to almost as great an extent as do men who patronize prostitutes, rock artists. by their own admission, see the groupie as a rather fetching device of roughly the same convenience quotient as a knothole, only more decorative and lots more fun; there are no demands, no wondering where you stand in the woman's eyes, no frantic posturing and juggling of stance — everything out front and the rules thoroughly understood by all parties involved.

Sure, it's exploitation: but I think that in such a situation as this, you just can't exploit anybody who so obviously *wants* to be exploited — for whatever reasons of her own. And much rock-journalistic fodder has been made, to date, of just what those reasons are. I don't pretend to know, outside of the obvious; but neither do I intend to protest too much, just because it may not be the way *I* do things — if deriving an identity of sorts from the men they ball makes them happy, fine, and welcome to it, but I could wish devoutly that rock musicians acknowledge the fact that there are indeed other-motivated women even in the rock and roll business. No slight on groupies, but there are even women who have their minds on the music as music and not on the musicians as groins. And I am sure that Karin Berg of the East Village Other and Anne Marie Micklo of Rock and Deday La Rene of Creem, to name a few, would back me up.

In It For The MONEY??

For a field that some claim is devoted to, supported by, and furthered for the interests of the women of the American alternative culture, the business end of rock and roll is noticeably sparse in women who are responsible for doing any of the prime moving that goes on. How often do you see a woman promoter putting together one of the monster festivals—not just serving as a sometime consultant, or a sop to Women's Liberation, but really *doing* it? How many women managers are there around, or booking agents, how many women who have any real responsibility or power in the running of giant talent firms, how many women engineers at recording studios, how many women producers, how many women disk jockeys or program directors, how many women are on the a&r staff of record companies like Columbia or Atlantic, how many women are involved in house advertising staffs for record companies, how many women run their own record-company executive positions the way they want and are regarded by their male co-workers as equal on all levels?

Though that last may be asked with equal validity of women in any field, it has particular importance in this one, which is supposed by popular belief and wishful thinking to be loose, free and easy, and not prone to the peculiar hangups of other, straighter business strata. (Though one group, Ten Wheel Drive, does have a female equipment manager, who schleps those amps as though she means it, women are as a rule regarded as not suited to such goings-on as lugging drum cases or sweating over a Scully 12-track or dragging the lead singer out of a bar at three in the morning.)

In fact, about the only thing that women appear to be thought of as good for in this business is p.r. Hype. Oh, I know about Alison Steele of WNEW-FM [*on-air personality*] and Tracy Sterne of Nonesuch [*label managing director*] and Dusty Street from KSAN [*radio show host*] in San Francisco and a few others. But these are clear and brilliant exceptions, or so the men who run everything else would have it. Everyone else is in publicity. Now, women are very good at hype, they do it all the time; they can brag about their groups the way they'd brag about their grandchildren. But that's like saying women are good at being secretaries because they like looking after their bosses. Men can hype very well too; gender is hardly a qualification.

And women writers. I do tire of flailing away at that ol' male chauvinism hydra, but I tire even more of going out to do an interview and being genteelly condescended to as not much more than a particularly well-connected groupie, and then, some time during the interview, having to watch the interviewee male drop his drink at a perfectly ordinary remark as to, oh, the influence of eighteenth-century Irish-Scottish broadside ballads in his work, or John Cage, or Django Reinhardt, or even non–musical things like the auteur theory of filmmaking, or just about anything having more intellectual content than "What's your favorite color?" Male reporters draw nary a raised eyebrow with questions having to do with pursuits intellectual, techniques musical, or just plain all-around mental information, but women journalists invariably pull down (a) suspicion ("Who coached YOU so well, little girl?") or (b) amazement ("My God! It thinks!"). Once the moment of truth is past and you are accepted as mind and not cunt, things go well, but there should never have to be even that momentary caesura of credibility.

And women artists. With my own ears I heard a member of a major British band [*Okay, the statute of sexist limitations has probably run out on this one, folks: it was Richard*

Thompson, then of Fairport Convention. He got better, I'm happy to say… – PKM] tell me that women in rock groups are bad news because they're "too emotional", whatever the hell that means. Does it mean that they miss gigs because they're drying their hair or had a fight with their old man, that they can't pull their weight musically, either playing an instrument or songwriting, that they evince unprofessional behavior patterns on tour? I have heard all of those charges laid to MALE group members, artists belonging to various groups at various times, so let's have no attitudes copped that female rock artists are any more emotional than their male counterpart prima donnas.

On the other hand, there appear to be only two roles for women rock artists to play. Joan Baez and Judy Collins and Laura Nyro can get away with much, under the cover of "art songs", but where does that leave Grace Slick and Tina Turner? Filling the—needless to say—male-specified roles of (a) Ice Princess, or (b) Down-Home Ball. So there we have Grace, gelid, brittle, bitch goddess incarnate—interestingly enough, she has never made any formal statement of position on the function of women in rock—at the one extreme, and Tina, or Janis Joplin—interestingly enough, neither have they—at the other, as the earth-mother, scratch-your-back, tiger-lady stone soul fuck. Not much in between, not much choice. And—

Women Is Losers, For Sure

If women as rock artists are severely circumscribed in their choice of role through which to communicate, then woman as the subject of rock lyricists merely reinforces the limitations.

Almost without exception, rock lyrics are dedicated to keeping women in their place, and we all know just where that place is: "Well, I know you must have heard it a lot/

But it's a fact/ Men always seem to end up on top." If men are on top, there's only one place left for the rock woman, no matter how much she does not like it.

There are a lot of reasons for this, not least among them the faggot attitudes of the male rock-appreciating populace (not for nothing did Jim Morrison recently complain during a concert, "The only people who rush the stage are guys"), or their wish-fulfillment fantasy trips ("Bet I'm better than *he* is anyway"). Nothing wrong with that, guys, just don't do it at my expense.

Women in rock lyrics are generally confined to, again, one of two very well-defined categories, and there is between the two absolute and utter dichotomy: the Conceptual Female and the Biological Female.

These two divisions tend to fit in pretty well with the functions assigned to female rock artists: they are at least as arbitrary, and they are certainly as rigid and as limiting, and they are probably a whole lot more insulting.

The Conceptual Female tends to be the province of the former folkies: Dylan, Tim Hardin, John Sebastian. She is idealized, romanticized, and she is held to function as either a hate object or a loved object: Martha Lorraine, who belongs to Country Joe, or the unnamed lady who's "got everything she needs, she's an artist, she don't look back" that Dylan missed so much, or even Mick Jagger's true beloved Ruby Tuesday, who is probably somewhere in between. The one thing that most Conceptual Females share is that they all got away from the men who celebrate them in song; their state is undoubtedly the more gracious for that, but it does somehow leave said dudes looking a bit like losers. You have to admire the ladies for it.

The Biological Female, on the other hand, exists in her creators' minds as nothing other than sexual object, and she is by far the more numerous of the two. From the Beatles

("She's A Woman") to the Stones ("King Bee", "Under My Thumb", "Yesterday's Papers", "Play With Fire", "Stray Cat Blues") to Hendrix ("Foxy Lady") to the Grateful Dead ("Little School Girl") to the Doors ("Love Me Two Times", "Back Door Man") to James Brown ("It's a Man's, Man's, Man's World") to Gary Puckett, even, for God's sake. The Conceptual Female may ball, but the Biological Female *gets* balled: it's an important and obvious distinction— active in the case of the former, passive in the case of the latter.

It's the real-life prototype of the Biological Female that all the leather pants and silk shirts of the onstage rock performer are aimed at; I see this not as specifically intended malicious oppression (I'm trying to be charitable), but purely stupid ignorance, and either it has to stop or it has to transmute. There's nothing wrong with sexism, provided it works both ways. For ex—

Coda and Conclusion

A rather well-known singer (male) [*yeah, yeah, we all know who it was… – PKM*] once asked me why I write and why I write about what I write about. Which is a perfectly legitimate question to ask any writer, but something there was about his…well, his *attitude* that caused me to make him a fairly snotty reply. And just so everybody can know, and to continue the point I was making somewhere above about sexism besides, the real reason I write about rock and roll is because I want to get up onstage at the Fillmore East, wearing a black leather jumpsuit and a silver-plated Telecaster, grab the mike, sneer at the audience, "You PIGS", and then get off forty-five minutes of the indisputedly finest rock guitar ever heard anywhere. And then retire from the rock and roll scene forever.

Now that's all very well, and it hasn't been done before, and it's just Patricia's private fantasy, no weirder than your own; but the point is that the way things are now, neither I nor any other woman will be able to do it, and not because we can't play guitar…if a man is free to do it, then so should a woman be free to do it, whether it's rock and roll stardom, or producing, or being the president of CBS or the United States; that's obvious. For all its self-hype to the contrary, rock is just another dismal male chauvinist trip, with one important difference: it's got the power and the looseness with which to change itself. It better happen quick.

Of course, it never did. Not really. And that's very sad. But enough other things happened to make it perhaps a little less sad, and these days I do see plenty of women onstage, though unfortunately they're always prancing around practically naked. (The boys too: Jim Morrison died for your sins, Marilyn Manson…) Autotuning and lip-synching, equally unfortunately (the boys too: Jimi Hendrix died for your sins, Justin Bieber…). Never a female Hendrix or Clapton or Lennon, but then again there was never a female Mozart, so there it is. I cannot possibly believe that such a lack is due to a severe and inherent lack of musical talent on the XX-chromosomal side, so I must then conclude that it has to be because no woman with the chops for it has decided that that's her priority. Which is strange, admittedly, but, again, there it is.

On the non-public front lines of sexual liberation, of course, things were very different. Sure, rock stars never got told no, but those were the days when even regular people never got told no. And good days they were, despite the lingering actuality that the sexual revolution just meant that women got screwed in brand-new ways of screwingness that now involved actual screwing as well as theoretical and figurative.

This was particularly prevalent and noticeable among male members of the Movement, who despite the presence among them of such firebrands as Angela Davis and Kathleen Cleaver and Susan Brownmiller, nevertheless still seemed to relegate revolution-minded females to providing coffee, typing and sex. Hey, just like their straight-world counterparts.

Well, fuck THAT noise, said I and many others, and started up feminism then and there. If the times they were going to be a-changin', then we damn well wanted to be a-changin' them to our own needs, specs and purposes, and no frizzy-haired, Army-surplus-jacketed dickbrains were going to tell us otherwise. We see how that worked out, of course: could have been a lot better, but actually not so bad at all, considering.

But as I mentioned way up front, apart from that, I didn't really encounter a ton of overt sexist crap, thankfully—mostly because the men I met in the course of doing my writerly job were my age or nearabouts, and had taught themselves, or had been taught, usually the hard way, how to treat women as human beings. More or less. At least face to face. I generally found them polite, engaging and quite human. (Yeah … "Apart from that, Mrs. Lincoln, how did you like the play?")

Nevertheless, imagine my dismay and astonishment to find that I encountered worse man-piggy behavior from some of the guys on Jazz & Pop than I did from any rock star I ever met…yes, including Mr. Robert Plant, who looked like Sir Lancelot du Lac by comparison to these louts.

It was generally the pre-war generation (though by no means all of them), and a couple of the younger jazz snobs as well, who were doing the dissing: older, cranky, superannuated and embittered hobgoblins who apparently didn't see why they should be respectful of or even courteous to some long-haired, miniskirted chit who nevertheless had the power to edit the balls off them if she so chose…and who could write the balls off them as well.

On their parts, perhaps it was explainable as equal doses

petulance, jealousy, resentment and sexism—the usual pernicious cocktail stirred up by things who walk in human guise who aren't fond of women, for whatever reasons. Or perhaps I, just by existing, reminded them of their inevitable and increasing irrelevance in the already churning revolution. In any case, not a pleasant mix. But I refused to stoop to their level, taking care to behave in a far kinder and more forbearing fashion to them, as both a woman and their editor, than any of them deserved.

Of course, some of our older writers were true gentlemen and great rock fans, for whom I had nothing but genuine respect: Ralph J. Gleason, Jay Ruby. The rest of them, not so much; or, let's say, I had at least as much respect for them as they had for me— yes, as much as that. I wasn't asking for reverence, or deference, or even friendliness: just common courtesy and the civility due my position. Frankly, I was a bit hurt and surprised that Pauline let it go on at all, let alone as far as it did: even to the extent that one of said louts kept me and my writings out of a book he assembled of notable J&P rock features and interviews—the only major person who wrote for the magazine to be so slighted. Which I found particularly galling, since in all sizzling modesty my work, and certainly my Doors feature, "When The Music's Over", here presented, could stand up to anything he did include or, indeed, had written himself—plus my being that, you know, EDITOR thing. But we had never really gotten on, so perhaps it wasn't such a surprise after all.

REVIEW:
ABSOLUTELY LIVE, The Doors

Once Jim and I were together, I perceived that it would probably look a lot better if I didn't write about the Doors anymore, though it didn't really bother Jim one way or the other but kind of amused him. (Rennie Stride, the protagonist of my rock mystery series, has the same difficulty with her own consort, superstud English guitarist Turk Wayland, and his band Lionheart...though apart from that, Turk and Rennie share very little in common with Jim and me.) But I loved the Doors and didn't want to give up reviewing them, and moreover did not trust anyone else to review them: still, as it turned out, there would be only two albums left for me to write about (L.A. Woman was released after I had left the magazine, saving me both the anguish and the angst).

So I adopted a pseudonym: Shamrock O'Toole. Not exactly the most opaque of aliases, but even so. We all had them, for whenever we felt we needed a bit of cover or plausible deniability: Pauline was Ringo Pasta, Sue Donoghue was Daisy Buchanan, Bruce Harris was Chris Reabur, Terry Towne was Rhapsody Packard. We all wrote our own bios, too. Shamrock's went thusly:

"Shamrock O'Toole is a freelance writer of half Irish, half Apache Indian ancestry, who trains pythons in her spare time and makes clothing out of the more unteachable ones. She is presently writing the definitive rock and roll dirty novel."

DOORS ♦ *Absolutely Live* (Elektra EKS 9002). Jim Morrison (lead vo); Ray Manzarek (or, b, backup vo, lead vo on *Close to You*); Robbie Krieger (g); John Densmore (d). *Who Do You Love*; Medley: *Alabama Song, Backdoor Man, Love Hides, Five to One*; *Build Me A Woman*; *When the Music's Over*; *Close to*

You; Universal Mind; Break On Thru, #2; The Celebration of the Lizard; Soul Kitchen.

Despite the fact that some of the tracks here performed were in the can for as much as a year after they were recorded, and despite the fact that *Absolutely Live* is the absolutely worst album title since and including *Absolutely Free*, and despite the fact that Ray Manzarek adds insult to injury by including (in addition to his lead vocal on "Close to You") a direct cop off the Stones' "Play With Fire" on the ride section of "Break On Thru, #2", and despite the fact that Jim Morrison's audience patter is a lot snottier than, say, John B. Sebastian's — despite all this, and maybe even because of all this, *Absolutely Live* is one of the absolutely finest live rock and roll albums ever made, and no mistake.

People are going to say, first off, that The Doors Are Back, meaning those old first-album Doors, and to a certain extent they will be right. (Have you noticed that it is invariably just this sort of record — this one, or *Volunteers*, or *Surrealistic Pillow*, or *Workingman's Dead*, or the first Doors — that is clutched to the collective rock and roll bosom, gaining showers of acceptance and glee and instantaneous nostalgia, but never the artistically demanding *Soft Parade*s or the *Aoxomoxoa*s or the *After Bathing at Baxter's*es? Not that there's anything WRONG with *Volunteers*, etc., it's just that that sort of record is more immediately and easily accessible than the other sort, and so automatically will elicit a wider reaction. Damn.)

But *Absolutely Live* is good. The sound quality is surpassing excellent, quite probably the best ever on a recorded-in-concert LP; crowd noise is at a gratifying high level throughout, and enough new songs are fitted in to make the double-record set less of a Doors anthology than an actual, carefully programmed concert caught on record, complete with rock-ya-sock-ya curtain-raiser ("Who Do You Love"); medley (three standbys and "Love Hides" — one of the most beautiful lyrics the Doors ever had); theatrics ("When The Music's Over"); production number ("The Celebration of the Lizard"); and encore ("Soul Kitchen").

Fine as everybody is — Morrison is in great voice and high spirits, Manzarek is unceasingly amazing on keyboard bass as well as on the more obvious organ, and Densmore comes across both solid and flash — it is indisputedly Robbie Krieger who is the real star of this album. Krieger, lurking insidiously in the far dark corners of the stage. Krieger, who has generally managed to be pretty badly under-recorded on previous Doors efforts. Krieger, who if he ever left the group could probably be the best studio guitarist in the world. Krieger, who if the group ever let him *do* anything could probably be the best stage guitarist in the world. To paraphrase Robert Plant: "Ladies and gentlemen, Robbie Krieger!" Oh, well.

Yes, and in addition to Robbie Krieger, this album does contain upon its last side "The Celebration of the Lizard", that somewhat legendary leviathan of a Doors 'theatre piece.' Now this is what I call poetry; its total effect is a truly vertiginous dazzle, and though it may not be the greatest work of poetic art in the history of civilization, it is possibly the most powerful piece of music and words ever recorded by any rock group, anywhere, and it alone is worth the price of the entire album.

Absolutely Live merely proves once again that the Doors are worth sixteen of Creedence any day of the week.

—*Shamrock O'Toole*

Not that there was a single damn thing wrong with Creedence, of course. Far from it. Though CCR themselves, weirdly, seemed to think there was: in December 1970, they flew about forty critics and writers from New York to Berkeley to hear their "new sound", putting us up lavishly at the fabulous old Victorian Claremont Hotel and giving us a private concert at their funky Oakland studio, Cosmo's Factory (sadly, recently burned down). We were appreciative, to be sure, and it was all terrific fun, kind of like a grownup elementary-school trip, only to the West Coast instead of to the Statue of Liberty. But it changed nothing—we still thought that Creedence were just great and that there had been nothing whatsoever the matter with their "old sound".

It was during this San Francisco junket, my first time to the West Coast, that I got my first tattoo, from Lyle Tuttle, who did Janis's ink: a black Pisces sign on my left wrist. When I flew down to L.A. afterward to see Jim, he was quite impressed with it, and more than a little turned on, but too cowardly to get one himself...

Anyway, Shamrock wrote this Doors review because by this point Patricia was beginning to feel rather uncomfortable showering public praise on her beloved's work, and I think rightly so. Nobody ever took me to task for it; it was strictly something that I felt on my own behalf. Such delicacy of feeling amused, and was appreciated by, the guy on the other side of the bed, at whom it was aimed...though His Majesty the Lizard King did think that "Shamrock O'Toole" (which he twigged instantly and teased me about endlessly) was maybe a bit over the top. But his loving Queen was just having some fun...something that was soon to be in rather short supply where we were concerned.

November 1970

Since I have lately been feeling about as generally relevant as Tyrannosaurus rex (the creature, not the group) with regard to the ostensible functioning category of "Rock Criticism", and since otherwheres in this same issue our distinguished Contributing Editor from up north, Ritchie Yorke, has placed fearsome judgment of his own on the practice, I thought perhaps the time has come for a spot of re-evaluation.

Though this is not, and never was meant as, riposte or put-down to Ritchie's views, many of which I share whole-soul, I nevertheless would like to use one of his comments as a jumping-off place: and that would be the fact that he appears to consider artistic criticism to be, in fact and in application, about as relevant and necessary as, well, Tyrannosaurus rex.

Like everything else, it all depends on what you know. In my First Annual Rock Criticism Rant, which took place in the August 1969 issue of this magazine, I made a certain distinction between criticism and reviewing, and subsequently attempted to define the present-day function and responsibility and attributes of true artistic criticism, and I quote:

> *Real criticism is a process of selection, a functional*
> *energy: it pulls in all the goods, considers*
> *all variants, and then goes on to pronounce*

conclusions. The best criticism concerns itself with direction and flow, general trends; and it logically follows that the best critics are the ones who can double as visionaries, who can see simultaneously where it's been and where it's going and how it is right now. I consider myself an observer [Still do—P.K.] *, not a critic; critics are people like Walter Kerr and H. L. Mencken and probably even Jimmy Breslin; people who perceive and then apply their own selves to the perception. Criticism is a reflection of both the artistic creation upon which it is based and of the society that fostered the creation; criticism provides insight, not doctrinaire pronouncements. No critic is infallible, and any who speak ex cathedra without having first considered all possibilities are only fooling themselves.*

End quote. I don't think it's changed much since then, but, if I may hark back for a moment to those dismal days in June at the Goddard College Alternative Media Conference, there was a workshop on the second afternoon of the conference which purported to concern itself with "Rock Criticism: Its Validity and Role". Hot dog, I figured, now we'll all get to see what everybody *really* uses for motives.

Predictably, it turned out to be more protective coloration than true colors: this particular congruency, of theoretically literate writer types, was the most disorganized, unproductive and acrimonious of all the workshops I attended. And to me the most interesting thing about it all was the nearly perfect dichotomy evidenced between the two opposing camps of rock criticism: the feelers and the thinkers, or the emotionalists and the academicists, or, yeah, why not, the Dionysians and the Apollonians. Fairly strange, but *very* logical.

Thanks to a number of people, we're all familiar enough by now with the Dionysian/Apollonian approach to rock music: Dionysian all smoky primeval and sensual and sexual and gut-level and gonadal and below the belt, Apollonian all cool and clear and logical and progressive and connected and above the neck. Now, much as I really dislike this sort of facile subdivisioning, I have to admit that indeed the D/A fandango does hold some kind of validity when applied to the music. However, I am not at all so sure that that same subdivisioning will hold when applied to the corresponding forms of rock criticism.

Working for the moment with the highly personal definiton of criticism that I quoted earlier, I think that the emotionalists are off the track: concentrating on one aspect of the whole does not make for criticism. And the same could be said of the hard-line academicians. Rock is a complex synthesis; one does not serve it best by extracting suitable elements and diffusing the remainder. (Maybe that's where the problem lies: the form — structure — of rock is Apollonian/intellectual, the substance — utilization and effect — is Dionysian/emotional? Possibly; if you find out, let me know.)

At any rate, the necessity of rock criticism is the same as the necessity for any form of artistic criticism, and this is apparently where Ritchie and I part company. Critics are not there, anywhere, to nay-say and negate, or to puff themselves at the expense of others, but rather to perform what I, at least, consider to be an essential part of the artistic experience: to serve as a conscientious liaison between artist and audience, or a sounding board, or a mediator. Call it whatever you like, but all it means is that a critic provides some personal sort of by no means infallible viewpoint that, ideally, should take into consideration both artist and audience. I don't see too much irrelevance in that.

The true irrelevance, in rock criticism or any criticism, would then appear to lie in a divergence toward one side or the other: in rock, a heavy slant toward either the thinkers or the feelers. Both are incomplete views and both lead to inaccurate critical viewpoints, yet neither should be ignored and neither should be overemphasized.

Artistic criticism has been going on for hundreds of years; rock criticism is only its newest manifestation, and only for about three years, so it is not to be wondered at that its practitioners have as yet to reach a successful mode. Balance is all.

A bit of an apologia pro vita mea, *I suppose. It was interesting that when, many years later, I was on set for the Doors movie with Oliver Stone, he told me that he was really glad I had given up criticism and had switched over to writing books, something creative of my own; that critics were pretty much parasites practicing a horrible profession. An attitude born, I would imagine, just making a wild guess here, of Oliver's own personal artistic run-ins with critics over the years. Ah, but then he hadn't met me yet, had he...still, I confess it was rather pleasant to hear him say so, and, given our other differences, rather decent of him to tell me.*

December 1970

"Just As Good As You've Been to This World…"

LOS ANGELES, OCTOBER 4: Janis Joplin was found dead in her apartment here at the Hollywood Landmark Motel at approximately 10 p.m. Dr. Thomas Noguchi, Los Angeles County coroner, attributed her death to an overdose of heroin. Needle marks and tracks were found in both Joplin's arms, and a hypodermic needle and unspecified amounts of heroin and marijuana were discovered in the apartment.

Joplin's death came only sixteen days after Jimi Hendrix died in London of an o.d. of barbiturates. The news that Janis had apparently been shooting heavily came as somewhat of a surprise to many admirers, as she had the reputation of being a dedicated juicer and had often spoken out against the use of hard drugs.

Born January 19, 1943 in Port Arthur, Texas , Janis described her life there as that of a "misfit", and ran away to sing the blues in California in the summer of 1965. Travis Rivers, an old friend from her Texas days, steered her on to a band called Big Brother & The Holding Company, who were functioning as more or less house band at Chet Helms' Avalon Ballroom, and that was how it all got started. Janis and Big Brother made their performing breakthrough at the 1967 Monterey Pop Festival, released one incredibly ethos-perfect but technically abysmal record on Mainstream label, came to New York in early 1968 to play at the Anderson Theater and then presided at the opening of the Fillmore East in March of that year—and became one of the top acts in rock and roll.

And Janis became a superstar. After that, the split with Big Brother wasn't long in coming: they were dragging her down, people told her, they weren't good enough to keep up with her [*No and no.* Emphatically. *— PKM*]. So she left them, right after their first album, *Cheap Thrills*, came out on Columbia, and put together a band of her own, which was renowned chiefly for its manifold personnel changes and state of chronic namelessness. It was one of these shifting assemblages which recorded with her on the second Columbia release, *Kozmic Blues*, and backed her up tumultuously at Woodstock in the summer of 1969.

After that, there were the appearances at most of the major rock festivals, the superhype, the gloomsayers who spoke of shuck and sellout, the obligatory Madison Square Garden supershow, and even a bust, for miscellaneous profanity and for telling a cop, in a burst of explosiveness, that she was going to kick his face in. Last year, the Janis Joplin Full Tilt Boogie Band was successfully put together, and Janis was back; it was this band which was working with her on a third Columbia LP at the time of her death [*the posthumously released* Pearl].

Like Billie Holiday, whom she greatly admired, Janis Joplin burned her candle at both ends and used a blowtorch on the middle. "I'd rather not sing at all than sing quiet," she said once, perhaps prophetically, and she never did sing quiet.

Until now.

Usually journalism students or beginning reporters start out writing obituaries as their first pieces, as a sort of rather grim drill or exercise in their craft. Though not a classic obituary in form, Janis's was the first real obit I ever wrote, and I wish to this day that I hadn't had to write it—indeed, I wish it had never had to be written at all.

Even though we knew about her drug use, and had on some level been dreading this, her death came as a huge shock; Jimi's death, two weeks before, had saddened us, but Janis's knocked us off our feet. We all loved her and Big Brother, and she was a good friend to us and to the magazine; she once gifted Pauline with an autographed bottle of Southern Comfort (only half empty), and gave me a string of beads off her own neck when I gave her a slice of pumpkin pie at one of Bill Graham's Fillmore East Thanksgiving dinners.

Our readers and critics were constantly voting her Best Female Vocalist in our polls, and it always, touchingly, made her feel happy and valid. I was glad to have known her, even as briefly and as casually as I did.

POP TALK:
ARTHURIAN ROCK

Like everything else in this feverish plane, popular music—whatever that somewhat overtired and always inaccurate concept has come to mean—tends to run in cumulative cycles. And all that means is that the corpus of pop music, being defined into phases as its wont, carries each phase through to some sort of conclusion, satisfactory or not, enters a hiatus of variable duration and then uses that just-completed phase to provide the kickoff into the movement of the next.

O.K. It is my considered opinion that we are—obviously—in the clutch of just such a hiatus at present, and though Ford alone knows when and where it is all going to start moving again, it seems that in such situations, things come back to their beginnings, almost for a refresher course, as it were: simpler stuff, but with the added difference of meantime experiences.

This totally unremarkable phenomenon manifests itself right now, this minutes, in what it pleases me to tag Arthurian Rock, though much of it is by no means so ancient in inspiration: your electrified balladeers, Blondel *cum* amplifiers. 'S interesting, and being the confirmed medievalist that I am, perhaps I place a tad more weight on it than it either merits or likes, but it does seem that enough people are doing it to make it worth noticing.

Of course, and needless to say, it's been around for a while: Donovan, that son of the Isles, has been doing it off and on for years, only now he's making more of it than before. (*He* calls it Celtic Rock.) It's the other practitioners of the art that make it notable.

As might be expected, some of it turns up in the most unexpected places. Like on the new Traffic album. Holding down the title spot, yet. "John Barleycorn Must Die", according to the liner notes, comes from Cecil Sharp's collection of English "folk" songs: the earliest known version dates to the time of James I, and there are an estimated 100-140 versions extant. The song itself is a very melodic, very minor-key, very conventional tune of its genre: mot Traffic's usual fare by any means, but interesting in itself and thoroughly astonishing in its context.

It's the groups that specialize in this sort of thing that are even more astonishing in their context: technically (and unimaginatively), you could call them folk-rock. But the sort of music they practice is so far removed in style and in sense from the musical category known in its heyday as "folk-rock" as to render the label practically meaningless.

Inevitably, all the bands involved are British: British traditional sound requires British people, or at least people who are thoroughly steeped in the Celtic-Anglo-Saxon medieval milieu. Not so inevitably, all the bands involved do not choose to make their music along the same lines.

Pentangle, perhaps the best-known of the medievalists and certainly the most musically innovative, seems also to be the first — or at least the first to achieve any degree of widespread recognition. Like their fellows, Pentangle does not feel obligated to restrict itself to one form of musical style. Bert Jansch, their dazzling lead guitarist, is probably responsible for most of this, but the other musicians (all of whom, it is interesting to note, have at least as heavy backgrounds in jazz as they have in traditional music) all contribute extensively. The overall sound, though, is distinctly and distinctively Middle-Aged. (Jansch once introduced what is perhaps their most overtly medieval number, a beautiful thing called "Hunting Song", with the remark, "This is a little thing we wrote back in the thirteenth century.") The jazz-swing element, however, in Pentangle's music, besides being quite valid on its own, undoubtedly provides welcome relief from too much medievalia (after a bit it does all start to sound alike).

Not so the other medievalist band currently popular on a mass scale: the Incredible String Band. In the first place, *everything* the Incredibles do sounds *exactly* the same. In the second place, though they are often described as such, they are not primarily British traditional, but rather Indian-Balinese in their general influences, instrumentation and tonal coloring. For four totally English lads and lasses, they have that ol' inscrutable Asiatic giggle down better than anyone.

But to return to the true traditionalists. The newest entrants in the class are Fairport Convention, a group of five stout-hearted Englishmen (there used to be a woman, Sandy Denny, of "Who Knows Where the Time Goes" authorial fame, but she now has her own group which will be discussed later) who bear not much musical resemblance to Pentangle, which is the group closest to them in actual spirit. Perhaps it's the difference between polished palace gleemen and roving street singers, but somehow Fairport comes off as twice as ancient: rough-hewn, all beards and leather leggings kind of thing. Like Pentangle, all of Fairport are consummate musicians, but the weight of the group is electric fiddler Dave Swarbrick. This boy is going to be a star: he plays his *ceilidh* music, Irish and Scottish jigs and reels, with such authority that in Los Angeles on their last tour he raised a conga-line going delightedly round the hall while he fiddled madly onstage; people were absolutely unable to sit still. Well, good on him, then: there are few musicians around with that kind of magic, and the more I hear of them the more it starts to sound to me that Fairport is, indeed, a troupe of Celtic minstrels reincarnate, going from hall to hall recounting their musical tales. Love it, love it...

Sandy Denny's new group, formed directly she left Fairport and yclept Fotheringay (presumably after the house which was Mary Queen of Scots' last mortal abode), sadly enough does not as yet fulfill the promise of its founder. Denny, during her tenure with Fairport, added a really original voice to some fine interpretations and some solid self-compositions and collaborations; her voice is not so rarefied as Jacqui McShee's (of Pentangle), and lends itself better to the realities of such tales as "Tam Lin" and "Matty Groves" (both on Fairport Convention's *Liege & Lief* album.) Fotheringay tends more to the old definition of folk-rock than any of the other bands here detailed, including in their repertoire even things like Dylan's "Too Much of Nothing"; hopefully, they will find a proper balance.

There are a few other groups who are getting into this area; for the most part, they are bagatelles, like Tyranno-saurus Rex, who have a fine flair for marvelous titles ("Nijinsky Hind", "Beard of Stars") and not much else. But then again, this is by no means simple music to play or to sustain, or for that matter, in which to interest oneself in the first place. It would be nice to see more groups involve themselves in it but not that many people are thusly motivated, and possibly the presence of such a mass-oriented saturation market as eventually evolved for, say, revival blues, would almost inevitably do in the far more subtle and evocative graces of this music.

Better to leave it as it is; it may be anachronistic and esoteric, but it's been around a long, long time, and if it continues to adapt itself to the rock idiom as successfully as it has to date, we may be in for a refreshing symbiosis.

A little too facile, a little too glib; a piece that could have been a lot better if I'd worked on it a little harder.

Funny how off I was in my predictions of stardom for Fairport Convention personnel: Swarb has done very well, of course, but it's Richard Thompson who really hit the gold. In spite of his then sexism, too (see "Rock Around the Cock").

But I give him a total pardon and pass and remit all penalties by grace of his heartbreakingly lovely performance of "The Flowers of the Forest", at the funeral of my beloved friend Mary Susan Herczog (a friend of Richard's too, obviously) in March 2010, at the gloriously over-the-top Hollywood Forever cemetery in Los Angeles. Before her death (after an inconceivably brave and valiant twelve-year battle with four recurrences of metastasizing breast cancer), he had offered to sing at the service, suggesting that particular song choice. She consulted me as to what I thought of it ("Saddest song in the world," said I, "we'll all be sobbing on the floor, rending our garments and beating our fists!"; and she was delighted to hear it), and he delivered. Voice and guitar. Spectacular. Not a dry eye in the chapel, and I made a point of thanking him after the ceremony.

And of course Sandy Denny, who died in 1978 at the age of thirty-one, has her own pedestal as the only guest vocalist ever to sing on a Led Zeppelin album: "The Battle of Evermore", which is my personal favorite Zep song and the only one I have on my iPod. She is absolutely superb on it, as is Plant, whose overrated sound I generally dislike (and no, not because he behaved like a jerk to me).

When I wrote this column I hadn't yet met or even heard of Steeleye Span, who by then had released three albums in a brace of different personnel configurations. In 1972, on their first trip to the States (for their brilliant Below the Salt *LP), Sue Donoghue, by then a publicist for Warner Brothers (who released Span's records over here), introduced me to them; along with our good friend Pamela Hannay, who was close to Sandy Denny and who knew Steeleye from London, we often got together when the band played New York or if we were in England.*

If I had seen or heard them before, of course, I should certainly have written them up in J&P, and been obliged to withdraw the palm from Dave Swarbrick and award it to Peter Knight instead. I think that Steeleye are the absolute best folk-rock group ever, though my favorite incarnation of theirs is the "heavy-mob" one of '72–'76.

Sandy and Susie and Pamela are all gone now, as is Tim Hart of Steeleye; I stayed on friendly terms with Steeleye right up into very recent years, when they pretty much stopped touring; Peter Knight and Bob Johnson dropped in on my East Village apartment for the occasional visit, and Maddy Prior and Rick Kemp had me to dinner at their house in Wood Green, London—a delightful evening, though there was, sadly, no music involved... And I've been in e-contact with some of them still, which is nice.

I used their splendid Royal Albert Hall show of October 1973— which Susie and I, on holiday with Noreen Shanfelter across Ireland and England, were lucky enough to attend—as the basis for a fictional folk-rock group's New Year's Eve concert appearance in my fourth Rennie Stride book, A Hard Slay's Night: Murder at the Royal Albert Hall. *Though my fictional band, Dandiprat, is not in any personal sense based on Steeleye, or on Fairport either: just the music in general and the extraordinary mummer's play with which Span often concluded or encored shows. And no murders either. Well, at least none that I knew of.*

January 1971

The very last thing I wrote for Jazz & Pop was the Pop Talk column "Season of the Witch", which appeared in this issue rather than in the February issue I meant it to run in, which was my last official one as editor. But since it was indeed the last piece written, and has the valedictory feel to it that I intended it to have, I have chosen to place it chronologically at the end of the February pieces instead. Confusing, I know, but it just feels right to have it be where I had meant it to be.

REVIEWS

DOORS ◆ *13* (Elektra EKS 74079): Jim Morrison (vo); Ray Manzarek (keyboards); Robbie Krieger (g); John Densmore (d). *Light My Fire; People Are Strange; Backdoor Man; Moonlight Drive; Crystal Ship; Roadhouse Blues; Touch Me; Love Me Two Times; You're Lost Little Girl; Hello I Love You; Land Ho!; Wild Child; The Unknown Soldier.*

Never call an album *13* unless you are prepared to back up your bluff.

Which, too bad, the Doors are not, in this alleged compendium of Greatest Hits, or Finest Moments, or what have you. Generally this sort of squalid anthologizing serves rock groups in lieu of death rattle; it remains to be seen whether this is so in the case of the Doors (no, no, hardly a deathbed vigil here, O'Toole is one of the all-time Doors loyalists, and proud of it, too, by God).

Sadly and ultimately, this album is like Hamlet, like Morrison: "fat, and scant of breath" (*Hamlet*, Act 5, scene v).
—Shamrock O'Toole

This was the review about which Jim good-humoredly remarked that he always knew when I was mad at him because all he had to do was read what I'd last written about him. I admit to a certain degree of anger at the time I wrote this, for very good reasons, but all I had to take it out on was a Greatest Hits album...hardly worthy of epic wrath...so there was only this.

By the time the final Doors album did come out, I had been gone from Jazz & Pop for several months—I had even been present at the recording and mixing of some of that album (L.A. Woman), when I was with Jim in L.A. in February. Just as well I was done reviewing...for many, many reasons.

———————————

ROLLING STONES ◆ *Get Yer Ya-Ya's Out* **(London NPS-5): Mick Jagger (vo); Keith Richards (lead g); Mick Taylor (g); Bill Wyman (b); Charlie Watts (d).** *Jumpin' Jack Flash; Carol; Stray Cat Blues; Love in Vain; Midnight Rambler; Sympathy for the Devil; Live With Me; Little Queenie; Honky-Tonk Woman; Street Fighting Man.*

For "Gimme Shelter", I would forgive the Rolling Stones anything at all, including this album, which, by no means bad in the usual sense, nevertheless winds up sounding more like great murder than anything else in particular.

Live albums are such iffy things, anyway: however "tight" they may chance to actually be, the connection between the live music and audience noise and the static grooves seems so tenuous as to be, indeed, fakey, on somewhat the same general level as the canned laughter on a TV situation comedy.

But, the Stones are the Stones, as we all know, and it is much to their credit that they can make this hurried anthology sound even as good as it does. Though I could wish for a heavier hand on the vocal mix and less on the instruments, that is merely a cavil, and though there is an obnoxiously cute little tease by Jagger about busting the buttons on his pants, that too is merely a matter of personal taste. Noting to make, nothing to mar: but too, nothing really gets moving until the second side, when the momentum gathers straight from first cut to last and ends up exactly nowhere, all that great climactic energy gone for naught.

The ultimate Rolling Stones tease. Damn.

Live albums, as I said earlier, present their own problems in reviewing; they can be either mangy or magnificent, and a reviewer can look a little silly either way. As it happened, I was at the Ya-Ya's concert in New York, Thanksgiving night '69, at Madison Square Garden, and though I thought it at the time a competent show—the Stones are too professional to offer anything else—in retrospect I have to say it merely confirmed my opinion of the band. Also they played almost no songs I liked.

Which opinion was: kind of boring in concert, and kind of spotty on records. I could always hear the competence on just about any Stones album, but again, like Hendrix, it didn't knock me out or give me joy. I just didn't care for them all that much as a band. If I was going to listen to music around the house, just throw something onto the turntable, it was never the Stones but the Doors (until Jim's death; after that, I just couldn't) or the Airplane or Quicksilver or the Dead (up to Workingman's Dead *and* American Beauty; *after that, they got too diffuse).*

February 1971

In spite of my longtime devotion to Jefferson Airplane and the many times I'd seen them and met them and talked to them and hung out with them, this was the first time, oddly enough, that I'd ever done a full-dress formal solo interview with one of its members. I chose Paul to talk to because we shared some major interests, like science fiction, and the album that the interview was in aid of was all sci-fi, and also because we'd never really talked at length before in a formal situation.

It was just the two of us present for the interview, at a big chain hotel on far West 42nd Street, which Paul had chosen because it had a top-floor pool. By this point we'd progressed in acquaintance beyond the need of publicists to oversee our meetings, though when Paul answered the door clad in nothing but a towel I must admit I was a little surprised. (Though not anywhere near as surprised as when Jim disappeared into his own hotel bedroom after we'd been out for our first date—lunch and a nice stroll in the park—then rejoined me in the living room apparently spectacularly glad to see me behind his gold corduroys and no underwear. Perhaps he just wanted to make sure I knew what he ultimately had in mind, and that I had no objections to it—as if! Messages, indeed...)

Not, I hasten to add, that I thought for a nanosecond that Paul was sending a remotely similar message, or any message at all; I just found it funny. Actually, his then-consort, Grace Slick, seven months pregnant with the future China Kantner, was trying to get some sleep in the bedroom, and offered cordial greetings but passed on the interview—quite understandable. Paul explained that while Grace was napping he'd taken a shower—nice to know that your interview subjects are squeaky clean—and then politely excused himself to get dressed.

The subsequent discussion centered around the about-to-be-released Blows Against the Empire...*one of my favorite albums, by the way. Well, the second side, anyway.*

The Doktor of Space

Paul Kantner's hotel room is not exactly the neatest place in the world. The living room looks like one big unmade bed: guitars, clothes, amplifiers, a portable synthesizer against one wall, lightbulbs, bottles of wine both full and empty, halves of loaves of bread, cake boxes, jugs of Poland water. *Blows Against the Empire,* the new Kantner solo album assisted by Jefferson Starship (Grace Slick, David Crosby, Jerry Garcia, Peter Kaukonen, Jack Casady, *et* a goodly number of equally heavy *al.*) is on the record player. Paul emerges from the other room wrapped in a white hotel towel and says that the record is to be listened to with total disregard for both the quality of this particular sound system and the level of the volume; he disappears and returns fully dressed in rock and roll fatigues, worn green T-shirt and pants, no shoes.

Paul is Pisces, Libra rising; the interviewer is Pisces, Virgo rising. As usual, the best stuff missed the tape...

Patricia: We've been doing some talking about the magic piano that appears on the album, and would you like to repeat that for the folks at home?
Paul: Oh, Superpiano. Wally Heider's studio. San Francisco. Hyde Street. They have this piano there that sounds like

nothing on earth; we didn't have to do anything to it, no electronic gimmicks or things like that. Some guy in L.A. put it together, and it just eclipses everything else, even the RCA pianos. That's what gives the record that churchy sound, gospel stuff. Grace and I did most of the piano playing for the album, and she can play, but I can't, but even the stuff I did do sounded wonderful because of that piano.

Patricia: *Blows Against the Empire* doesn't sound particularly like Airplane music, even though most of the Airplane plays on it.

Paul: It's just basic tracks. That's what my basic tracks always sound like even if they don't come out like that.

Patricia: Would that maybe be because of the musical background you in particular have? You were originally the folky member of the Airplane, banjos and things, and I notice you play solo banjo on "The Baby Tree".

Paul: There's a lot of that on there, lot of acoustic guitar. Also the progressions and the way it's all put together make it sound like that. One of the tunes on the first side starts off with the riff from "Let Me In."

Patricia: Right, and you have bits from "We Can Be Together" and "Volunteers" the song on "Starship."

Paul: Yes, it is, it's the same guitar tuning.

Patricia: Who plays lead guitar on Starship? It sounds a lot like Jorma.

Paul: Not a chance. Jerry Garcia. Grace did this illustration on the inside sleeve, of Jerry when he was trying to figure out just how to play that particular thing, how to do the chord changes, fiercely concentrating.

Patricia: I notice Grace did most of the illustrations.

Paul: Yeah, the ones that appear in the libretto thing that will come with the record. We printed all the words out, because otherwise nobody would be able to understand them.

Patricia: One thing I noticed, though you can't really tell from just one hearing —

Paul: No.

Patricia: No.

Paul: I haven't even heard it all myself yet. We'd be in the studio recording along, and all of a sudden we'd hear new stuff we'd forgotten about, like a month later, "Oh yeah, what's that? Far out, I don't remember doing that." There's stuff on there now that I still don't remember recording.

Patricia: How long did it take you to do it all?

Paul: Three or four months, on and off. It just involved getting everybody into the same studio at appropriate times. The Dead were recording upstairs, Santana was down the hall, Quicksilver was recording there also; everybody just moved around. Whenever anybody wasn't busy doing something, I'd just grab them up. I even got Graham Nash to mix it down for me. I had spent two and a half weeks trying to get it all together, had two-track tapes going up to the ceiling, and Graham came in and did it all in two days. He did it all with headphones on. I hated him for it. But that made the mixed album fantastic for headphone listening, all these little weird things you can't pick up otherwise. What we want to do next is to have Grace and me and Crosby and Jerry and Phil Lesh and Graham and Neil Young and some more people all get in the studio and make a sequel album.

Patricia: My God. What will you call the group?

Paul: Oh, Crosby Garcia Slick Kantner Young Lesh… The studio scene in California is sort of ridiculous anyway. We have a room about the size of this one gone floor to ceiling with tapes that happened in all possible combinations when all these people fell by the studio.

Patricia: You record in San Francisco now?

Paul: Yeah, we haven't recorded in L.A. since way before *Volunteers.*

Patricia: Where does the basic starship philosophical idea come from that you use on *Blows Against the Empire*? There were a couple of stories about the idea's genesis—what's the *real* story, Paul? [*Laughter*]

Paul: I haven't any idea. It started getting together somewhere and then it was there.

Patricia: No, why specifically a science-fiction concept?

Paul: Oh, 'cause I like science fiction. If you're familiar with science fiction...you are...well, there are pieces of *Dune* in it, also *Stranger in a Strange Land*, two Theodore Sturgeon books I really liked, some Pooh stuff, Edward Lear... The last three lines "At first I was iridescent/Then I became transparent/Finally I was absent" are a transmutation by Grace of what Jean Genet had to say about the Chicago Convention of 1968—which I can't remember, what he said, but he said it, whatever it was, about Chicago, and Chicago had to do with why we're doing the starship.

Patricia: There's been some talk about your doing a movie based on the album.

Paul: Nothing definite on that. Though I did talk to Kurt Vonnegut today; if I decide to pursue it, he may have something to do with the screenplay. He's doing a movie version of *Sirens of Titan*, and I might do the soundtrack for that, maybe even use pieces of *Blows Against the Empire* for it. Vonnegut's the only new writer I've found that *writes* new: he writes like a singer, a lot, as far as weighing words, phrasing... But the movie: I tend to see it in levels, like a nuclear submarine down below, with Crosby's sailboat above it, and a saucer hovering over both of them to cover all three levels.

Patricia: That's a very visual image. It seems as though the movie itself will have to be purely that: no real script or action.

Paul: Well, yeah, because it'll be mostly just little bits and pieces of conversation. For instance, having Grace and Garcia and Crosby sitting on the deck of the starship one day coming up on the chrono-synclastic infundibulum, and the dialogue would go, "[*Sniff*] Well, Crosby, what do you think of that thing out there?", and just picking up from that. That's the way we did the album. "Well, Crosby, what are you going to play here?", and Crosby would just pick up with a riff.

Patricia: So you might just as well call it a visual album as a movie.

Paul: Right, right. And the starship is going to be basically an Earth; we'll be able to create another Earth right from the starship itself. There'll be an ocean Crosby can sail his boat on, hydroponic forests where the Grateful Dead can play free concerts; and different levels and decks, from the force deck up through the marijuana deck — probably three decks for marijuana [*Laughter*] — on up to "A" deck, which will be the top deck. Like in the song on the album, go up to "A" deck and watch the stars…

Patricia: Paul, I hate to say it, but you're mumbling…

Paul: Paul's got the mumbles again, is that it? [*Laughter*]

Patricia: Yeah… It seems that this album would be an easy one to stick subliminals into.

Paul: Any album would be, really.

Patricia: Right, but somehow this one in particular, just the way it's layered.

Paul: Actually, there is subliminal stuff there, but you can hear it if you listen close enough; sort of marginally subliminal. Mostly words, underneath noises that are sung or spoken in the far background, and they're there, but if you don't know they're there you'd just pass right over them.

I'd like to play you this Al Capp thing; it's his statement about Jefferson Airplane on a mailer that he sends out to all his fans. We got it on tape from a radio station in Boston, and we play it at all our shows and the kids go wild. If you turn it all the way up it sounds like God talking. The next voice you hear will be that of Al Capp, folks.

TAPE OF AL CAPP'S STATEMENT ON THE JEFFERSON AIRPLANE: " [...] The Jefferson Airplane ... has messages for your kids in their songs: their big hit, 'We Can Be Together' [*Paul: Big hit!?*] has one line repeated — 'Up against the wall, mother!' [*Paul: Finish it, man!*] Now your kid knows what that line means: it means KILL COPS. [*Insane laughter in the hotel room*] [...] Acid rock is composed by stoned musicians, played by stoned musicians, to generally stoned audiences. 'Stoned' is defined as 'dominated by other than normal consciousness, loaded on drugs'; acid rock is just another form of dope peddling."

Patricia: Solid! [*Laughter*]

Paul: Right on, Al, right on. Hard on... [*Laughter*] We're thinking of using that as the opening for our next album, and then when he sues, we'll double whatever settlement he gets if he wins and give it to the Black Panthers. We may also sue him, too, for libel, but it's probably not worth the bother. Send him a copy of the records, though... When [*Vice President Spiro*] Agnew came out with that three-year-old insight about "Eight Miles High" and "White Rabbit", we got together and sent him all our new albums — the new Dead with that cocaine train song, new Quicksilver, Crosby Stills Nash & Young with "Ohio". Made up a nice big thick package and sent it with a letter saying, "Here, get up on our new shit." We never heard anything from him.

Patricia: Probably gave the records to his daughter. Did you have any censorship problems with this record?

Paul: No, not a bit. We're giving RCA another record, and that should finish them. "Saucers" and "Mexico" will be on it, probably live versions; Marty [*Balin*] has a couple of songs, Joey [*Covington*]'s got a song called "Bludgeon the Bluecoats" — social protest.

Patricia: There you go, taking sides again.

Paul: No, listen. Quote: "Don't think I'm on your side, I'm on nobody's side/I'm a battlefield/Burn me or mark me, explode me and beat me/ I, we, you will live." That's easy. Maintain yourself and everything maintains itself around you.

Patricia: There's an ad on the back of the booklet that comes with your album that lays out what seems like a plan of action: "We intend to hijack the first sound interstellar interplanetary starship built by the people of this planet. We need people on earth now to begin preparing the necessary tools. There will be room for 7,000 or more people. If it seems that your head is into this please write & talk about something for a bit. You will not be contacted immediately." Is this for real?

Paul: Sure. Want to go?

Patricia: Oh, absolutely!

Paul: You gotta get ready, though. But you have twenty years or so. We'll have drugs to keep everybody young, develop astral traveling , get rid of your body altogether if you like. The starship thing is really political action and reaction, the natural outgrowth of *Volunteers*. Having done *Volunteers* and seeing nothing get done, we decided to do this. You can't just sit around and make protest albums all your life; eventually it comes to the point where you have to *do* something. What we're saying now is you have a choice: you can stay, or you can go away. You can go out to sea, as in "Wooden Ships", or you can go out into space, as in "Starship". Ultimately, it'll be getting away from the concept of ships altogether; maybe what we'll do is get out into space, hit a time warp, come back, and funnel back through the Sixties.

Patricia: I think it may have already happened.
Paul: Right, and now we just have to go to the other end to find out.

Not bad for a couple of stoned Pisceans sharing the initials P.K. ...

Al Capp, in case some of you were wondering, is indeed the cartoonist of Li'l Abner and Daisy Mae fame, who had jumped on the moralizing bandwagon at that time being driven by the same sort of Rally for Decency folks who were railroading Jim. I had to redact hugely, as he did go on so about the Airplane. The entire text of his noxious comments is available online, should anyone care to take the chance of losing their lunch.

This was the last interview I did for Jazz & Pop; I quit as editor in February 1971, and went out to Los Angeles to spend some time with Jim before he left for Paris. (Though while out there I did do a Curtis Mayfield interview, which Pauline refused to run, for reasons of her own...)

We used some of Grace's charming liner-note drawings (sketches of Paul, David Crosby, Jerry Garcia, herself)—precursors to her present career as a portraitist and painter—to illustrate this cover piece, my last work for the magazine, published three years to the month after I joined the staff as editorial assistant. I was going out as editor; chiefly because the music didn't interest me so much anymore, didn't engage me on that deep personal level. And I think that my work reflected that, so clearly I was going at the right time.

My relationship with Jim continued, of course, only now I wouldn't have to worry about favoritism or unprofessional journalistic conduct.

And one of my only consolations, come July, was that at least I didn't have to write his Jazz & Pop obituary...or read it, either...

POP TALK:
SEASON OF THE WITCH

My final Pop Talk column, and the last thing I wrote for Jazz & Pop, so even though it actually appeared in the January issue, I'm placing it here in the chronology. With the February issue, which headlined my cover interview with Paul Kantner (done in November) as a Pop Talk piece, I left the magazine, exactly three years after I had joined it. Pauline ran an old rejected column in the March issue, perhaps to get as much mileage out of me as she could (especially annoying, since my name had by then been taken off the masthead as editor and I didn't like the suggestion of demotion this gave), but it was nothing special, just filler.

This one, though—this one was different...

It's the bad last end of a bad past year that never should have happened: many changes, much grief, and though none of it is—ultimately—useless, so goddamned much of it was avoidable.

Who wants to be Cassandra in rock and roll land, and in any case Agamemnon's already cold, but what can be seen ahead by the light of what has taken place is looking by no means good.

The Scene has reached an age of real decay. It's my party and I'll die if I want to? Well, maybe, but the party is really Trimalchius', *Satyricon*-scary, getting fast and decadent— and getting decadent fast. And decadence is not fashionable, and decadence is not good.

Your drugs are only part of it. The running as fast possible through as much as possible while as high as possible may be indeed a tremendously appealing modern-day neo-Byronic attitude, but that's all it ever is: an attitude, bearing little resemblance to workable reality, then as now. And its sidekick corollary of you've only got so much to spend so better do it quickly and gloriously rather than be pushed around in a bath chair at seventy is just as invidious.

Softly, softly. "It was haste killed the Yellow Snake that ate the sun." And it was cocaine Romanticism that killed Janis and Jimi, and appears bent on doing in any number of others.

Not just rock and roll stars, either, friends. Supergroup in the Sky may need bass and drums, but that's no reason to go rushing along to audition. It never fails to astonish me, that if it is as simple as it appears for rock performers to lead great masses of young people one way or another, as if they were a pig on a string, then why is it so difficult to lead them into some kind of sense? There has, naturally, been a good lot of pious exhortation on how the deaths of Joplin and Hendrix are going to *teach* us all not to fuck around with drugs, but you know, even as I know, that that just isn't the case. On the contrary: now everybody's gonna want to *die* like Joplin, too.

Where then is the example? It lies, I think in where the distinction fails to be made. The pressures on a rock performer are not like the pressures on you or me: we can sit in our seats, safe and happy in our wish-transference, at our crucial remove, but the Hendrixes and Joplins are the ones who are up there onstage doing it for us — and for themselves. For also it has much to do with the inner pressures that put them up on that stage in the first place: the insecurity, the ego or the shyness or both, the need for approval and applause that all of us have and that all of us handle by one means or another, in varying forms and by varying degrees. What it all comes down to it, finally, is different strokes for different folks; or, don't treat yourself for pneumonia if all you've got is a cold.

Which is by no means to condone the drug method of dealing with your problems, or the drink method, or any method, for that matter, that the practitioner of which demonstrates that he or she cannot handle. Evidence recently accumulated would seem to indicated that Jimi and Janis were probably accidents, just a little too much when they were a little too low, but it was no accident that they were into that sort of thing in the first place.

Joplin just didn't suddenly wake up one morning with a needle stuck in her arm, far *out*, how did *that* get there: it was on all levels a conscious choice and a conscious act, each and every time it happened. All right, she may have had her reasons, but it seems that in such a situation, the reasons almost never balance the rewards, and the risks *absolutely* never balance the rewards. There are other ways to handle yourself in bad times.

The rest of it is not so simple. Morbidity rules. Rock has always had that underlying streak of mass necrophiliac tendencies going all the way back to "Tell Laura I Love Her" and the Valens-Holly-Big Bopper plane crash; deathwish, not so hidden, a fascination with fatality which has unpleasantly evolved into a desperate need for heroes and a concomitantly desperate need to have them die.

Nor is it new, nor is it limited to rock: in Mother's day, it was movie stars, the Carole Lombard/Marilyn Monroe/ Clark Gable ultimate Method. For a while there, and sickly, it seemed to be white politicians and black reformers. Now it appears to be rock's turn: Jim Morrison's been trying to get himself killed for three years now. If rock in is truth an art, as some of us have been earnestly claiming all this time, where then is the classic channeling of the self-destructive impulse into genuine creativity that is one of the marks of the true artist? Hendrix, it would appear, was, after real creative setbacks, on the point of reaching this sort of artistic transmutation, and that makes his death doubly tragic; but even so, evidences of it happening elsewhere are few and faint.

But those evidences *are* there: God forbid ill-fate or mischance, but I cannot imagine waking up to hear of a Zappa or a Slick or a Garcia, to cite only a few, dead of an o.d.: they seem to have too strong and clear a sense of themselves, as individuals as well as artists. The health of the music demands the health, in every sense, of its proponents and participants: the interaction of rock insists upon it, it cannot function without it. It would seem to go without saying that messed-up minds are going to be capable of producing only messed-up music, but apparently not too many of either the creators *or* the consumers have gotten the equation down.

Yeah, it's the Season of the Witch, all right, an oppressiveness that's been building for a long time. Heavy heavy hangs over our heads, and we are the only ones who can do anything about making it go away. Jagger, as usual, has the right of it, in a song ["*Memo from Turner*"] from *Performance*: "The baby's dead, my lady said, and you gentlemen [to paraphrase a bit] are ALL going to work for me." We'll have to see about that.

I've always considered "Season of the Witch" to be my swan song with J&P, and to my original love of the music as well. It reflects personal grief too, and, tragically, predicts more; while for me the worst was still to come. Predicted all too accurately: why else had Jim started telling people (including me, which pretty much tore my heart out every time he did) that "You're looking at Number Three"? I knew it, and he knew it, and he didn't seem willing to do anything to prevent it. Which was why I made the reference to it that I do here—a desperate attempt to get through publicly where I seemed unable to do so privately.

I used some of the more somber insights set out here for my Rennie Stride books, particularly when she, my protagonist, is reflecting on the rock stars she knows, especially her boyfriend and future husband, Turk Wayland, a superstar English lead guitarist whom I present as a sort of Clapton clone without the drug problems. (Hey, it could have happened...)

Back in those early days, there was no personal blueprint for the kind of pressures world-class rockers were subjected to, and frankly, it's only surprising that more of them didn't end up dead or insane, or at the very least severely disillusioned. For which we can all only be grateful. Though that doesn't help us get past the grief we feel for those who were not so lucky as that...and who still aren't.

I wrote a song about it, even, called "Dark Angel"—a song dedicated to Jim and Janis and Jimi, and to Brian and to Kurt and to all the rest who couldn't get out of it alive. As Jim sang, no one here ever does; but it would have been wonderful if more of them could have gotten alive through a bit more of it than they did...

And Out to Fade...

Well, that's it: pretty much my entire rock-critic output. I left some stuff out because it just wasn't that good or interesting: a few less than exciting interviews (some of them my fault, some of them my subjects' fault, some of them where the blame is shared equally), several lesser Pop Talk columns and reviews that just didn't measure up, the three non-J&P pieces. So in that sense this is a curated collection. But even so, the material here is truly representative, of both me and the Sixties, and I'm not ashamed to be judged by it. (No, not even Shamrock's stuff — 'Chris Reabur' named her as his favorite critic, by the way…quite a compliment, and ever so meta.) The Sixties can speak for themselves.

It's been a long time since Jazz & Pop flourished, and even then it never flourished on the mass level of, say, a Rolling Stone; we were more caviar to the general, pleasing not the million. But we damn well did please, and were respected by, the discerning reader, and, more importantly, the artists. Which is why I thought it was important to collect at least my own writings and make them available to those who read and remembered and especially to those who weren't there and thus have never read them. I wish I could have collected *all* the great pieces we ran: that big Airplane interview by Tom Phillips and Pauline; David Walley's monumental MC5 interview, a classic of Sixties rock reportage; Lenny Kaye's history-making doo-wop piece (the one that hooked Patti Smith) and Arthur Lee interview; Jim Marshall's Janis Joplin and Joan Baez photo portfolios; Jay Ruby's sweetly lyrical Donovan interview; so many more.

It makes me sad that some of those, not to mention all the rest, are already lost and gone forever, dreadful sorry; there is no Jazz & Pop online archive, and now that Pauline and David and others have gone to that great Fillmore in the sky, there probably never will be—it would be impossible to sort out the rights. I see issues turning up from time to time on eBay, but that's pretty much the only posterity the magazine now exists in, and I suppose I should be thankful for that at least.

Overall, I am not sorry or regretful for anything; or if I am, it's only because it didn't turn out as felicitously as I had planned, or had dreamed—that it wasn't my best, or our best. Which is a legitimate regret to have on any human's part. But anyone who sneers that the Sixties and what we did there were irrelevant can please just shut it and keep it shut. We may not have prevailed utterly, as once we were so sure we would, but we got a HELL of a lot done.

Just, oh, you know, little things. Little insignificant bagatelles like civil rights for blacks and other racial minorities, liberation for women and gays, raised consciousness in all manner of things from the environment to sex to health to nontraditional spirituality. Mere fluffy trivialities like music, art, dance, politics, literature, fashion, cinema, television, technology. Jim once said that he thought that we the people of the Sixties were going to look very good to future generations, very Romantic, and he was right; what he didn't see, or never said, was how envious those generations would be of us and what we accomplished.

So anytime you hear anyone try to tell you that the Sixties failed, kindly pop them one in the eye for me, and for all my people too. The Sixties never failed and the Sixties never stopped. They just transformed. They became the baseline, the touchstone, the seedbed, the wellspring for everything that came after—things the world now perceives as taken for granted, not things for which young men and young women, and those who stood with them, once fought fang and claw to make possible and real. And all you other people who didn't keep the faith and who sold out to The Man and who now say you're mad at the Sixties? Well, the Sixties are mad at YOU!

I still listen in the past—my personal soundtrack goes dead air not far beyond the years of this collection, just a few songs here and there taken from intervening decades. I have links and associations to just about every song on my brain playlist, my music of choice forever. I didn't stop loving my particular brand of music once I stopped writing about it for Jazz & Pop, or even once I'd stopped writing ads for it at RCA and CBS. And now with Rennie Stride and Turk Wayland and their friends to play with, I still haven't stopped, either writing about it or loving it. I never will.

Bottom line, I was so incredibly lucky to have been there, to have been the age I was, to have had the job I had, to have met the people I met, whose music I so loved. Like Rennie, I was in it to meet the music; meeting the musicians was merely the icing on the cake. Lucky…or fated. Or maybe I just had really, really good karma from my past lives.

But this life, karma gave me music. It gave me words. It gave me Jim. Asking for anything more would have been purely, completely, greedy. In *Strange Days*, I wrote that I wanted my tombstone to read "She kept the faith." Now, besides that, I want it to say "ROCK CHICK."

Dark Angel

for Jim, Janis, Jimi, Brian, Kurt...

Something that we never expected
Something that came as no surprise
Hand on our shoulder hard out of nowhere
Closing our dreaming, opening our eyes

We only had you while we had you
Should have understood you could never be owned
You were just here on a one-day passport
We never guessed you were only on loan

None of us ever thought you could leave us
We watched you bank your magical hours
Coining your blood to buy time on installment
We should have known you could never be ours

You weren't meant for long-term duty
Just dropping in for the midnight shift
Wasn't gonna be any gold-watch party
Your time was the present, but you were the gift

We only had you while we had you
Should have realized you could never be owned
You were just here on a working visa
We should have seen you were only a loan

[bridge]

Sometimes we think that we have all the answers
But we can't learn what we don't want to know

If life's a debt without an obligation,
there's no way to repay what we don't owe
and so…
you came to go…

Never found yourself a place to shelter
Crashed with us when you needed a friend
Hardly even got to unpack your baggage
None of us dreamed there was so much to mend

Who could have thought you'd run the table
That's just the way your loaded dice were thrown
Got off the bus for a quickie gamble
Back on board, destination unknown

We only had you while we had you
Didn't understand you could never be owned
You were just here on a one-way ticket
Even in our arms you were always alone

We only had you while we had you
Nobody saw you get sliced to the bone
Nobody heard you bleed out silent
Nobody noticed you leaving alone

We only had you while we had you
Couldn't accept you weren't meant to be owned
You were just here on a one-way ticket
Even in our arms you were always alone

We only had you while we had you
That's just the way the rolling dice were thrown…

[hook out to fade]